WHO IS OZYMANDIAS?

has written eighteen collections of poetry, most recently *Pebble & I* and *Song & Dance*, both chosen as Poetry Book Society Recommendations. His 1996 collection, *Stones and Fires*, won the Forward Prize; his 2004 collection, *Ghosts*, was shortlisted for the Whitbread Award for Poetry; *The Space of Joy*, published in 2006, was short-listed for the Costa Poetry Award. He is an Emeritus Fellow of Magdalen College, Oxford.

ALSO BY JOHN FULLER

Fiction

Flying to Nowhere
The Adventures of Speedfall
Tell It Me Again
The Burning Boys
Look Twice
The Worm and the Star
A Skin Diary
The Memoirs of Laetitia
Horsepole
Flawed Angel

Poetry

Fairground Music
The Tree That Walked
Cannibals and Missionaries
Epistles to Several Persons
The Mountain in the Sea
Lies and Secrets
The Illusionists
Waiting for the Music
The Beautiful Inventions
Selected Poems 1954 to 1982
Partingtime Hall
(with James Fenton)
The Grey Among the Green
The Mechanical Body
Stones and Fires
Collected Poems
Now and for a Time
Ghosts

The Space of Joy
Song & Dance
Pebble & I
Writing the Picture
(with David Hurn)
Dream Hunter
(Opera, with Nicola LeFanu)
New Selected Poems 1983–2008

Criticism

The Sonnet
W.H. Auden: a Commentary

For Children

Herod Do Your Worst
Squeaking Crust
The Spider Monkey Uncle King
The Last Bid
The Extraordinary Wool Mill
and Other Stories
Come Aboard and Sail Away

As Editor

The Chatto Book of Love
Poetry
The Dramatic Works of
John Gay
The Oxford Book of Sonnets
W.H. Auden:
Poems Selected by
John Fuller
Alexander Pope:
Poems Selected by
John Fuller

JOHN FULLER

Who is Ozymandias?

And Other Puzzles in Poetry

VINTAGE BOOKS
London

Published by Vintage 2013

2 4 6 8 10 9 7 5 3 1

Copyright © John Fuller 2011

John Fuller has asserted his right under the Copyright, Designs
and Patents Act 1988 to be identified as the author of this work

First published in Great Britain in 2011 by
Chatto & Windus

Vintage
Random House, 20 Vauxhall Bridge Road,
London SW1V 2SA

www.vintage-books.co.uk

Addresses for companies within The Random House Group Limited
can be found at: www.randomhouse.co.uk/offices.htm

The Random House Group Limited Reg. No. 954009

A CIP catalogue record for this book
is available from the British Library

ISBN 9780099541691

Typeset by Palimpsest Book Production Ltd, Falkirk, Stirlingshire

The Random House Group Limited supports The Forest Stewardship
Council® (FSC®), the leading international forest-certification organisation.
Our books carrying the FSC label are printed on FSC®-certified paper.
FSC is the only forest-certification scheme supported by the leading
environmental organisations, including Greenpeace. Our
paper procurement policy can be found at
www.randomhouse.co.uk/environment

Printed and bound in Great Britain by Clays Ltd, St Ives PLC

CONTENTS

PREFACE

This book is intended to comfort readers who find poetry difficult by showing that everyone, including professional critics, can find it difficult. I should say at the outset that I myself find a lot of poetry hard to construe and consider myself by comparison with others (in group reading, for example, and poetry workshops) rather slow on the uptake. I claim, however, that this doesn't matter. It doesn't matter for one thing because poetry is a form of writing that deliberately employs puzzles as a means of engaging the reader in the pleasurable business of solving them, and that therefore we might as well take our time. In our era this deliberate puzzling is a commonplace, almost an obsession. 'I've put in so many enigmas and puzzles,' said James Joyce about his ground-breaking poetic novel *Ulysses*, 'that it will keep the professors busy for centuries arguing over what I meant, and that's the only way of ensuring one's immortality.' And, indeed, sometimes there can be no final agreement about the answers, and no definitive interpretation of everything that is going on in a poem. The critic can be just as much at a loss (or mistaken) as the ordinary reader.

The book is largely built, not so much upon theories about all this, but on a number of briefly considered examples of individual puzzles that cast light on different aspects of how we read poems. I hope that most readers will already be familiar with some of them, and be curious enough to delve deeper. The major examples are taken from poets such as Shakespeare, Pope, Shelley, Keats, Tennyson, Browning, Arnold, Hardy, Yeats, Stevens, Hulme, Pound, Eliot, Empson, Auden, Bishop, Jarrell, Lowell, Larkin and Merrill, so that there may be no possibility that the puzzles are a matter of carelessness or incompetence. There is, after all, a great deal of difficult modern poetry that is obscure almost by accident or through wilfulness. I may have something to say about this phenomenon in passing, because it has its own grim interest, but my basic position is this: if a poem has not in the first place earned its claims upon us in some way, by getting into our head and charming us, teasing us or impressing us, then we are hardly guilty of anything if we put it aside.

It will be noticed that a few poems do double duty and that certain topics (such as Oedipus, the *Aeneid* or Egypt) appear several times: the intention is to supply an undertow of extra interest. Sometimes I rehearse received opinion on the puzzles, but more often the argument or solution is my own. The book is not the sort to be burdened with footnotes, but I hope that I have properly attributed the original ideas of others within the text. After forty happy years of reading poetry in the company of ingenious students it is hard to be quite sure where one's knowledge comes from. I have made use of some material from lectures not only given at Oxford, but also for the Royal Society of Literature and for the British Council, and from various articles.

It need hardly be said that in the text the generalised male pronoun stands firmly for the female one as well.

JOHN FULLER

1

THE BRICK-WALL MOMENT:
WHAT IS THIS POEM ABOUT?

For many readers this is often the primary puzzle: what is this poem *about*? If only they had a clear signpost (they feel) they would know roughly where they were going. The title can barely be trusted, since the poem's opening may seem to have nothing to do with it, nor with its subsequent development. It may be hard to tell what the poem's setting is, if it has one at all. It may be almost impossible to disentangle the metaphors, so as to be certain of what is being compared with what, and which of them is the thing under scrutiny (the 'tenor') and which is the thing being brought in by way of analogy (the 'vehicle'). There are all sorts of minor difficulties of language and reference that may come into play at any moment. All in all, readers may justly complain that their journey is unnecessarily impeded. Don't we all sympathise with Jane Carlyle when she said of Browning's *Sordello* (a poem of 5,982 lines) that she had read the entire thing through without being able to work out whether Sordello was a man, a city or a book? Her complaint indicates a profound puzzle indeed, and this as early as 1840. Something of Carlyle's problem (accepting her exaggeration for the moment as licensed by irritation) is common to our experience of much twentieth-century poetry. At one extreme we sometimes wonder how we are meant to know if it means anything at all.

It is worth having a couple of examples here, both from much-admired living poets, both at the less challenging end of the spectrum and chosen pretty much at random. The impediments to the reader's journey in these cases are not severe, and the reader is not unduly pessimistic about eventually making it, but there are some undeniable frustrations on the way. The first example is Geoffrey Hill's 'The Humanist', whose opening stanza runs:

> The *Venice* portrait: he
> Broods, the achieved guest
> Tired and word-perfect
> At the Muses' table.

The second example is James Fenton's 'Here Come the Drum Majorettes!', whose first stanza is as follows:

> There's a girl with a fist full of fingers.
> There's a man with a fist full of fivers.
> There's a thrill in a step as it lingers.
> There's a chance for a pair of salivas –

We have to know what a humanist is, or a drum majorette, and if we don't know we can look them up. But we soon discover that the openings of the poems stand at a confidently oblique angle to the titles (with a good deal of weight in the latter on the secretive assumptions behind the article 'the') and we have to begin to track the poets' intentions. Quite soon we begin to see that Hill must be writing about a particular Renaissance man of letters (but he is going to make us guess who it is) and that Fenton is associating his cheerleaders with the selling of erotic favours (the title is in effect giving full licence to the exciting musicality of his poem).

Who is to say what is necessary or unnecessary in the matter of textual obscurity? We know very well that most obscurities in poetry soon or eventually begin to respond to the light of the reader's intelligence, and that it is an intrinsic part of the pleasure of poetry to be able to unravel difficulties and to solve puzzles. This is the position established by Mallarmé, for whom as much as three quarters of the enjoyment of poetry lay in discovering, little by little, what it means ('To *suggest*, that is the dream,' he said in an interview with Jules Huret). This pleasure (which I take as agreed) endorses recognition, since the answer to a puzzle ought to be satisfyingly obvious. Poetry surprises us with what we already know. Yes, we have all seen sixteenth-century portraits of self-assured scholars (Hill) and we recognise the hectic inter-involvements of sex (Fenton).

Despite this comforting principle, there are a few problems about wilful obscurity in poetry, and I shall deal with some of them in the course of this book. For the moment it remains to examine a little further the reader's relationship with the poet who is responsible for the puzzles that for a time confound him. Is the poet in some sense a superior person to the reader, leading him on just for the sake of it? Is it possible that the poet sometimes doesn't know what he is doing and is asking for some sort of mindless complicity on the reader's part? Is it all serious and worthwhile? Or is it a pointless game? Such needling questions are often, I believe, lurking behind the reader's occasional impatience with poetry, and though they may be irritating to poets, it is important that they be addressed.

What is this poem about? 'About' has two distinct senses which link *meaning* with *purpose*. And the word links them rather firmly, one would think, and much in accordance with readerly common sense, for to discover the true subject of the poem (what it is 'about') must, we feel, lead us to the heart of what the poet is up to (what he is 'about'). If, then, we are not at all clear what he is up to – beyond the playful exercise of his medium – we are free to blame either our capacity for interpretation or his intentions in the matter. Until we know more, that is to say, we may always be in the position of mistrusting the poet's intentions. Not that we suppose that he intends no meaning at all (though we may distressingly come across examples of such literary nihilism), but we fear that he may have failed to take something into account, led us up the garden path, got something wrong himself. If he were the setter of a crossword puzzle, such a blind alley would cause us to write angrily to the editor. But setters of crossword puzzles don't often get things wrong, and they rely very much on the addict's pleasure in patient solutions and sudden revelations. Araucaria of the *Guardian* is much more of a poet than the hired versifiers of Hallmark greetings cards. There is no puzzle in the facile birthday wish, and not much pleasure either, though the pleasure of skilled verse is quite another matter.

Related to this dual sense of 'about' in the protestations of the reader is the dual sense of 'mean' (what does a poem 'mean', and does the poet 'mean' it?), linking the reader's act of decoding with his estimate of the poet's sincerity. This is a popular misunderstanding of the value of meanings, since a poem is quite unlike a promise or a lover's vow or a street direction. You cannot act on it or expect anything further from its author. You do not even need to know who the author is. It may be deliberately fictive, even misinformed. It is quite likely to be hypothetical. The poet is often in today's parlance 'only joking', out to get our attention for propositions that are closer to wild surmise or philosophical paradox than to vital truth. This doesn't at all suggest that such poems are not worth our attention, or that they have nothing to do with truth of any kind. But you can't ask whether the poet 'means' them any more than you can ask whether a composer 'means' a symphony. Fenton's poem, for example, is a self-generating verbal performance that earns its weary conclusion (*'And it's hard for a heart to put up with'*) rather as a piece of music earns its final chords. 'Here Come the Drum Majorettes!' is not entirely an anti-sex poem in a polemical sense, because the words take joy in it, and the weariness seems to be as much a vocal as a temperamental weariness.

There are, curiously enough, other words like 'about' and 'mean' that share this duality of implication, linking a challenging quality in a poem with the character of the poet who produced it. For example, if there are things in a poem that we don't yet 'know', we may feel that the poet seems to be too 'knowing', appearing to take pleasure in the things he knows that the reader doesn't (that *'Venice* portrait' in the Hill poem). It's odd that the word should have become an accusation, since any poem surely intends to convey its knowledge. After all, in ordinary life, a 'knowing' look is designed to make you think twice before interpreting it. It is directed at someone in order to enforce a certain response. It establishes a complicity. Do we resent this challenge to our mental resourcefulness? A poem shares with the reader the matter that must be interpreted. That, indeed, is what the poem is 'about.' If the poem is good enough, it will send us off to find out, for example, about that portrait.

The ideal reader understands all this. To be sympathetic to a poem that one may not yet fully understand is surely to be 'understanding'. And further, in taking up a poem to be read it could be said that one enters into an 'understanding' with its author. In this case, the poet can be no more 'understanding' than the reader can be 'knowing'. Of course, the poet may appear to understand something that we recognise in our acknowledgement of it. Thus, 'understanding' is shared and becomes empathy or compassion, while 'knowing' is felt to be purely intellectual and entirely challenging. But we have already seen that 'knowingness' intends complicity. We are paid the compliment of being presumed to know what the poet knows. It should be part of the understanding between us. But is it always? The invitation flatters us by asking us to get ahead of our experience of the poem, to meet the poet halfway. For example, we might feel that we have to read 'Here Come the Drum Majorettes!' as a poem specifically weary about sex between men and women. Is there a touch of revealing hysteria in its tongue-twisting high jinks? A knowing poem challenges those who do not know what the poet already knows, whereas what the poem really should do is lead both poet and reader to a state of knowledge. The poem can be an experiment in self-discovery.

All this shows how deeply we expect cognitive enlightenment from our reading. And why not indeed? What else is reading for? The classic statement on this issue for our age comes in Fenton's 'The Manifesto against Manifestoes': 'Imagine a poem that was so intrinsically interesting that it never occurred to people, when discussing it, to mention treatment, method, tradition, influence, form or any of the usual critical categories. The only thing people wanted to talk about was the subject. Would not that be, in its way, revolutionary?'

Well, it would be indeed. Because I think in fact the usual things that people want to talk about when they read a poem are its puzzles. They don't want to be the only reader who doesn't get the puzzle, just as they don't want to be the only member of a nightclub audience who doesn't get the joke. But it is more than this earning and parading of consumer credentials. It is the recognition that the poet is intending to entertain you by making it puzzling and it is the wish to respond in the same spirit. If we are entertained by Fenton's drum majorettes, as surely we are, then we can engage with its puns, its word chimes and its puzzles, and in the process begin to talk about the poem's subject.

In the light of this unsigned human contract between poet and reader, let's look again at 'about.' The suspicion is generally and often rightly held that poetry is 'about' something other than its ostensible subject, and that there is a reason for its concealment. It's as though we are dealing with a conspiracy ('We came to know what he was *about*; we were let into his secrets'). This concealment might not be deliberate, of course. Indeed, it might be all too plainly part of the whole difficulty of the poet's gearing himself to the enterprise ('He set *about*, with all due deliberation . . .'). We know that will and intention have a crucial role in writing, as well as mere futurity ('It has not yet come *about*; it is *about* to happen'). And what the mere situation of sitting down to write may cause to avowed intention is well known to Freudian theory. The poet may not be fully aware, we often feel, of the conflicts within him ('He's *about* to make a fool of himself'). The poem he set out to write turns out to be something else entirely more revealing. The drum majorettes may begin to look as though they were written on a hazardous psychological fault-line.

But whatever the degree of fruitful self-knowledge in the poet, or confidence in his putting a plan successfully into operation, from the reader's point of view the poem does often remain a kind of puzzle. 'What *is* he about?', archaic as the formulation is, links the unknown intention of the poet to the modern sense of the intrinsically difficult subject, 'What is *it* about?', where the 'it' may stand quite closely for the whole enterprise, and not merely for the present result of that enterprise, i.e., the 'text'. It is this question that leads us to try to discover Hill's temporarily occluded attitude towards Renaissance humanism.

Sometimes a poetic text is quite clear, but we hardly feel that the poet could possibly 'mean' it, as when W. H. Auden and William

Empson (sensible poets, both, and down-to-earth critics) simply didn't believe that W. B. Yeats in 'Sailing to Byzantium' (1927) could have meant that he wanted after death to become a mechanical bird. This is hardly a failure of reading, unless you feel the need to continue to search for something else that the poem might be 'about'. Empson's endeavours focussed on proving that the magic of an automaton is a sufficient symbol of the powers desired by the poet (this appears in *Using Biography*, 1984, pp. 176ff.). He was scornful of the common view that Yeats's Byzantium represents the Christian afterlife and that the Emperor is a symbol of the deity. We should perhaps be ready to see that Yeats's proposition might really 'mean' something else, quite regardless of whether he 'meant' it or not. And he may have meant to suggest (as Auden's own solution to the unsatisfactory message implied, in his 1939 elegy for Yeats) that he really wanted to turn into his own perfected poems, to become, as it were, 'his admirers'.

The crucial stanza in 'Sailing to Byzantium' is the final one, after the aged poet has established that he has rejected the hauntingly sensual world of youth and fecundity in order to sail to Byzantium, where his soul can study 'monuments of its own magnificence' and be taught to sing by 'sages standing in God's holy fire'. It is easy to see how it appears to propose a metamorphosis after death:

> Once out of nature I shall never take
> My bodily form from any natural thing,
> But such a form as Grecian goldsmiths make
> Of hammered gold and gold enamelling
> To keep a drowsy Emperor awake;
> Or set upon a golden bough to sing
> To lords and ladies of Byzantium
> Of what is past, or passing, or to come.

But the easier and more moving reading involves not the achieved sublimation of a poet's oeuvre (which the aging poet might well have had in mind, thinking back to what a mediaeval Irish bard could have learned from the traditions of the holy city of Justinian) but poetry's essentially unsatisfactory nature as a secondary world. Behind the confidence of 'Sailing to Byzantium' might be the sickness of a quite different emperor, who in Hans Andersen's story 'The Emperor's Nightingale' could not be cured by a clockwork bird, which, after all, could do nothing but simply imitate the real one. Art, however fascinating, is no substitute for life itself. Did Yeats mean this? Or rather, once we have thought up this 'meaning', what shall we do with it? Yeats's bird is not said to be a nightingale (a Byzantine bird is more likely to be a peacock, though a peacock can hardly sing) and Andersen's emperor was Chinese.

Yeats's modernism is not the same as the modernism that notoriously allowed words and images a free play regardless of any intended meaning, like Dylan Thomas letting (as he willingly admitted) an image be made emotionally in him; letting it breed another to contradict the first; making – of the third image bred out of the first two together – a fourth, contradictory image; and then letting them all conflict. Such procedures can lead to a dangerous confidence in technique and can also result in a sterile formalism. It is certainly possible to admire technique and to be dazzled by verbal implications thrown up by the accident of contiguity. But after a while the reader longs to re-establish the traditional communication of felt truths in art. This was certainly true of Auden in the late 1930s when he made his comment on Yeats's belief in a spirit world, and found him 'silly'. There were important things to be said about the suffering of the decade in which Auden himself had developed from ostentatious obscurity to forceful simplicity, and Yeats had once happened to set a benchmark for such poetry.

Auden looked to the artist for an attitude to his material that defined his subject, and he occasionally felt safer in sounding off about this in painting than in poetry. He made an effort when in Brussels to appreciate painters like Rubens, for whom a classical subject like Daedalus and Icarus in flight was simply an excuse for a virtuoso performance of flesh, drapery and perspective. 'The daring and vitality take one's breath away,' he wrote to a friend apropos of such a small Rubens oil sketch, 'but what is it all ABOUT?' He preferred Bruegel, who could portray the life of his own time and dramatise the human emotions he found there. The result was his own poem about Icarus, 'Musée des Beaux Arts', which begins with the all-important word that is at the heart of this discussion: 'About suffering they were never wrong, | The Old Masters . . .' The poem goes so far as to propose that the poet's real subject may – like the human suffering that lurks unnoticed in the scenes of our daily life – be itself hidden away in his poem. It may be a subject that the poet hardly dares acknowledge or wishes the reader to hunt out and discover for himself, but it is there. In 'Musée des Beaux Arts' this subject is Christian revelation, surprisingly enough. Comparing it with the Christian gestures thrown up by Dylan Thomas's self-generating images, for example, we can see a poet's mind at work. In Thomas, we can only see the images at play.

Still, the puzzles in Thomas are often enticing enough to require our attention. If we can find more meaning in them than we suspected was there, we dignify the poem. If it is in some sense more our own meaning than the poet's, we are usually generous enough to wish to share it with the poet, as though we could let him know that his own half-conscious instincts have been successful. In the matter of intention, we want to give the poet the benefit of all doubt. And he, in turn, is felt to sanction our interpretation. Until, that is, we encounter the brick-wall moment when we may temporarily concede the puzzle. The reader will probably recollect experiences of this unhappy state of affairs, perhaps with the work of early Thomas or late Hill, perhaps much of the time with John Ashbery (though these are by no means extreme cases).

I shall examine brick-wall moments in poets generally rather clearer than these examples, as well as in other cases where we may well feel that we have solved a puzzle and yet not seen the problems that a false solution will lead us into. Although there is little overarching argument, the book is arranged in loosely convenient chapters. I begin with the importance of using images as a key to the 'story' behind a poem and proceed to the crucial habit of riddling in poetry. Then I look at a variety of puzzles that relate to our mistrust of poets and of believing what they say. Finally, there are chapters on problems that occur when poets borrow from myth or other literature, on problems related to a poem's title, and on problems in identifying mysterious central characters in poems.

The pleasure of poetry resides in moving from one state of understanding to another. We can return to it and feel different pleasures as our own understanding shifts according to the changes in our knowledge and experience. The pleasure is in the poem and the way it works upon us, but our contract is with the poet. And, of course, he has insisted upon inserting the clause that allows him to conceal the meaning for dramatic purpose.

2

POUND IN THE METRO:
IMAGE AND STORY

IMAGE AND STORY

What is poetry about? The question has been asked already, and it will be asked again. We may leave aside for the moment narrative or didactic poems, which offer the reader an unmistakable primary subject. You can embark on Spenser's *Faerie Queene* or Thomson's *The Seasons* with reasonable confidence of identifying what is being proposed, though even in such cases you soon begin to suspect that there are suggestive, even distracting, political allegories or subtexts to take into account. This is because poetry is in its very nature beautifully adaptable to secondary meanings.

Poems create images. Objects real or imaginary, scenes and situations, qualities that suggest personality, abstractions that perform vigorously within their syntax: the 'thinginess' of images can be elusive sometimes, but we know when we are dealing with them, for they convey the drama of the poem. We are happy to take them for granted, since this is how poetry works on us. 'I had a little nut tree'; 'While shepherds watched their flocks by night'; 'My titillations have no foot-notes'; 'How sleep the Brave, who sink to Rest': in different ways these opening lines compel the mind to attempt a picture, with varying degrees of success.

However, it is not the 'how' of this process that I'm concerned with here, but the 'why'. Very literal-minded readers are unhappy with poetry's habit of making images that clearly evoke a thing that turns out to be significant of something else altogether, or even, disconcertingly, of something else *as well*. How can we possibly decide what this something else is, they ask?

In Imagist poetry (and in the Symbolist poetry which precedes it) the image is deliberately isolated from all applications and conclusions, not so much to create an insoluble puzzle as to allow the reader the unhindered pleasure of solving it, often fairly quickly, but sometimes not at all quickly, and on occasion never quite. T. E. Hulme, because his poems are brief, is a useful example. Here is his poem 'Autumn':

> A touch of cold in the Autumn night –
> I walked abroad,
> And saw the ruddy moon lean over a hedge
> Like a red-faced farmer.
> I did not stop to speak, but nodded,
> And round about were wistful stars
> With white faces like town children.

There are two 'likes' in the poem, giving the reader the benefit of simile. There is a harvest moon, and there are the early stars paler than the moon. And there is the figurative 'story' of town children deprived of the healthy vigour of the country wanting something from the farmer that they are too shy to ask for. A glass of milk? Is this too much story for what may be simply a description of a rising moon? Perhaps. But the description isn't all that simple, and it isn't the end of the story, for at the heart of it we find the poet himself, who nods at the moon in a way that the excluded stars wouldn't dare to and who has no intention of mediating between them. He simply gets on with his walk. He must be a countryman, too, we think. And, of course, his profession as a poet allows him to choose which heavenly bodies are at any moment of numinous significance to him. Think of all the poets who have been on a much more than nodding acquaintance with the moon.

It is important to establish from the outset that it is poetry's privilege to say as little as this, just as it is Hulme's privilege to show himself thoroughly acquainted with the populated autumn sky and able to treat it lightly. The poem's subject requires examples, but these examples need no more elaboration than to evoke it.

It is quite the other case with fiction, where it is the priority of the example that allows generalisation to follow. Auden made a concise distinction of this kind in an early journal: 'The novel – talking of Mrs Snooks reminds me of kleptomania. The poem – talking of kleptomania reminds me of Mrs Snooks.' Fiction naturally has its own real story. Here is another example of what we call an 'image':

> When Farmer Oak smiled,
> The corners of his mouth spread till they were
> Within an unimportant distance of his ears,
> His eyes were reduced to chinks,
> And diverging wrinkles appeared round them,
> Extending upon his countenance like the rays
> In a rudimentary sketch of the rising sun.

I'm afraid that this isn't a poem, but the first paragraph of Thomas Hardy's novel *Far from the Madding Crowd* printed with line breaks. Oak is a character in a narrative, so that whatever Hardy chooses to write we know that it is 'about' him. He is Auden's 'Mrs Snooks'. Hulme's poem isn't about a farmer, but perhaps also not about the moon (just as Hardy isn't writing 'about' the sun). Hulme's subject (Auden's 'kleptomania') seems to be elusive, however pleasurable the invention and texture of the comparisons it makes. Even the title ('Autumn') doesn't quite indicate the subject, since it has nothing to say about the powerful feeling of privilege ('nodded') and contrasted alienation ('wistful') that we find at its emotional centre. Sometimes, of course, a title may indeed be a calculated key to meaning, and in another Hulme poem we will find this to be so, even though the puzzle remains (see my discussion of 'Conversion', p. 185).

These examples are not particularly difficult, and exhibit the writers' fancy in ways that are common to much description in literature. But they may be usefully remembered when considering the naturally puzzling character of poetry compared with the forthright purposes of prose (Oak in this case is established as an easy-going character to whom challenging events will occur, but who is likely to survive them, just as the sun, however obscured, will undoubtedly rise again). We may have no such clear idea of what Hulme may be up to, but our individual reading will wish to come to a conclusion of sorts. Perhaps his subject can be said to be not autumn so much as the transience of autumn and the onset of winter. There is a touch of cold in the air. The poet recognises the harvest exertions of the 'farmer' moon, sharing as he does our human sense of what is appropriate to a season measured in months. But the stars work to other timescales, some of them incomparably vast. Do we imagine them wishing ('wistful') that they might be more involved in human calculations?

TWO MEETINGS

Hardy himself was both novelist and poet, and incorporated into his fiction many of the evocative and suggestive techniques of poetry – as, famously, when Angel encounters Tess at Talbothays dairy, and the meeting is described in the rich and subtle terms of an Eden under threat, and innocence lost. The reader may judge the imagery of such a narrative passage in the full light of the elaborated history of his characters. In the case of his short poem describing a similar encounter of sexual thrill and fore-boding, 'Once at Swanage', we are told nothing much at all about the participants. The poem moves towards its presentation of the couple in its final line as a pair of dramatic pronouns ('I and she!') in some ways comparable to his presentation of Angel and Tess as the primal pair ('she regarded him as Eve at her second waking might have regarded Adam'), but without their personal history and with the universalising power of anonymity:

> The spray sprang up across the cusps of the moon,
>   And all its light loomed green
>   As a witch-flame's weirdsome sheen
> At the minute of an incantation scene;
> And it greened our gaze – that night at demilune.
>
> Roaring high and roaring low was the sea
>   Behind the headland shores:
>   It symboled the slamming of doors,
> Or a regiment hurrying over hollow floors . . .
> And there we two stood, hands clasped; I and she!

There is only a slight puzzle here, but it may prove a good example of how tricky it can be to read a poem, in particular to 'read' the story evoked by the imagery. The story of Tess and Clare unfolds before our eyes in the plainest terms, but the story of 'I and she' (about whom we know no more than that they are holding hands) must be constructed from the way that Hardy has chosen to describe the moon and the sea. Far from contributing to an idyll, as we would expect, moonlight provides an implicit curse. The sea, too, is inimical to the couple: its sounds suggest quarrels and (bizarrely!) the billeting of soldiers. The speaker is conscious of this prophetic colouring, so that the final line may be read in two quite different ways: 'And there we two stood, doomed!' or 'And there we two stood, nonetheless defiant!' The time scheme of the poem indicated by the title may help us here: the occasion happened 'once' upon a time and 'now' the speaker may be presumed to know the outcome. We reflect that 'once' the hand-clasp and the implicit exchange of vows would have been everything, and that it is only 'now' that the landscape is described in such baleful terms. We are forced to conclude that the fatal outcome (whatever it is) is being read back into the past, when the pair was ironically unaware of it.

One crucial piece of the puzzle (so often there is a missing piece, and you look everywhere for it, on the floor or back in the box) can be provided by the real story of Hardy and his first wife Emma, for in the many poems written after her death he revisited the early days of his wooing in the light of the later domestic estrangement he came so bitterly to regret. It is a clue quite outside the text of the poem, of course, but it is nonetheless a powerful light shone by Hardy's perhaps most celebrated body of poetry, and it reveals the military image to be a total red herring.

All this is telling us that however powerful the images of a poem, and however forcefully they convey meaning, we still look for the story. And images do convey story, if they are read with attention. Take 'Meeting at Night', a poem by Browning that is similar in some respects to Hardy's, in that the details of its seascape setting lend emotional value to a situation from which the actual elements of the story are dramatically withheld:

> The grey sea and the long black land;
> And the yellow half-moon large and low;
> And the startled little waves that leap
> In fiery ringlets from their sleep,
> As I gain the cove with pushing prow,
> And quench its speed i' the slushy sand.
>
> Then a mile of warm sea-scented beach;
> Three fields to cross till a farm appears;
> A tap at the pane, the quick sharp scratch
> And blue spurt of a lighted match,
> And a voice less loud, thro' its joys and fears,
> Than the two hearts beating each to each!

Many readers find no puzzle here, or at least will ask no questions, requiring no narrative context. The sensuous excitement of the achieved assignation seems to be enough. But ask them what happens next, or even what might have happened earlier, and the puzzlement sets in.

The point is that some sort of context is supplied by the language and images of the poem. Its mode of description (which could have been conducted in some quite different way) underlines everything that is unusual and furtive in the encounter. The yellow half-moon (like Hardy's 'demilune') is a baleful presence, and there is a restless, erotic imagination at work in the remaining lines of the first stanza. It is impossible not to feel that, like the waves, a woman is going to be startled from her sleep. Startled, moreover, not with reluctance but with a passionate response ('fiery') that is somehow conditioned by the light of the moon reflected in the ringletted waves that represent her. A different sort of anticipation (definitely the speaker's this time) is suggested by the tactile, even sexual description of the boat's arrival ('pushing', 'quench', 'slushy').

In the second stanza, the matter-of-fact details seem designed to convey a different aspect of this story. A mile of beach and then three fields to the farm? Why, therefore, come by boat? Surely there must be a direct road to the farm? The tap at the window and the spurt of the match are both signals of the secrecy that must be maintained by making the least noise. Why is this? Why are the lovers conscious of the loudness of their beating hearts (louder than a whisper)? These puzzles are momentary. We realise that the love-making ('joys') can't take place here because of the possibility of discovery ('fears') and that, therefore, some kind of elopement is taking place. We can imagine the couple retracing the three fields and the mile of beach. Is it likely that after such a journey he will do so alone?

It will be replied that he might very well be alone. He might be making this journey every night, for all we know, and if so it would be evidence of an heroic commitment to a forbidden or illicit amour (not unlike Browning himself insistently attendant upon Elizabeth at Wimpole Street). If you choose that explanation you are perfectly entitled to do so. But my point is that the poem requires us to be alive to all of these speculations, which are directed by the details and imagery of what is, after all, a very short poem. And, as ever, we speculate in order to resolve momentary puzzles.

POUND IN THE METRO

Working out the implications of the images of even quite short poems is, as we have just seen, a traditional pleasure. Perhaps the complexities of Browning and Hardy might be seen as preparing the ground for a movement like Imagism, where the taking of some kind of 'story' for granted – however elusive it might have become in the tradition that Hardy represented – is generally abandoned. What remains, however, is likely to provoke the idea of 'story' in some way in the reader's mind, as we have seen in the poem by Hulme.

Possibly the most celebrated Imagist poem is Ezra Pound's 'In a Station of the Metro', first published in 1913 and collected in his volume *Lustra* (1916). Here is the complete poem:

> The apparition of these faces in the crowd
> Petals on a wet, black bough.

I shall take it as an example of a puzzle about a poem that is ostensibly a standard-bearing example of formal borrowing. But I don't want to minimise the significance of its metrical form, since there turns out to be a puzzle about that as well.

The formal borrowing is (or is commonly said to be) from the seventeen-syllabled Japanese haiku, an ascription taking up a hint from Pound himself. Writing of the experience of seeing a succession of 'beautiful' faces as he left the Parisian Metro at La Concorde, and of attempting to find an artistic equation for his emotion, he concluded: 'The "one image poem" is a form of super-position, that is to say, it is one idea set on top of another. I found it useful in getting out of the impasse in which I had been left by my Metro emotion. I wrote a thirty-line poem, and destroyed it because it was what we call work "of second intensity". Six months later I made a poem half that length; a year later I made the following *hokku*-like sentence.' But his equation was first embodied as 'little splotches of colour', and he had a vivid sense of what it might have been to be not a poet, but a painter, and to found a new school of painting that would speak only by arrangements in colour.

Poetry is not, however, abstract. Moreover, the haiku or hokku has its own structural rules of pause and cadence, and its own tradition of evoking seasonal transience. Pound's poem approximates to all this (as do the poems surrounding it on its page of his 1928 *Selected Poems*) and, in particular, it provides a vision of the ephemeral nature of beauty. The blossom has been reduced by storm to its individual petals pasted on (or at least seen against) the now rain-soaked branch of the tree they once grew on. Soon they will exist no longer.

To notice a face in a crowd is not to identify it, but the sense of searching it out as if to locate an identity is a significant element in the current sense of an 'apparition' as an immaterial appearance, as though of a real being. A crowd of indiscriminate ghosts under the ground inevitably evokes the world of Homer, Virgil or particularly Dante, whose lines '*si lunga tratta | di gente, ch'io non averei creduto | che morte tanta n'avesse disfatta*' ['So long a train of people that I would never have thought death had undone so many'] is now better remembered in T. S. Eliot's own dispirited encounter with commuters in *The Waste Land*. This may perhaps have affected some readers of Pound's poem, who interpret it as a celebration of beauty in ugliness. But whether there was anything particularly ugly about the Metro is doubtful. The particular station where Pound's epiphany took place was noted for a distinctively tiled tunnel spelling out the Declaration of the Rights of Man and of the Citizen. This might lead a reader to imagine that the poem is somehow attempting to recreate individuals with political identities out of a massed crowd of commuters, though it would not be sensible to do this. Does the Underground, a place where you might be regretfully uncertain of ever again meeting someone that you have loved and perhaps

betrayed, put us in mind of the classical underworld? Perhaps.
But this would merely be to substitute a moral poetry of loss for
a painterly sense of the attractive but elusive; a Eurydice or a
Dido for any passing anonymous beauty.

Pound's theory about the poem ('trying to record the precise
instant when a thing outward and objective transforms itself, or
darts into a thing inward and subjective') has something of the
sacramental about it, but the idea of 'super-position' is still undeniably metaphorical in implication. And the metaphor in the poem
– as we have it after Pound's savage and deliberate reduction –
suggests not that the faces are beautiful as in the recounted 'Metro-
emotion', but that their bloom has gone. Even so, of course, the
startling contrast of blossom and bough reminds the reader of beauty,
the ephemerality of beauty, the former beauty of the dead.

Super-position is a structural notion, but in poetry structure is
indicated temporally rather than spatially. The earliest magazine
text of Pound's poem was:

> The apparition   of these faces   in the crowd;
> Petals   on a wet, black   bough .

It doesn't work. A poem without a verb is one thing, but a poem
that pretends that prepositions aren't in fact struggling to relate
one phrase to another across the imposition of asyntactical gaps
is simply confusing poetry with painting. Spacing in poetry is
nothing to do with space and everything to do with time. There
have been experiments in spatial arrangements of words. There
is one by the sculptor Giacometti, for example, called 'Poem in
Seven Spaces', which plays with sounds as well as colours, and
the eye is invited to scan it as it might scan a painting. But such
a thing looks on the page entirely like what it is pretending to be:
simply an imitation of a canvas.

POEM IN SEVEN SPACES

2 golden   a drop
  claws   of blood

                                                    the yellow
                                                    field of
          white   spiral   folly
          of wind upon
          two great
                  breasts

              3 galloping black horses

the legs of   all   objects   have   gone
chairs break   far   away and the sound
with a dry   of a woman's steps and
    crack   the echo of her laugh
                               fade out of hearing

ALBERTO GIACOMETTI
(Translated by David Gascoyne)

Pound returned to a more conventional typographical arrange-
ment, whereby a masterly semi-colon fully restores the way in
which the two parts of the metaphor are held in a suggestive
interrelationship. There was always something entirely traditional
lurking in the two lines of the poem that makes us speculate about
the nature of the original thirty lines. Were they pentameters?
What we have is a hexameter followed by a tetrameter, linked by
the assonance of 'crowd' and 'bough'. It is undeniably a couplet
of some sort, in which one could view the first line as poaching

a metrical foot from the following one. Despite Pound's resolution to 'break the pentameter', this is a poem that has contorted it, but not yet broken it. Traditional structure is more powerful than one expects it to be. It has even been suggested that this poem of fourteen words is thus a kind of 'sonnet of words', broken into an 'octave' of eight words and a 'sestet' of six. Such a notion, bizarre as it is, does have the virtue of recasting Pound's spatial 'super-position' as a sonnet's familiar rhetorical 'turn'.

The twin puzzles in this poem arise, then, from differing expectations of Pound's avant-garde aims in poetry. They are both formal puzzles in their way. We have no idea of the role of classical allusion in the poem, since the purely painterly aesthetic runs counter to it; and we have an insufficient grasp of its revolutionary minimalism, since its avowed japonaiserie is undercut by a lingering addiction to Western form. Much has been written about this miniature, and more could be said of it here, but as is the case with all puzzles, what we have to do is understand the occasion and read for the sense.

POPE'S HIDDEN METAPHORS

There are several puzzles about the poetry of the Augustans, at least as it tends to strike readers coming across it after Donne and Herbert (or perhaps going back to it from Coleridge and Keats). The most obvious is their almost exclusive fondness for the heroic couplet. Another is their liking for generalising and expository poetry: readers wonder what has happened to the poetic imagination, or more particularly to the actual imagery. We have seen the subtle suggestiveness of imagery in dramatic situational poems by Hardy and Browning, and in Pound we have found the image itself elevated to an unusual prominence. In this section I am going to deal with the puzzle of imagery that is so deliberately buried that you are hardly aware of it.

But first I should say something about the couplet. Its astonishing predominance is probably after all indefensible, but there have been other periods of literary history with recognisable default modes of verse (the four-stress alliterative line of the Anglo-Saxons is an obvious example) and there are usually reasons for it. There is beauty in concision, and in the balanced exposure of contrasts and anomalies. The couplet is a fine medium for the rhetorical display of aphorisms, where close rhyming both isolates the successive examples and prompts a continuation of them. And it works well in the barest of language, so that the natural tendency of couplets is towards an undeniable truth.

Here is a good example of the superiority of the couplet in this respect, bearing in mind that these qualities inevitably bear some responsibility for the second of the two puzzles, to which I will then pay more attention. The refrain of the *Pervigilium Veneris*, 'The Vigil of Venus', a fourth-century Latin poem, is: '*Cras amet, qui nunquam amavit; quique amavit, cras amet.*' The twentieth-century American poet Allen Tate translated this finely chiastic line as: 'Tomorrow let loveless, let lover tomorrow make love.' Tate himself was a strong and confidently rhetorical poet, but here his desire to unpack the Latin and still to keep it in one line has made him too condensed. 'Loveless' as a noun, without any article, is initially hard to grasp, and spoils our pleasure at the anapaestic bounce of his line. '*Cras*' certainly means 'tomorrow' if you look it up in the dictionary, but in context this lacks immediacy. At the time of a vigil, on the evening before the celebrated day, one can reasonably be expected to refer to 'tomorrow', I agree, but on the other hand the poem is a passionate hymn to erotic love, and 'tomorrow' has an unnecessarily 'next year, sometime, never' flavour to it.

As a line appearing eleven times in the poem, 'Tomorrow let loveless, let lover tomorrow make love' has several irritating defects.

When we come to the eighteenth-century poet Thomas Parnell's version of it we are immediately in a quite different world of ease, control and clear thinking. Parnell renders '*cras*' not by 'tomorrow' but by the urgent word 'now', and uses the greater space of the couplet to distinguish between the past and future love of those who are already initiated, which is an encouraging bonus:

> Let those love now, who never lov'd before;
> Let those who always lov'd, now love the more.

To my ear, this version, with its subtly varied caesura, has dated less than its twentieth-century counterpart, since it bears a relationship to the spoken language (never, I suppose, claimed by Tate's). In its considered organisation of language, paralleling the effect of the Latin but with different rhetorical devices, it belongs to the general family of wit.

Of course, it could be said that Parnell's version lacks enthusiasm. It is a reasonable injunction rather than a thrilling anticipation. It is to poetry of this sort, of rational conviction and admonitory example that I turn now, poetry that intends to expound truth. Alexander Pope is famous for saying of himself in his *Epistle to Dr Arbuthnot* that 'not in Fancy's Maze he wander'd long, | But stoop'd to Truth, and moraliz'd his song', and it is relevant to the nature of submerged metaphors that we should misunderstand this. You might easily think that the image is of getting lost in a labyrinth and then bending down and accidentally finding the lucky clue that will lead you to the centre of it (or out of it altogether). But Pope actually used 'maze' to indicate a circling movement (compare 'the Mazes of the circling Hare' in *Windsor-Forest*) and 'stoop' to mean swoop. The image is, in fact, of a falcon circling for its prey, admirably appropriate to the career of a moralising satirist.

In his poem *An Essay on Criticism* (1711) Pope frequently makes use of metaphorical allusions to landed occupations like falconry, as if to suggest that the critical faculty is properly available to any gentleman of taste. And it is true that preceptive poems in the eighteenth century avoid taking as subjects those that are primarily the concern of a profession or vocation. John Philips suggests that anyone who owns land may consider the making of cider (*Cyder*, 1708), and William King's *The Art of Cookery* (1708) is as much the concern of hosts as it is of cooks. Poems such as John Breval's *The Art of Dress* (1717) or John Gay's *Trivia; or the Art of Walking the Streets of London* (1717) are much more obviously the province of the knowledgeable amateur.

Similarly, much of the time in the *Essay*, when Pope is talking about criticism he is talking about the sort of activity which any well-read member of society might be tempted to take up, and is continually directing his precepts towards the reader himself, the informed, literate, typical member of this social audience. It is not so much an essay on formal or theoretical criticism as we would understand it, but an essay on literary sympathy, an essay on how to read, an essay on how best to share one's understanding of literature.

The imagery frequently conspires to suggest this, but with the slightest of touches. War, courtship, falconry, fencing, sailing, horsemanship and so on: these energetic, upper-class pursuits elevate the purely literary, and make it seem to be a matter of heroic endeavour. There is a fine passage about coming to terms with one's limitations that takes the falcon idea a stage further into history:

> Like Kings we lose the Conquests gain'd before,
> By vain Ambition still to make them more:
> Each might his *sev'ral Province* well command,
> Wou'd all but *stoop* to what they *understand*.
>   First follow NATURE, and your Judgment frame
> By her just Standard, which is still the same. (64–9)

We duly note the simile of the king who does not know when to stop (and Pope may be referring to Charles XII of Sweden, who was defeated in this way in 1709, the year the poem was completed), but the continued military imagery is likely to slip away from us. Pope italicises some of the key phrases, however, just as he was to do in a passage in his *The Art of Sinking in Poetry* about starting a metaphor, running it down, and pursuing it, like a hare. This is a deliberate clue. The Roman *provinces* were controlled by the discipline of the legions who *stood under* Roman authority, with the eagle (implied by 'stoop') as their *standard*. Nature, then, is as all-powerful as the Emperor, and if you are a poet who is faithful to the truth of nature, then your reward may be a province, a fine outcome for a neo-classical poet.

Comparing Pope's *Essay* with Parnell's *Essay on the Different Stiles of Poetry* (1713) shows that without an overriding allegorical framework such as Parnell employs, Pope was bound to use his key images in marginal ways. As it turns out, his imagery hints at much the same sort of allegorical implications as Parnell does, and we would expect the later poem from the lesser poet to be at once more obvious and derivative. Readers of Pope's *Essay*, puzzled or not, will acknowledge their memory of such submerged images as the mounted rider or the mountain to be climbed. A single almost barely metaphorical word such as 'curb'd' in the lines 'Nature to all things fix'd the Limits fit, | And wisely curb'd proud Man's pretending Wit' gives you the idea that the control of the poetic imagination is equivalent to equestrian skill. Any fox-hunting squire might, then, feel that he understands something about poetry.

Parnell, however, spells it out. Wit for him *is* Pegasus the winged horse; the Poet *is* his rider; and the various poetic styles of his title *are* the countries that they encounter on their journey. So we are, in turn, introduced to the barren terrain of false wit; the frigid land of 'starv'd Conceits that chill the Reader's Mind'; the land of cliché, 'open, unimprov'd, and low', and so on, until the Poet reaches his final destination, the 'Palace of the *Bright* and *Fine*'. Once there we have some ingenious representations of individual rhetorical figures seen as courtiers or lovers in the palace, but these subdued metaphors don't really illuminate the central conception of literary exploit, as Pope's do when he rings the changes on Roman, military or sporting metaphor. The subtle implications lie discreetly just below the surface of the verse's impeccable clarity.

MISREADING

All first readings of poems are uncorroborated interpretations, leaps of faith about what is going on, assumptions about nuance. Without a duty to share our view of a poem, we may live with a misreading all our lives, hoarding an unrecognised puzzle. We can be shocked by readings different from our own. We may even disbelieve them. At our most generous, when politeness or curiosity overcomes habit, we cheerfully allow them. But whether or not these new readings ever quite replace our first thoughts is doubtful, since our long possession of a poem is an emotional investment of a kind, and our understanding can be defiant. Much depends on the tone of authority accompanying a rival reading, and its appeal to traditions of interpretation.

To encounter a flagrant misreading is to be suddenly thrown back on one's confidence of being unquestionably right, and for this reason a guarded diplomacy is common amongst professional critics. The celebrated formula of critical dialectic proposed by F. R. Leavis ('This is so, is it not?' – 'Yes, but . . .') allows for polite accommodation, and the cautious building of a tradition. To encounter a brilliant novelty is, on the other hand, more dangerous. How can we tell whether it is right or not? Why has no one thought of it before? Much depends, of course, on whether it is you or the other person proposing the unusual reading. Tolerance, like truth, is relative. It is possible to be quite proud of one's mistakes, and common to be resistant to anything new.

Take my example, in the previous section, of a familiar word that can be unpacked to reveal its latent metaphor: 'curb'd'. If any reader rebels here against the requirement to read 'Wit' and imagine a horse, finding 'curb'd' instead a perfectly familiar word in its plain and general sense, no amount of quoting the dictionary will help. Yes, a curb does happen to be a chain or strap passing under the lower jaw of a horse, and fastened to the upper ends of the branches of the bit, and it is used for checking an unruly horse, but we are by now used to unthinkingly 'curbing our passions' and few of us ride horses any more. The word is no longer attended by an image.

It happens that the very next passage in Pope's *Essay* after that couplet about curbed wit provides an excellent example of common misreading, and one which is indeed an elaborate analogical simile and not a question of revived cliché:

> As on the *Land* while *here* the *Ocean* gains,
> In *other Parts* it leaves wide sandy Plains;
> Thus in the *Soul* while *Memory* prevails,
> The solid Pow'r of *Understanding* fails;
> Where Beams of warm *Imagination* play,
> The *Memory*'s soft Figures melt away.

Pope is no doubt making his own sense of current philosophical thinking, such as Locke's inquiry into whether memories continue to exist when we are not thinking about them. The faculties of memory, understanding and imagination are so different and have such exclusive claims upon the mind's attention, that they do not have free play together at the same time. Commentators on the poem will tell you that these soft figures are wax melting in the sun, without recognising that Pope's seashore metaphor demands to be extended, indeed is incomplete without this extension. When the tide is in (i.e., when memory floods in upon us) the land is covered (present understanding suspended) and this much Pope spells out. But the second of the quoted lines is often overlooked. The tide is variable, and will in some places leave shallow pools and patches of abandoned sea, ready to evaporate in the sun. The application is precise: as we manipulate these involuntary memories, our understanding of them comes back into play (and all is sand again). It is crude psychology, perhaps, but it appropriately accords the imagination a crucial role in making comprehensible shapes of the otherwise inchoate force of past experience. Not wax, but ocean.

Sometimes a poem's subject itself can be misread. I once saw an old photograph in a museum at Keswick in the Lake District of a group of formally dressed black men posed behind a kind of roughly hewn xylophone made of local stone. The incongruity happened to suit my surrealist interests, so I wrote a brief poem about it (this was fifty years ago, and I used the language of the time):

> O Lakeland Musical Stones! Played by
> Negroes in faultless evening dress circa 1900!
>
> Listen to the chopping clinks as felt
> Hammers bounce on the slabs!
>
> Like Debussy at the Odeon . . .

Those ubiquitous exclamation marks were picked up from Gregory Corso, whom I had met in 1958, but there was nothing substantively American (or African-American) about the poem. This didn't prevent my being commended, when I gave a reading a few years later at the University of Buffalo, for having written evocatively about the Modern Jazz Quartet. I protested that they were not at all the subject of the poem, but was not believed because had not the MJQ appeared that very semester on the campus, playing to a large audience in the sports hall? It was no use my reminding my kindly admirer of the title of the poem ('In the Keswick Museum'), because it was obvious to him that I had been describing the vibraphone of Milt Jackson.

I give this personal example because it allows me to vouch for my intentions. But, of course, it doesn't prevent readers eager to promote their own interpretations from saying that I couldn't know my own subconscious intentions, and that in any case if someone chooses to believe that the poem is about the MJQ, then *for that reader* it is unquestionably what the poem is about. And, moreover, a poem may be about two (or more) things at once (see my discussion of the poem about Crinog, p. 44). Does all this constitute a misreading? I take the common-sense view that it does.

As for cases of argument between mere readers, where the author has no chance or wish to cast his authorial vote, the notorious example of T. S. Eliot's Pipit comes to mind (see p. 212). It will be apparent elsewhere that although Eliot liked to drop clues, he was happy for readers to be in charge of meanings (see p. 238). When a poet is professedly invisible, as Eliot was, then his interposition might be an embarrassment, a case where the author should not attempt to be authoritative. Differing views must rely on evidence to settle the matter, and since almost any good line of poetry can throw up a puzzle for a reader, criticism can often sound like a law court.

I remember once arguing with a pupil about a passage in Keith Douglas's '*Vergissmeinnicht*', one of the most celebrated poems of the Second World War. Douglas returns to a place of combat after three weeks to find a dead German soldier 'sprawling in the sun'.

> The frowning barrel of his gun
> overshadowing. As we came on
> that day, he hit my tank with one
> like the entry of a demon.

The brilliant pathos of the poem is yet to come, and Douglas prepares for it by curiously neither admitting nor enquiring who exactly has killed the soldier. For the moment his memory is confined to the effect of the German shell on the armour-plating of his tank.

Is there a puzzle here? I wouldn't really have thought so. I take the entry of the demon to be a simile drawn from pantomime, where the Demon King traditionally makes a trapdoor appearance accompanied by a puff of stage smoke. For a moment the poem is both inside the tank ('he hit my tank') and outside the tank (seeing the smoke from the shell's explosion). But this isn't a puzzle, merely a bit of cinematic montage.

My pupil was having none of it. He simply couldn't see it. As we talked it over, I tried to guess what alternatives he had in mind, since a simile is a simile. The shell hitting the tank wasn't itself the entry of a demon. It was *like* the entry of a demon. So what did he think this entry of a demon could be? Was it some biblical thing, perhaps like John 13:27 ('Satan entered into him') or the devils entering the swine in Mark 5:12? I don't think that my pupil was much taken with this either. What we didn't have time for was a look at Douglas's memoir *Alamein to Zem Zem*, where stage and circus imagery is widely used, and where we would have found, for example, this: 'Looking to the left I saw a dark grey blur of smoke, shaped like a tree, but many times a tree's height, standing up silently from the ground, like a djinn who had suddenly materialised.' A djinn is not unrelated to a demon. I don't now remember what interpretation my student favoured, but I believe that although he eventually became a distinguished scholar and editor of seventeenth-century poetry, for him this poem of Douglas's either contained an unresolvable puzzle or no puzzle at all.

This is perhaps a case not so much of misreading, but of not reading enough. The most intelligent and interested readers of poetry sometimes simply don't notice the obvious, even in their favourite poems. This inattention can be part of a rapt reinvention or appropriation of the text. We sometimes want to see poems in our own terms.

Take the novelist Rachel Cusk's reading of Coleridge's 'Frost at Midnight', for example. The poet presents himself on a still winter's night meditating alone over the cradle of his newborn son Hartley, and vowing to give him an education in a natural environment very different from what his own had been. This poem is, Cusk claims (in *A Life's Work*, 2001), one she has always loved, and yet she admits that she hadn't realised that it had a baby at its centre. An imaginative novelist might have been expected perhaps to observe that Hartley proved to be something of an educational disappointment, losing the chance of an Oxford fellowship through persistent drunkenness, once being found in a ditch in what is now Parks Road. So much for the beneficent powers of Nature. But as a baby in his father's poem he is an iconic presence. It would be wayward not to notice him.

Which brings us to the positions of professional critics, who have a different duty towards poems. They are surely the acknowledged detectives of poetry. We rely on them to give significant help in solving puzzles, but perhaps no more than will be useful, since it is, of course, possible for a critic to create his own puzzles and leave us no less in the dark. This is particularly true of critics who are also poets.

Empson's openness to varieties and nuances of meaning is a famous case. His style of criticism seems to have been invented hand-in-hand with his own multi-layered poetry, and with him we always end up seeing more in a poem than we expected. What we struggle to keep in our head after reading Empson's criticism does not always feel like a solution, but simply more poetry. As a critic he seems to have been necessarily created in the wake of the greatest lexical endeavour of modern times, the Oxford English Dictionary, although he was a Cambridge man himself. The semantic niceties of the Cambridge tradition – continued in the work of Christopher Ricks or Eric Griffiths – often centre on wordplay that is itself poetical (like the puns of Ricks, for example).

A newer development in the sort of criticism that exists in symbiosis with poetry itself is the associative method of Paul Muldoon. For him, not merely words, but certain letters, chains of letters or anagrams can contain allusive meaning. Lecturing in Oxford in October 2003, for example, he found in some lines of Arnold's 'Dover Beach' ('Where the sea meets the moon-blanched land' and 'Its melancholy, long, withdrawing roar') the ghostly appearance of one of King Lear's dogs ('Blanche') and the letters of the name 'Darwin' (in 'withdrawing'). The audience, as yet unused to Muldoon's by now well-established and widely published critical practice, were somewhat bemused. Such observations do, to a degree, help the reader a little with the ludic practices of Muldoon's own poetry, but they do not solve any of the puzzles in Arnold's poem (for one of these, see p. 120).

HIGH WINDOWS

Now for a more detailed look at a well-known, powerful and yet puzzling image. The title-poem of Philip Larkin's final collection, finished on 12 February 1967, seems to occupy a special place in his readers' affections, as it must have for the poet himself, in so choosing it for the volume's title. And just as the title of the poem became the title of the book, so the mysterious symbol of the high windows in the final stanza became the title of the poem itself. The symbol is Chinese-boxed in such a privileged way that it tends to receive a concentrated focus of readers' attention. And rightly so, for it arrives in the poem 'immediately', literally out of the blue.

> When I see a couple of kids
> And guess he's fucking her and she's
> Taking pills or wearing a diaphragm,
> I know this is paradise
>
> Everyone old has dreamed of all their lives –
> Bonds and gestures pushed to one side
> Like an outdated combine harvester,
> And everyone young going down the long slide
>
> To happiness, endlessly. I wonder if
> Anyone looked at me, forty years back,
> And thought, *That'll be the life;*
> *No God any more, or sweating in the dark*
>
> *About hell and that, or having to hide*
> *What you think of the priest. He*
> *And his lot will all go down the long slide*
> *Like free bloody birds.* And immediately

Rather than words comes the thought of high windows:
The sun-comprehending glass,
And beyond it, the deep blue air, that shows
Nothing, and is nowhere, and is endless.

The poem takes a characteristically no-nonsense view of untrammelled sexual relations as though they were childish turns on a playground slide that for 'everyone old' now seems forbidden and therefore deeply enviable. It proposes a bleak version of an earthly 'paradise' free from the constraints of religion. But if an earlier generation had thought much the same thing of the younger Larkin, then the envy might be merely a perennial commonplace. The meditating mind of the poem is therefore faced with choosing between such an infinitely regressive argument about a commonplace or deciding that in our era of the death of God it is a disturbingly new phenomenon.

It is at that moment, when the discursive words for such a choice fail him, that the symbol of the high windows enters the poem as abruptly as it enters his mind. In the logic of the poem the symbol should be an answer to his question in line 9, 'I wonder if . . .' Did the old always think this about the young, or is it something new? Is it part of the way in which society has always dealt with the generational possession and envy of sexuality? Is it something merely subject to historical development, like combine harvesters? Or have we thrown out moral absolutes together with religious belief? The answer is not given. We simply get the vision of the high windows.

Symbols can be the most puzzling kinds of poetic images, because they are self-contained and not obviously compared to anything else. However, in interpreting them the reader always has to bear in mind the context. What are these 'high windows'? If the context seems merely to be 'Larkin', then the critic might

as well exclaim 'the windows of Larkin's top-floor flat' (Tom
Paulin). This is about as unhelpful as Maeve Brennan facetiously
using the phrase 'high windows' in the caption of a photograph
of Larkin looking out from 32 Pearson Park, Hull, or my own
feeling once when I visited the top floor of the Brynmor Jones
Library that I had never been quite so high up as to see nothing
but sky from a window, a feeling trumped by a subsequent visit
to New York's World Trade Center. The high windows in the
poem are of the essence of window, in which the transmission
of light is everything. They are 'sun-comprehending' in this
absolute sense, and the way in which that word seems barely able
to contain the word 'uncomprehending' struggling out of it
tells us that the process is itself a mystery, as much a mystery as
nothingness or endlessness.

Confronted with the symbol's own mysteries we might for a
moment forget that suspended question and attempt to order our
puzzled thoughts. One such thought might be that the blue air
is hardly nowhere; it is at least 'out there' uniquely surrounding
our planet; and far from showing nothing, it shows us where we
are within our planet's belt of oxygen. Another thought might
be that blue air is not in fact endless. It ends both when the sun
sets and the sky turns black, and when, travelling outwards, you
have reached the limit of the oxygen belt. We quickly decide that
these practical objections are not intended to have any force. The
symbol is content to exist within a framework of mystery.

As such it is all too easily accessible to a reader's own context
or existing line of critical argument. Let us look at a few existing
explications of the high windows. Perhaps the windows simply
parallel the envied situation of the young in the first stanza? If
so, they represent 'ideal freedom and happiness' (A.T. Tolley). But
perhaps they point not to the young but to the resentful observing
Larkin. Then they must embody a 'haunting sense of difficulty

and pain' (Janice Rossen). But they can't do both. If the theme of life's disappointments is the critical context, then they are 'typical of Larkin's way of verbalising oblivion' (John Bayley). Or if the negatives in the final line seem to be the real point, then the windows represent 'ecstatic nullity' (Steve Clark) or 'a translucent nihilism' (Stan Smith). It might seem quite a feat of conjuring to move from 'a translucent nihilism' to 'the Dantesque vision of paradisal beauty' in the same critical article, but Smith manages it. A more practical approach is to relate the poem to Larkin's first visit to Coventry Cathedral six months earlier, on 10 August 1966, even though he 'wasn't greatly impressed' (Christopher Fletcher). What emerges from any overview of the critical consensus is that it can't be said to be a consensus at all. The most eagerly accepted view of the matter is that of Barbara Everett. For her Larkin is a post-modernist who incidentally provides a revisionary critique of symbolism, and 'High Windows' is a kind of argument with Stéphane Mallarmé's '*Les Fenêtres*'.

The Larkin persona on offer in this poem may indeed be not unrelated to Mallarmé's '*homme à l'âme dure*', but in what way the windows represent a transfiguring path to Beauty (or any ironical version of this Symbolist redemption) is unclear. Larkin once let me set up a very early poem of his on my treadle printing press, and publish it in a broadsheet series. 'Femmes Damnées' turned out to be a free imitation of Baudelaire, and Larkin engagingly told me that I could let it be known that it was evidence that he had read at least one 'foreign poem'. Since then Larkin's notorious cultural insularity has been tempered by the notion that he was in reality a secret Francophile. But 'Femmes Damnées' still seems to me more like Betjeman than Baudelaire.

I don't believe that a source of any kind is needed for the high windows. To suppose so is to be tempted (as T. S. Eliot warned) into inventing a puzzle simply for the pleasure of trying to discover the solution. The puzzle is how we are to read the symbol as part of the interrupted argument (about whether the freedom from religious constraints is unique to our time). But it so happens that a famous passage of an English writer does provide both of these things, a source and an argument.

The second chapter of De Quincey's *Autobiographic Sketches* contains the celebrated account of his mystical experience after the death of his three-and-a-half-year-old sister Jane. He goes up to her bedroom and looks for her face, but finds that her bed has been moved. All he sees is 'one large window, wide open, through which the sun of midsummer at midday was showering down torrents of splendour. The weather was dry, the sky was cloudless, the blue depths seemed the express types of infinity; and it was not possible for eye to behold, or for heart to conceive, any symbols more pathetic of life and the glory of life . . . A vault seemed to open in the zenith of the far blue sky, a shaft which ran up for ever. I, in spirit, rose as if on billows that also ran up the shaft for ever; and the billows seemed to pursue the throne of God; but *that* also ran before us and fled away continually. The flight and the pursuit seemed to go on for ever and ever.' At this point he appears to fall into a trance. Later, at the funeral, he raises his eyes to the 'upper windows' of the church galleries. The stained-glass side windows were a mingling of heavenly emblazonries (the sun's light) and earthly emblazonries (the colouring of art), but 'through the wide central field of the window, where the glass was *un*coloured, white, fleecy clouds sail[ed] over the azure depths of the sky'. He associates these clouds with the beds of dying children, and in later dreams imagines the faces of angels clustering round the pillows of dying children in the 'blue heavens, the everlasting vault' (*Collected Writings*, 1896, I.38, 42, 47, 49).

Even if Larkin was not remembering this account, it seems clear that his high windows do function more or less as a symbol 'pathetic of life', just as his 'long slide | To happiness' has its own pathos. Endlessness links them. Larkin's deep blue air is notably lacking the objective at the end of De Quincey's ever-receding vault: the throne of God. '*No God any more*' is what triggers the unspoken thought in the poem. The vault is everlasting, but empty.

De Quincey's context is death, and Larkin's powerful symbol seems to most readers to be redolent of such a finality. It can hardly suggest mere happiness or paradisal beauty, but it seems nonetheless (like his 'Church Going', where God is also not to be found) to be some sort of a negotiation with the 'seriousness' of the religious point of view. I think that De Quincey may help us to see that.

3

WHO IS THE EMPEROR OF ICE-CREAM?: THE HABIT OF RIDDLING

WHAT IS IT?

At the heart of the poetic enterprise is a little game where the poet needs the reader to identify something from a teasing description of it. This is traditionally known as a riddle, and the teasing consists of an alternative solution, which has to be discarded. This alternative is often more immediately obvious or attractive than the real solution, and it is not always possible to put it out of mind. The two answers to the riddle may continue to coexist in the mind, and there is pleasure to be had in accommodating them and distinguishing them. Indeed, at its most complex, the supposedly 'false' answer can lend a metaphoric intensity to the thing described, but it is the thing itself that is ultimately important.

In the Anglo-Saxon period, for example, riddles about armour, ploughs, vegetables and the weather were very common, and many of them had false solutions of a sexual kind. The trick was to animate or personify some common thing to show how marvellous it really is. Here are a couple of the riddles from the Exeter Book in my own translation:

I saw four creatures on the march: their black
And curious footprints made a single track.
Sometimes he dipped beneath the wave, and fast
As birds, swifter than scudding air he passed,
That restless hard-worked warrior who controlled
All four in paths across the splendid gold. (No. 51)

The generally accepted answer to this riddle is 'a scribe's hand'.
Not very difficult to guess, perhaps, though there are still arguments about it. It has attracted solutions such as 'alchemy' or 'a
horse and wagon.' The second riddle's answer is 'ice', less contro-
versial because common across many cultures:

I saw this sea-born marvel move alone:
A strange thing happened. Water turned to bone. (No. 68)

In the eighteenth century Matthew Prior, Thomas Parnell,
George Crabbe, William Cowper and many others all composed
riddles. The form had inevitably tended to become a mere parlour
game on traditional topics, but you can see from a range of
riddles by Jonathan Swift (on gold, a pen, a corkscrew, a flea, the
gallows, ink, time, reflections, dice and two on the anus) that not
only can a society's interests be represented by riddling, but something of a poet's character too. In Swift's case we sense that the
eternal verities are significantly on a level with good living or
physical discomfort. On the other hand, some of Prior's (on the
Knave of Clubs or a pair of skates, for example) have a more
playful air, in character with his poetry in general.

The riddling habit may be stylised into brief formulae such as
the Anglo-Saxon kenning or Augustan periphrasis, where the alternative solutions are mere ghosts of exaggeration or disproportion
('hwaeles eþel' – what road does the whale use? Answer: the sea;

'the Sylvan War' in Pope – what kind of war takes place in woods? Answer: hunting; or in our era, 'the folded lie' in Auden's 'September 1, 1939' – what kind of lie is folded? Answer: the headline of a newspaper tucked under the arm of a commuter). Whatever else you may interpret them as will have some kind of dramatic force, but the 'right' answer can be a revelation.

A riddle should ideally focus its poetic force in the revelatory moment when the true answer becomes apparent and we realise that our emotions have been misled. A particularly beautiful example was recorded by Iona and Peter Opie in *The Lore and Language of Schoolchildren*, told to them by a nine-year-old Birmingham girl:

> The King of Cumberland
> Gave the Queen of Northumberland
> A bottomless vessel
> To put flesh and blood in.

We can make a story out of this. It has a ballad-like concentration suited to its suggestion of pre-Conquest dynastic rivalry, and might be an ironic gift ('This is what you're going to need when the fighting's over'). The true answer (a wedding ring) is in complete contrast to our first impression. Our thoughts of warfare, even of cannibalism, are resolved like a joke as a tragedy is turned into a comedy (one opposite of war is marriage).

A celebrated example of erotic riddling is the tenth-century Ulster poem in which the speaker recounts his relationship with the beautiful Crinog ('of melodious song' in A. P. Graves's translation), sleeping with her from the age of seven. The poem tells how Crinog left him and took up a similarly chaste relationship with four other men before returning to him in old age. He claims that this virtue of sinless sisterhood is a saintly example, a path to the living God. We can be sure that there is a degree of deliberate titillation in this theme of the *virgo subintroducta*, testing the virtue of monks or hermits by making them share their bed with a young woman. This practice is said to have survived only in the Irish Church at the time of the poem, but our era is perfectly familiar with it from, for example, the case of Mahatma Gandhi, who slept naked with his nineteen-year-old grandniece to test his vow of *brahmacharya* or total chastity.

There are elements in the Crinog poem that point to a puzzle, however, and we are not surprised to discover the 'real' answer: the melodious lady is a book of psalms that the speaker lost when he was a boy and which he came across again late in life with the signatures of four other owners on the flyleaf. Or is she? It is impossible to read the poem without re-entering the false trail afresh, and the two solutions live together in a metaphorical tension not unlike that of the saint and his virgin.

The demands of the riddle are exactly like those of the puzzle: the search for an answer. But it is clear that our experience of metaphor in poems tends to familiarise us with ingenious relationships between the subject and the thing introduced to represent it, and we are well-used to negotiating priorities. The appearance of riddles in poems tends not to hold up readers for long if their function is largely metaphorical. There is a rich example in the third canto of Alexander Pope's *The Rape of the Lock*:

> For lo! The Board with Cups and Spoons is crown'd,
> The Berries crackle, and the Mill turns round.
> On shining Altars of *Japan* they raise
> The silver Lamp; the fiery Spirits blaze.
> From silver Spouts the grateful Liquors glide,
> While *China*'s Earth receives the smoking Tyde.

Here the 'Altars of *Japan*' and '*China*'s Earth' insinuate themselves as real altars and real national territory. The lamp raised in the ceremonies appears to invoke 'fiery Spirits', deities who manifest themselves in response to the ritual. The false answer to the riddle suggests that Japan is praying to her gods to inundate her enemy China with earthquake and flood, a prayer that is answered in the last cataclysmic line. Even the berries and the mill are pressed into service as something like incense and prayer wheel. The vignette is the equivalent of a small narrative in willow pattern.

But this is what is really happening: the aristocratic residents of Hampton Court are making coffee. The 'shining Altars of *Japan*' are lacquered tables; the 'Mill' is grinding coffee beans; the 'Spirits' fuel the spirit lamp beneath the silver urn; and '*China*'s Earth' is porcelain. Pope is describing a social ritual in terms of a religious oblation because he is parodying such events in epic poetry, and the diction is correspondingly periphrastical. The eighteenth-century critic Owen Ruffhead later suggested that in such a mock-heroic context the words 'cups' and 'spoons' were too low, that is to say, too prosaic: 'They ought to have been mentioned with a periphrasis to have preserved the mock dignity of the piece.' Ruffhead's offended concern with decorum is a bit of a red herring, however. The cups and spoons are 'wrong', if they are wrong at all, because they make no contribution to the attractive false answer to Pope's riddle.

There are many examples of metaphors in poetry where the foregrounding of the substituted term can lead to momentary confusion. In such cases we get something like a wrong answer. It is quite possible, for example, for a careless reader of John Keats's 'On First Looking into Chapman's Homer' to think that it is after all merely about the discoveries of travellers, since paying attention to the title (which gives the answer to the riddle) can be the first casualty of carelessness:

Much have I travelled in the realms of gold,
   And many goodly states and kingdoms seen;
   Round many western islands have I been
Which bards in fealty to Apollo hold.
Oft of one wide expanse had I been told
   That deep-browed Homer ruled as his demesne;
   Yet did I never breathe its pure serene
Till I heard Chapman speak out loud and bold.
Then felt I like some watcher of the skies
   When a new planet swims into his ken;
Or like stout Cortez when with eagle eyes
   He stared at the Pacific, and all his men
Looked at each other with a wild surmise –
   Silent, upon a peak in Darien.

The 'wild surmise' of Cortez and his men staring at the Pacific for the first time is a specific enough emotion to require a geographical interpretation: you sail westward across the Atlantic believing that it is a more convenient way to reach the Indies (that crucial eastern source of trade) only to find that there is yet another unknown ocean to cross to get to them. The sonnet builds its drama around seafaring and the wonder of discovery, and there is (as there so often is in metaphor) a slight strain between what Keats really wants to say and the runaway demands of his chosen metaphor. The clearest interpretation seems to be that if the desired Indies represent Homer's epic poetry, and ships are used to reaching them laboriously round the Cape of Good Hope (the translations of Pope, say), then the whole adventure of a western route across the Atlantic must be Chapman's translation (a novelty to Keats, though in fact a much earlier translation) and the consequent vista of the Pacific must be the realisation that Homer's original is still hauntingly out of reach (Keats does not know

Greek). But the sonnet has already set up a riddlingly complex metaphor for his experience of poetry (including the many 'western islands' which poets hold in fealty to Apollo, evoking not only the classical tradition, but the *Odyssey* itself) so that the geography is itself a slight puzzle to the reader, rather more of a puzzle, in fact, than the more celebrated one of why Keats substitutes Cortez for Balboa (he was confused between two separate incidents in William Robertson's *History of America*).

WHO IS THE EMPEROR OF ICE-CREAM?

As we shall further see, there is almost no clear dividing line between riddles in verse (the literary 'enigma'), poems where the real subject is unstated, poems where the subject is only indicated by the title, and poems where (in the manner of the enigma's false solution) it is easy to mistake vehicle for tenor.

Wallace Stevens is a poet who liked to tease in this way. The first poem in his *Collected Poems*, 'Earthy Anecdote', is a perfect example of an enigma on the Anglo-Saxon model – a natural force fictively animated:

> Every time the bucks went clattering
> Over Oklahoma
> A firecat bristled in the way.
>
> Wherever they went,
> They went clattering,
> Until they swerved
> In a swift, circular line
> To the right,
> Because of the firecat.

Or until they swerved
In a swift, circular line
To the left,
Because of the firecat.

The bucks clattered.
The firecat went leaping,
To the right, to the left,
And
Bristled in the way.

Later, the firecat closed his bright eyes
And slept.

Stevens is writing long before Walt Disney animated fire as something conscious and wilful, but the idea is the same. The bristling
and the leaping of the flames seems designed to intercept the
stampeding deer even as they try to avoid them, and the eventual extinction of the prairie fire is described as the grateful slumber
of a sated predator. 'There's no symbolism in the "Earthy Anecdote",' Stevens wrote to an eager anthologist. 'There's a good
deal of theory about it, however; but explanations spoil things.'
When the anthologist arranged for a symbolic illustration to
accompany the poem, Stevens was put out. He had, he said,
intended actual animals, not 'original chaos'. In the light of these
objections, drawing a further conclusion about the role of his
riddling fire is perhaps beyond the mark, but the reader will note
the contrast between the indiscriminate 'clattering' and the beauty
of the symmetrical 'swerving' and he will also note an implicit
self-satisfaction in the final sleep of the personified and playful
fire. And he will surely infer a typical Stevensian analogy, that of
the creative artist.

Another of Stevens's early anecdotes is the much-anthologised 'Anecdote of the Jar'. (Stevens wrote half a dozen 'anecdotes', which were not so much the amusing biographical incidents that you might expect, but something more like fables.)

> I placed a jar in Tennessee,
> And round it was, upon a hill.
> It made the slovenly wilderness
> Surround that hill.
>
> The wilderness rose up to it,
> And sprawled around, no longer wild.
> The jar was round upon the ground
> And tall and of a port in air.
>
> It took dominion everywhere.
> The jar was gray and bare.
> It did not give of bird or bush,
> Like nothing else in Tennessee.

Here the analogy of art is more immediately striking, although the ceremonious stateliness of the jar and its ultimate sterility suggest a criticism of all man's works in the face of the profusion of nature (the jar surely feels empty rather than full of anything). It is not the place here to rehearse the extensive puzzled commentary that this poem has received, but a small reminder of the attraction of false answers in enigmas may be in order. In our possibly futile search for a true interpretation of the jar, we are bound to take more than a passing interest in the early settlers' treatment of the Tanasi ('Tennessee') Indians, or (as Roy Harvey Pearce triumphantly demonstrated) in the 'Dominion Wide Mouth Special' canning jar, provenly in use in Tennessee in the year of the poem's composition. But readings of this sort bear witness to the ingenuity of scholars rather than to the force of symbolism, and this may well be another case where, in Stevens's words, 'there's no symbolism'. A jar is always, whatever else it may import, a jar.

While we are on this domestic note, one of Stevens's most notorious puzzles comes to mind. Who is 'the Emperor of Ice-Cream'? The two-stanza poem of that title invokes the laying-out of a corpse and the summoning of mourners in a setting of particularised plainness and poverty:

> Call the roller of big cigars,
> The muscular one, and bid him whip
> In kitchen cups concupiscent curds.
> Let the wenches dawdle in such dress
> As they are used to wear, and let the boys
> Bring flowers in last month's newspapers.
> Let be be finale of seem.
> The only emperor is the emperor of ice-cream.
>
> Take from the dresser of deal,
> Lacking the three glass knobs, that sheet
> On which she embroidered fantails once
> And spread it so as to cover her face.
> If her horny feet protrude, they come
> To show how cold she is, and dumb.
> Let the lamp affix its beam.
> The only emperor is the emperor of ice-cream.

The appearances of things in this poem look very like the observations of a fastidious and fanciful writer who is for once slumming it. When selecting the poem as his favourite for another anthologist, Stevens stressed its 'deliberately commonplace costume' and wrote of it as an example of him letting himself go, although he had no memory – eleven years after its publication – of the circumstances under which it was written. But most readers of the poem are made very conscious of the celebratory realities of the poem's details and the conclusions drawn: although life may to a philosopher be a matter of appearances ('seem' in line 7), we are happy to take 'being' (be) as what finally ('finale') matters, not death. And, after all, being is always in powerful denial of death, until that moment when one can say no more.

Stevens was often pestered for clues about this poem, not least by the US Amalgamated Ice Cream Association. A professor at the University of Ceylon complained that for his own students ice-cream was a luxury, but so perhaps it is intended to be in the poem. It is, at any rate, a perfectly sufficient refreshment to provide at a poor woman's wake. Stevens claimed it as 'an absolute good' and representative of the libido that necessarily animates life. But what about that emperor?

'The Emperor of Ice-Cream' is one of Stevens's great poems of celebration, not so much in the celebration of the wake itself (a Faulkneresque scenario, with its specific and uncontrived details that perhaps suggest a brothel), but the celebration of its striking metaphysical injunction 'Let be be finale of seem' and the whole complex of contrasted and weighed values which impose upon the reader the process of so contrasting and weighing them. After all, 'Let be be finale of seem' is little more than a philosophical adage, self-sufficient in itself and unexceptionable in its implication, but in the poem's details Stevens is more generously saying that everything must happen as it must do, however limited or impoverished it may be. The girls have no smart dresses, the flowers are poorly wrapped, the funeral meats are nothing but ice-cream. But the 'concupiscent curds' are a symbol of survival, a guarantee of the generative energy that is really all we can bring to our battle with death. If, as Stevens once said, they 'express or accentuate life's destitution' this can only be because of the essential pathos implicit in the weighed values of the poem: ceremony and poverty, decoration and comfort, beauty and toil. The ice-cream is inevitably a kind of tawdry treat, yet its sufficiency in the poem's context is almost sacramental.

'The only emperor is the emperor of ice-cream' is a line, a phrase, that must be decoded into providing a context for the ice-cream as a symbol of survival, a kind of charm against death even at the very moment of the acknowledgement of death. And it comes from the moment when Hamlet has killed Claudius's councillor of state and is being quizzed by the king:

King. Now, Hamlet, where's Polonius?

Ham. At supper.

King. At supper? Where?

Ham. Not where he eats, but where 'a is eaten. A certain convocation of politic worms are e'en at him. Your worm is your only emperor for diet: we fat all creatures else to fat us, and we fat ourselves for maggots. Your fat king and your lean beggar is but variable service – two dishes, but to one table. That's the end.

King. Alas, alas.

Ham. A man may fish with the worm that hath eat of a king, and eat of the fish that hath fed of that worm.

King. What dost thou mean by this?

Ham. Nothing but to show you how a king may go a progress through the guts of a beggar.

Hamlet's food-cycle works ingeniously both ways. In one view the worm ('your only emperor for diet') is the final consumer of everything else, even of a real emperor. In the other view it may initiate an alternative upward cycle that leads not to any emperor at all, but to a beggar. This paradox allows no consolation to wealth or power. Stevens's allusion subverts Hamlet's egalitarianism by proposing another. If it is not the worm but ice-cream that is the only emperor for diet, then not only putrefaction but poverty is transcended in the preparation and consumption of it.

Ice-cream is truly democratic, being the national food of a country which has eschewed emperors. And eating it at a wake is one way of keeping the worms away, one way of asserting the life force, one way of defying diminishment. So long as it is eaten, the woman is not yet buried and the worms may not have their way with her.

MISSING THE OBVIOUS

I well remember the first time that I was fooled by the power of metaphor in a poem into thinking for a moment that the metaphor itself might be the subject. At the age of twelve at school we all copied poems into our exercise books: James Flecker's 'Old Ships', John Masefield's 'Cargoes', T. S. Eliot's 'Preludes' and one by Ralph Hodgson which begins:

> Time, you old gipsy man,
> Will you not stay,
> Put up your caravan
> Just for one day?

No, the poem is not 'about' a gipsy (as I thought at the time), though the speaker goes on to offer Romany bribes to him not to hasten away (silver bells, a golden ring, peacocks, may blossom) and these are as distracting to the reader as to the 'gipsy'. At this point, his wanderings are given a pointed symbolic extension:

> Last week in Babylon,
> Last night in Rome,
> Morning, and in the crush
> Under Paul's dome;
> Under Paul's dial
> You tighten your rein –
> Only a moment,
> And off once again;
> Off to some city
> Now blind in the womb,
> Off to another
> Ere that's in the tomb.

Of course, the poem is about the headlong passage of time and the collapse of empires. 'Time' is the very first word of the poem and Hodgson is putting his cards unequivocally on the table. But it's worth noting that the poem is an example of the kind that economically and unhelpfully use the first line as a title.

How is it that we miss the obvious? One reason is that in ordinary discourse familiar abstractions very often need concrete expression of some kind (look at that familiar metaphor in my casual phrase 'passage of time') and we become habituated to a narrow range of figurations for them. Step outside this range, and we are thrown. In the case of Hodgson's poem, the powerful appeal to a characterised physical presence is helpfully signalled by an identification from the very beginning, but I had obtusely read this as shorthand for something like '[It is] time [that you stayed] . . .' or even '[Take your] time . . .', in other words a telescoped colloquialism. A mistake, but puzzles in poetry are fuelled by such obtuseness. Hodgson is producing a considered variation on Andrew Marvell's 'wingèd chariot': we regret the passage of time not because it seems to hurtle by, but because its measurement in epochs seems so deceptively leisurely.

Would the ideal reader see immediately all that is going on in a poem? According to Mallarmé's theory (see p. 3), a good deal of pleasure would be lost if he did, because there would be no puzzling. In most cases of symbolised abstractions, where the subject is deliberately withheld, the point dawns on us at some point or other. Take Stevens's 'The Plot Against the Giant':

First Girl

When this yokel comes maundering,
Whetting his hacker,
I shall run before him,
Diffusing the civilest odors
Out of geraniums and unsmelled flowers.
It will check him.

Second Girl

I shall run before him,
Arching cloths besprinkled with colors
As small as fish-eggs.
The threads
Will abash him.

Third Girl

Oh, la . . . le pauvre!
I shall run before him,
With a curious puffing.
He will bend his ear then.
I shall whisper
Heavenly labials in a world of gutturals.
It will undo him.

With as much story as this, based on motifs from folk tales, we are close to allegory. But allegory (where Spenser's Red Cross Knight is the Anglican Church, Una is the true religion and her protecting lion is England, and so on) is usually a systematic performance with a concealed, local and tendentious argument to be decoded. Stevens's giant, like Hodgson's gipsy, is an unarguable familiarity, a constant in all human existence. His version of Death as a clumsy murderous peasant somehow to be 'checked', 'abashed' and finally 'undone' by Beauty is so brief and powerfully dramatic that we barely reflect on the outrageous claims it makes or the curiously elitist presentation of that familiar triad Nature, Art and Poetry.

This elitism, constituted of an extreme fastidiousness and refine-ment of taste ('civilest', 'unsmelled flowers', 'besprinkled with colors') and a dash of salon patronising ('le pauvre!'), doesn't seem likely to us to have any effect whatsoever on the whetted hacker of Death. Indeed, once we have solved the primary puzzle of identifying the giant, a process strictly analogous to that of a riddle, this ineffectiveness becomes the core of the secondary puzzle: what is Stevens really saying about the power of the aesthetic faculty?

We sense an irony in the Lilliputian heroism of the three girls. Take the phrase 'arching cloths besprinkled with colors'. It's an odd way to describe a painter's canvas. It's much more like the way you would describe the preparation of a cloth sprinkled with chloroform in an attempt to 'anaesthetise' the giant, a hopeless prospect given his size and the fact that she is running ahead of him. It is, in fact, knowingly hopeless: 'arching' is itself arch. There is irony, too, in the final postulated triumph, since in the human language of poetry gutturals (sounds produced in the throat) must obviously be employed as well as labials (sounds produced by the lips). The evident truth of this preference for labials has, inci-dentally, recently been concisely explained by the linguist David

Crystal: 'You're in a spaceship approaching a planet. You've been told there are two races on it, one beautiful and friendly to humans, the other unfriendly, ugly and mean-spirited. You also know that one of these groups is called the Lamonians; the other is called the Grataks. Which is which? Most people assume that the Lamonians are the nice guys. It's all a matter of sound symbolism' (*Guardian Review*, 18 July 2009).

Stevens's Giant is obviously a Gratak, but this isn't the end of the story. Just as poetry must use worldly gutturals as well as 'heavenly' labials, so our sense of the value of human life must also encompass the fact of death. Elsewhere, Stevens unequivocally attributes our sense of beauty precisely to the fact of mortality ('Death is the mother of beauty'). And the girls run before him not only because he is in murderous pursuit, but because they could not be aesthetes at all without the sense that death will inevitably catch up with them. In Stevens's philosophy the giant is not only whetting his hacker; he is whetting our transient appreciation of beauty.

DOUBLE ENTENDRES

My students would sometimes report back to me (or simply incorporate into their own essays) a fellow-lecturer's challengingly proclaimed interpretation of the opening of Tennyson's *Maud*:

I hate the dreadful hollow behind the little wood,
Its lips in the field above are dabbled with blood-red heath,
The red-ribbed ledges drip with a silent horror of blood,
And Echo there, whatever is ask'd her, answers 'Death'.

The description, they said, obviously betrayed Tennyson's phobia about menstruation. When I complained that the speaker of the poem hates the hollow because it is where his father committed suicide, and for that reason among others is already himself (as Tennyson said) 'on the road to madness', they were unimpressed by the facts of the story. It had to be about menstruation *as well*. The lecturer had told them so.

I learned to be polite about such theories, since most of them were by no means as outlandish as they might be. I was once, for example, faced with an essay that claimed that Maud herself – far from being a vigorous young beauty who could be overheard singing popular martial ballads by the cedar tree in the meadow below the hall where she lived (her 'wild voice pealing up to the sunny sky') – was nothing other than a total figment of the deranged hero's imagination.

The lecturer who titillated his young audience with extended Freudian double meanings soon moved on to Browning, whose 'The Last Ride Together', with its imagery of the world rushing by and the soul unscrolling in the wind, and its metaphors of vain military endeavours appropriate to riding 'side by side' on horseback was, it appears, not so much one of his great metaphysical lyrics of 'the instant made eternity' and of the strange experience of the perpetual in the very idea of a goal once it is envisaged – but an account of an act of sexual intercourse lightly agreed to by the woman because she will soon be rid of her lover.

In such cases, where words like 'lips', 'blood' or even 'ride' inevitably suggest carnal meanings to the carnally minded, we have nothing but another reader's arguments as a defence. Or perhaps Freud's own commonsensical (though probably apocryphal) remark to an overzealous student: 'Sometimes a cigar is just a cigar.' Did the Victorians want to suggest such things, being prevented by social decorum from writing about them directly? Did they introduce them unconsciously? Are there cases where our generally sceptical sensibilities should, after all, admit sexual scenarios and double meanings? What about the erotic attraction in Clough's '*Natura Naturans*' or the orality of Christina Rossetti's 'Goblin Market' (all that sucking of fruit)? What about the strange disgusts and compulsions in the dream landscape of Browning's '"Childe Roland to the Dark Tower Came"'?

This business of a poem meaning something *as well* has to be confronted. I have mentioned the sexual false solutions of the Old English riddles. Here is an example (my translation), where we learn that sometimes an onion is not only an onion:

> I am of general use, a wonder though
> Especially to one half of the nation
> (Women), harmless unless they prove my foe.
> Stiff in a bed's my shape and situation,
> With secret hairiness somewhere below.
>
> Now and again some pretty girl will try
> To pluck her courage up (and me), her hands
> Around my red skin, pulling my head away,
> Gripping me hard: and the encounter lands
> My pig-tailed wrestler with a brimming eye. (No. 25)

Innuendo is enriched by taboo, as anyone old enough to have seen Max Miller on stage can attest. Freedom to say what one likes spoils the point: in such conditions there can be little shock, embarrassment or delight. The point is saying it without admitting to saying it, which is something that poetry can also do. Our then finding it all a puzzle merely attests to our innocence.

A couple of poems by Elizabeth Bishop show different ways of writing about one thing in terms of another, both of them examples of the great third thing that a poet in quest of the truth about life must always have in her sights. Bishop's desire to be absolutely truthful is rooted in observation. It is the sureness of observation that allows her strange flights of fancy, presenting the sea in 'Wading at Wellfleet' as an Assyrian chariot. The chariot had knives on its wheels to cut down the warriors it advanced against. There is nothing riddling or puzzling about the analogy. It is an extended comparison, subtended from her painterly and museum eye. You wade into the sunlit sea, and it is like knives against your legs.

But this masterly aesthetic sense of hers is also challenged by other needs, of a more schematic and hypothetical kind, and her poetry at key moments does have more than an aesthetic, it has a religious or metaphysical dimension. How could it be otherwise, one reflects, bearing in mind her apprenticeship to the emblematic writers of the seventeenth century, Herbert, Crashaw, Quarles and others? Even in the midst of an apparent caprice like 'Wading at Wellfleet' she can't resist quoting Herbert's 'my thoughts are all a case of knives' in order to give a little interpretative nudge to her text: the blades on the chariot's wheels are not only like the glitter of the waves, but they have a psychological force as well. The sea becomes an emblem of the existential, the world that waits to be enacted, with all its seductive dangers. But wading is not a serious encounter with the sea, it is merely wading, and the 'war' is postponed.

The decorative charm of 'Wading at Wellfleet' is elaborated in a more specific direction in the poem immediately following it in the *Complete Poems*. 'Chemin de Fer' has a similar truth embodied within it in more obviously parabolic terms:

> Alone on the railroad track
> I walked with pounding heart.
> The ties were too close together
> or maybe too far apart.

> The scenery was impoverished:
>   scrub-pine and oak; beyond
> its mingled gray-green foliage
>   I saw the little pond
>
> where the dirty hermit lives,
>   lie like an old tear
> holding onto its injuries
>   lucidly year after year.
>
> The hermit shot off his shot-gun
>   and the tree by his cabin shook.
> Over the pond went a ripple.
>   The pet hen went chook-chook.
>
> 'Love should be put into action!'
>   screamed the old hermit.
> Across the pond an echo
>   tried and tried to confirm it.

Walking dangerously along the railway track in girlhood and wading into the dangerous sea in 'Wading at Wellfleet' are linked here. Wellfleet was Bishop's Massachusetts summer bolt-hole from Vassar, where she had friends to stay, including Margaret Miller, the greatest infatuation of her student days. The explicit sense of something not yet 'put into action' is common to both poems, something attractive yet feared. The difference is that 'Chemin de Fer' is implicitly, or riddlingly, sexual.

It offers landscape as the body, like sixteenth-century Flemish puzzle-pictures. Unlike Tennyson's little hollow, her 'little pond' is insistently genital. She sees it, with 'pounding heart', beyond the foliage of the bare landscape, and when the 'dirty hermit' who lives there 'shoots off', it ripples. The orgasmic moment seems somehow shameful, not only because the hermit is dirty, but because the peremptory stridency of its onanistic demands ('Love should be put into action!') seems to find no rational echo in the poet. Somehow it would be a gamble to import this solitary sexual pleasure into a friendship whose ties, like those of the railway, might be 'too close' or 'maybe too far apart'. The pun in the title links the railway tightrope walk with playing a card game that one can't consistently win. This might be an admonition against play, against recreational sex between friends as a kind of toy instead of the real thing, but the parable requires the sexual urge to be ironically both the regretted but inevitable recurrence of masturbation (the old tear lucidly holding on to its injuries) and its own vain cry of 'action'. The frustrated echo is an echo of *both*, the location of a frustrated solitariness.

Once we have solved what may well have seemed to some readers a stubborn puzzle, the small narrative events of the poem's parable seem to fade, like a theatrical scrim, under the spotlight thrown on to the solution behind. But they can never disappear, for they are the events that contain the subject. We shall always approach it through the story of the roaming child and the crazed hillbilly. The poem is that *as well*.

It is in the nature of the imagination to lead only to hypothesis. The tear image, by the way, recurs in Bishop's most famous poem of surrealist frustration, 'The Man-Moth'. This creature of dreams is a type of artist, exploring the Max Ernst-like moonscape and (significantly) trainscape of his poem. His tear is his only possession, 'like a bee's sting'. If you don't pay attention he will swallow it, but 'if you watch, he'll hand it over, | cool as from underground springs and pure enough to drink'. This purity is akin to virginity, that strangely vulnerable erotic weapon that, like the bee's sting, is only possessed once, and which makes

Pope's *The Rape of the Lock* a riddle-poem of epic scope. It has also, however, become a symbol of the poem, that requires attention from the reader and (as the bee image suggests) the willing yielding of the poet of her laboriously sought-for truth. Which is also like the generosity of love put into action.

FINGERS IN THE SANDCASTLE

As with Bishop's risky autoerotic game, the riddling poem more often conceals a sexual subject than flaunts it. But once the reader is on the track of the answer it seems clearer and clearer that it means to be found out. Suppose that a twentieth-century poet – intellectually resourceful but physically reticent – wants to write a poem about frustrated foreplay and build into it arguments in favour of the real thing. His mind will be full of his reading, and if he admires John Donne the poem will reflect the earlier poet's manner of robust address and strange inclusivity. The poem will be something like William Empson's bewildering 'The Scales', written in 1929:

> The proper scale would pat you on the head
> But Alice showed her pup Ulysses' bough
> Well from behind a thistle, wise with dread;
>
> And though your gulf-sprung mountains I allow
> (Snow-puppy curves, rose-solemn dado band)
> Charming for nurse, I am not nurse just now.
>
> Why pat or stride them, when the train will land
> Me high, through climbing tunnels, at your side,
> And careful fingers meet through castle sand.

Claim slyly rather that the tunnels hide
Solomon's gems, white vistas, preserved kings,
By jackal sandhole to your air flung wide.

Say (she suspects) to sea Nile only brings
Delta and indecision, who instead
Far back up country does enormous things.

The poem's argument ('But . . .'; 'And though . . .'; 'Why . . .';
'. . . rather . . .') will strike the reader as something of a front,
since what this rhetorical glue appears to connect actually sits
rather oddly together. It is not my place here to unravel all the
obscurities of the poem, which, like others of its decade, was felt
to require notes provided by the poet himself (in the volume in
which it appeared there were ten pages of notes to 34 pages of
text, a proportion comparable to that in *The Waste Land*). The
literary and geographical distractions of the poem (Lewis Carroll,
Homer, Rider Haggard, the source of the Nile) provide analogy
and illustration, but at the core of the puzzle is the simple question of what it is that they are illustrating.

'The Scales' might be thought to be 'about' its title (what else
are titles for?), but the title itself seems to be only a way of
isolating and then generalising what in the poem alludes insistently to the disproportion between the unthreateningly small
grown suddenly surprisingly large. After all, how many 'scales'
can there be of this kind? In the plural they might turn into a
different kind of alternative, one of comparison and judgement.
But the basic disproportion is sexual.

A sandcastle is usually some sort of model of a mountain, and
a mountain can be like a breast (and up close a breast can be
like a mountain: Empson claims that only a baby should really
be that close, patting it as it feeds). But you make tunnels in a

sandcastle as fingers make sexual investigations, and when careful fingers meet they are like the sensitive attention to varieties of female pleasure that Empson was daringly to refer to at the time of the controversy about *Lady Chatterley's Lover*: 'she can get pleasure from the inside of the whole ring of bone through which a child is born; the chief cause of her birth-pangs is also one of her deepest areas of satisfaction. To awaken her all round in this way is not a sordid ambition, and the hands may well be working on it while the normal act is in progress' (Empson in *Essays in Criticism*, xiii, 1963, p. 103). The man is seen as always wanting to explore.

The bough that hid Ulysses's manhood from Nausicaa is gifted to Carroll's Alice to ward off the puppy that suddenly seemed so enormous when she had eaten the mushroom that made her tiny. If this puppy becomes in Empson's plan a kind of eager penis, it seems entirely justified that there should be something both comical in its wooing effrontery ('An enormous puppy was looking down at her . . . and feebly stretching out one paw, trying to touch her') and yet exciting enough to give the woman confused feelings (Alice is 'terribly frightened' as she keeps it at bay with the twig like a bullfighter, but afterwards reflects: 'And yet what a dear little puppy it was!'). There is a telling condescension about such a decisive way of evading sexual feelings, and Empson's summary ('wise with dread') conveys such dismissiveness beautifully. Alice's wisdom throughout her adventures depends upon quizzical practicality. It is a form of defensiveness. The woman is seen as always wanting to retreat.

Both the man and the woman, then, are performing their customary roles, by turns tentative, reductive, prissy and devious. Empson seems to be even-handed in his criticism of this level of experimental foreplay not far developed from childish curiosity, but the poem concludes magnificently with allusions to the neural mysteries of the sexual relation. 'Delta' is classically the female genitals (mathematically, the area of a triangle) where the man might have no real idea what to do ('indecision') and yet the force of female sexuality almost necessarily produces the idea of the origin of a mighty river seeking its end in the sea and creating a life-giving fertility in the process. The long-unknown source of the Nile gives Empson back his heroic role as a sexual explorer, in contrast to the initial Homeric comedy of teasing concealment and condescension.

There is now some sort of conspiracy between the pair ('she suspects') to agree to this new scale in mapping their relationship. There is the demeaning scale of patting (close to 'petting', where the substitute can be a kind of put-down) and on the other hand the enlarging scale of deeper biological needs. Both might well be excuses for reserve, given Empson's celebrated anxiety about the presumptuousness of wooing ('boy being afraid of girl').

To write about all this in 1929 is daring enough (Lawrence again comes to mind), but the habit of puzzling in Empson gives him a form of cover which poetry had long had, though not in so extreme a form. 'The fashion for obscure poetry, as a recent development,' he blandly remarked in his 'Note on Notes' to his volume *The Gathering Storm*, 'came in at about the same time as the fashion for crossword puzzles; and it seems to me that this revival of puzzle interest in poetry, an old and natural thing, has got a bad name merely by failing to know itself and refusing to publish the answers.' Today the practice of the poet supplying his own notes has, probably rightly, been on the whole quietly dropped. For one thing, where would you stop? For another, it so much looks like a confession of indecision or, as Marianne Moore bluntly put it, 'evidence of an insufficiently realised task'.

The reader of Empson's poem who is struggling with difficulty may quite soon solve its primary sexual puzzles, but may be left with incidental obscurities that can impede the natural flow of interpretative reading. The obvious examples of these in 'The Scales' are 'gulf-sprung', 'snow-puppy' and 'rose-solemn' in the second stanza, where the number of extemporised, hyphenated epithets suggests an imagination beginning to take brisk shortcuts. These tiny momentary puzzles do feed into the larger argument, of course, but they seem to overload it, or to be insufficiently absorbed into the verse lines. We find ourselves almost inclined not fully to bother with them. Yes, the breast is a channel for milk and a freshly nubile girl may have puppy fat; but though the colour of the nipple's aureole may be rose it isn't quite clear that an aureole could be described as a dado, or why rose should be solemn (though a manuscript note of Empson's suggests that it is the mountains that are seen as pink). A critic's professional reading will have to give an account of them, but the reader will tend to take them on trust.

WHAT HAPPENS TO THE BALL TURRET GUNNER?

Sometimes in a riddling poem the puzzle consists not in identifying the subject, but in discovering what exactly is going on in the metaphorical subtext. There is no question of confusing the vehicle of the metaphor with its tenor, and no doubt at all as to what the poem is actually about. The puzzle arises because the reader knows that something else is going on, but hasn't been quite able to put his finger on it.

It happens that a great deal of metaphor is elusive in this way, and it is tantalisingly true that much of language itself is metaphorical without being fully recognised as such. I have already dealt with some aspects of dead, secret or submerged metaphor in the case of Pope in the previous chapter, but here I want to focus on an example of hidden metaphor that helps to shock the reader without making itself quite clear.

Randall Jarrell's most anthologised poem is perhaps appropriately 'The Death of the Ball Turret Gunner'. Appropriately,
because he is the best of the American poets of the Second World
War, though unlike most of his British counterparts he is not
merely a poet of war. And, appropriately, also because the poem
is more than a war poem: brief as it is, a mere five lines, it
becomes what most good war poems become. It becomes a political poem:

> From my mother's sleep I fell into the State,
> And I hunched in its belly till my wet fur froze.
> Six miles from earth, loosed from its dream of life,
> I woke to black flak and the nightmare fighters.
> When I died they washed me out of the turret with a hose.

The poem moves to its grisly end so quickly that the reader can
lose track of the subtext. When Jarrell supplied the technical facts
behind the fate of the gunner, he also felt obliged to underline
this subtext, as though the reader might need some help with the
machinery of metaphor as well as with the machinery of warfare.
Although Jarrell's note was a response to the poem's unusual
popularity – rather than a note in the Eliot or Empson mould –
it is worth seeing it as evidence of the modern poet's nervous-
ness about his complex effects. It is far from being mock-scholarly,
and far from the sometimes drily triumphant tone that attaches
itself to the Empsonian business of jotting down material that
never quite made it into the poem itself. However, it does remind
us that Jarrell was also a university teacher as well as a critic, and
that his desire to enlighten readers was genuine. Indeed, he is (as
are many poets when introducing their work at poetry readings)
quite prepared to give the game away. He wrote: 'A ball turret
was a plexiglass sphere set into the belly of a B-17 or B-24, and

inhabited by two .50 caliber machine guns and one man, a short, small man. When this gunner tracked with his machine guns a fighter attacking his bomber from below, he revolved with the turret; hunched upside-down in his little sphere, he looked like the foetus in the womb. The fighters which attacked him were armed with cannon firing explosive shells. The hose was a steam hose.'

The poem itself, while in its own way conveying the gist of these documentary facts, is a paradigm of the awakening from political innocence that all citizens must in some sense undergo. The poem nudges us into accepting its singularity as really also a generalisation about what all such awakenings might at one extreme involve.

The crucial transference is multiple and irrevocable. It takes the gunner not only from sleep to awakening, but from Nature into Society. It takes him not only from his own sleep into a consciousness of his political obligations, but from 'his mother's sleep', a condition in which he is inseparable from her. It there-fore takes him from a female world of passivity into a male world of action.

This movement is also conveyed with deliberate paradox. The 'fall' into the State is lapsarian, as from the Eden of the womb into the guilt of male institutions, and yet it is embodied as a *further* foetal condition, icy and constricting where the mother's natural womb was sleep-inducing. The political 'State' is repre-sented by the bomber, which we know is really a machine but which becomes in its role as a surrogate womb something monstrous in an organic sense.

Jarrell's poetry is full of such paradoxes. In 'Siegfried', the gunner is both innocent and guilty. In that poem the dreamlike 'leather and fur and wire' represents the gunner's helmet, but are also part of his strange organic metamorphosis within the womb of the bomber. In 'The Death of the Ball Turret Gunner', the gunner is 'hunched' in the bomber's 'belly' with frozen 'fur', so that after his natural birth he is ready to be born again as a beast. Moreover, the bomber represents a 'dream of life' because its mission is intended to be liberating and life-affirming, even though its means are necessarily destructive. The gunner, dreamless in the womb, has been given this dream of life as a specific instance of the idealism which institutions are designed to teach citizens. A further paradox is that he wakes from this dream to a nightmare which reminds him that he is, after all, merely mortal. He is neither machine nor beast, nor capable in this instance of preserving the institutional ideal.

The solution to the puzzle of the metaphorical subtext is now unfolding, and we knew it all along. The final image is, of course, of the one kind of birth absolutely appropriate to a beast or a machine, i.e., an unnatural birth: 'When I died they washed me out of the turret with a hose.' This is both a final paradox (the second metaphorical birth turns into a death) and a symbol of the way in which war is the absolute and extreme violation of Nature by Society, and a form of moral sleepwalking. The cannon of the nightmare fighters more or less perform dilation and curettage, and then the job is completed by the steam hose: the gunner is aborted.

WHAT IS THE SPHINX?

Not the oldest, but perhaps the most celebrated riddle in literature, is the one proposed by the Sphinx to passers-by at Thebes: 'What walks in the morning on four legs, at noon on two, and in the evening on three?' The Sphinx was herself a challenging hybrid, with the head and breasts of a woman, the body of a lion, an eagle's wings and a tail with the head of a serpent. It was no wonder that travellers became confused: was the question perhaps something to do with this intimidating creature herself? Were they self-possessed enough to count the legs? They failed to answer the riddle and were appropriately strangled ('sphinx' is from σφιγγειυ, 'to draw tight') and then eaten.

Why is it that human development and aging seem such a puzzle? The riddle does not seem difficult to us, certainly no harder than the supplementary one sometimes supposed to have been asked by the Sphinx: 'There are two sisters; one gives birth to the other, and the second then gives birth to the first.' This one, like the Elizabethan rhetorician George Puttenham's single example of the enigma ('It is my mother well I wot, | And yet the daughter that I begot'), is merely an example of the apparent mysteries of physical matter. We take delight in the passage of night into day, or of ice into water, and it becomes our pleasure to remind ourselves through riddles of unnatural birth that such, after all, perfectly natural occurrences are at heart matters of wonder.

The central riddle of the Sphinx is, however, a matter of pain rather than of wonder. Because it was solved by Oedipus, in blithe ignorance of his own future fate, the generalised answer ('mankind') is sometimes taken as a kind of prophecy of his own self-blinding, when the oracular prediction that he will kill his father and marry his mother is fulfilled and he finally realises it. This is doubly satisfying. It tells us – as the earliest riddles do – that our would-be control of the world is, in fact, imperfect, and it embodies this dismaying discovery – as many riddles also do – in an alienating myth of incest. Moreover, Oedipus is made king of Thebes precisely because it is he who has defeated the Sphinx. A king may well be a king if he appears in this way to have profound knowledge of human nature, but a true philosopher knows only that he knows nothing. The tragic destiny of Oedipus in Sophocles is intimately bound up with a cruel teasing through ignorance and discovery, and it leads to suffering.

And yet there remains a puzzle about the Sphinx's riddle that has haunted poets ever since. The answer to the riddle was not in fact 'Oedipus', however dramatically satisfying that might have been, since her question was put to all travellers, and the answer concerns us all. It is an answer that involves the generation after generation who will inevitably crawl in babyhood and end life with the support of a stick. The riddle is, therefore, in a sense about the apparent futility of having children, who themselves will merely repeat this process. It is a riddle, then, not so much about mankind as about the cycle of generation and mortality.

The knowledge of this process is represented in the myth of the Sphinx as a secret guarded by a monstrous version of the female. And well it might be, if we presume a male fascination with sexuality (awed as well as repulsed) as the only means of seeking some sort of eternal life. Monstrousness is the sign of our animality. It is unwelcome to a creature of high ideals, but is the only guarantee of the organic perpetuity that is our frail substitute for eternity.

Something like this sense of delusion is conveyed by Jorge Luis Borges's sonnet 'Oedipus and the Riddle', when 'inconstant' man faces the unchanging Sphinx as in a mirror, as if to decode his true nature, the 'falling off' that is his destiny:

> It would annihilate us if we saw
> The enormity of what we are; God's law
> Allows us succession and forgetfulness. [my translation]

There is a further puzzle in many poems about the Sphinx which make her not so much the challenging poser of questions, but a strange symbol of whom herself questions might be asked. Ralph

Waldo Emerson's drowsy Sphinx metamorphoses into the whole of Nature ('Who telleth one of my meanings | Is master of all I am'). Carl Sandburg's silent Sphinx has refused entire processions of questioners, suggesting that they know the answers already. Oscar Wilde's Sphinx suffers a torrent of interrogations of her exotic and sensual past, only to be finally dismissed as a 'loathsome mystery'. What such poems (published between 1841 and 1916) characteristically share is a sense that we do not need supernatural sources of wisdom at all: even though we are still haunted by oracles, we should be able to find the answers elsewhere. Their authors presided, then, over a dawning ambivalence about these mysteries, but they were also (following the Regency craze for all things Egyptian) more familiar with the Sphinx of Gizeh than with the Sphinx of Thebes. Wilde's cavalcade of names and rhymes culminates with Ammon as the Sphinx's still-living divine lover, whom she is encouraged to rejoin ('Back to your Nile!'). Ammon was, confusingly, the local deity of not the Grecian but the Egyptian Thebes, a town on the east bank of the Nile, near the present Karnak.

Poets in the last century tended to be openly ambiguous or cheerfully inclusive about which Sphinx they might have had in mind. Empson's poem 'Four Legs, Two Legs, Three Legs' of 1935 spends eight lines weaving ideas about the conceptual triangulation of the point at which Oedipus killed his father, but then changes gear abruptly to Gizeh ('The wrecked girl, still raddled with Napoleon's paint, | Nose eaten by a less clear conqueror, | Still orientated to the average dawn, | Behind, Sahara, before, Nile. . .') as though this time-worn guardian of a Pyramid could be equated with the self-destructed riddler of Thebes.

Perhaps in Empson's mind she could. All he ever said about this was: 'Of course the Egyptian sphinx has nothing to do with the mysterious demigod who put the question to Oedipus. But I don't know, why should you not say that this sphinx is still there?'

In the poem itself, however, there is the ghost of an argument: Napoleon, though not yet acclaimed Emperor as Oedipus was acclaimed King of Thebes, was just as capable of 'wrecking' the Sphinx's quizzical aplomb by firing his cannon at her nose as Oedipus had been by guessing the riddle. However, in proper secular spirit Empson suggests that the erosion of the nose could have been accomplished by time alone, and time that brings bodily decay over a man's lifetime is, as we already know, a crucial constituent of the answer to the riddle.

But I want finally to focus on a Sphinx poem that was written three years later than Empson's, W. H. Auden's 'The Sphinx'. Here it is as it was first published in *Journey to a War* (1939), the travel book about the Sino-Japanese War written with Christopher Isherwood:

Did it once issue from the carver's hand
Healthy? Even the earliest conquerors saw
The face of a sick ape, a bandaged paw,
A Presence in the hot invaded land.

The lion of a tortured stubborn star,
It does not like the young, nor love, nor learning:
Time hurt it like a person; it lies, turning
A vast behind on shrill America,

And witnesses. The huge hurt face accuses,
And pardons nothing, least of all success.
The answers that it utters have no uses

To those who face akimbo its distress:
'Do people like me?' No. The slave amuses
The lion: 'Am I to suffer always?' Yes.

It will be immediately clear that much of what might be puzzling here can be explained by the way in which earlier poems have confused the two Sphinxes. As in the examples given above, Auden's Sphinx encourages questions rather than asking them. But this would not in itself mean that Auden did not have Oedipus somewhere in mind, even though the poem is a response to a specific geographical opportunity.

Auden and Isherwood were en route to China when their ship docked at Port Said on 25 January 1938 and Francis Turville-Petre drove them to Cairo. Not yet clear about what his contribution to *Journey to a War* was going to be, Auden made use of the arresting, observant, conversational free verse of D. H. Lawrence to get down his feelings about Egypt as the uncomprehending cradle of Western culture, and about the Sphinx itself as a symbol of that ancient and alien self-sufficiency. The result was a kind of provisional travelogue, an eighty-one-line exercise in cultural fastidiousness about a 'land of inertia and death'.

Seeing Egypt, Auden would have been naturally reminded of the theories of G. Elliott Smith and W. J. Perry, who had argued for its being the origin of all archaic civilisations. Auden had used Perry in the poem 'O Love, the interest itself in thoughtless heaven' in 1932 (see p. 136) and was still using his ideas when writing about Spain and China in 1937–8. The contrast between Egypt's history and its present reality led him to revisit Perry's theory in terms of a cartoon view of contemporary materialism, where the country is 'like an anarchical Woolworth's' looking balefully towards brash America, 'denying Progress'.

Auden claimed that every good poet should be more than a bit of a reporting journalist, but he forgot to notice the orientation of the Sphinx. A fellow-passenger on the boat told him that it faces west, prophesying the importance of the New World. It actually faces east. When Auden came to distil his eighty-one line poem into a sonnet for *Journey to a War*, he consulted someone at the Egyptian Embassy in London and corrected the mistake.

This distillation is an instructive example of poetic concentration: virtually five-sixths of the poem disappears, with many perfectly good ideas ruthlessly discarded (the suburban setting of the Egyptian monuments, the Sphinx's refusal to believe in 'progress', a potted history of the imperialist nations, and so on). It is the difference between a journalistic poem and a philosophical one.

The residual puzzle of the sonnet that Auden ends up with can be fairly said to arise from these somewhat thwarted expectations of the ordinary reader of a travel book (and similar puzzles throng the final sonnet sequence of the book, 'In Time of War'). The key phrases that feed the first ten lines of the sonnet had been lovingly elaborated in the longer poem, and they benefit in the shorter one from being themselves, as it were, carved to the bone. The one really new idea in the sonnet is the summary symbol of the oracular dialogue in the sestet: 'The slave amuses | The lion.' Most readers will think of Androcles and the lion, perhaps even of Shaw's play where in the Roman arena the lion recognises the Christian slave who had pulled the thorn from his paw and happily waltzes with him into the terrified presence of the Emperor and his gladiators ('ANDROCLES: [*naïvely*] Now I wonder why they all run away from us like that. [*The lion, combining a series of yawns, purrs and roars, achieves something very like a laugh*]').

Androcles as a lucky innocent would have appealed to Auden (something of the whole donnée of Shaw's pantomime gets into his and Isherwood's own play *The Dog Beneath the Skin*, whose hero was based on Francis Turville-Petre). But the questions asked of the Sphinx are hardly those asked by an Androcles. In the first drafts for the sonnet, the sestet launches a contrast between the

Sphinx (who is silent) and 'the beautiful', who 'always answers' by accusing. There is something here of Hölderlin's lines in his poem '*Sokrates und Alcibiades*' about the wise being susceptible to the beautiful, which Auden often quoted at the time. But this was clearly too complex an idea for the rapidly foreshortening opportunities of the sestet. We might think that a beautiful slave would have something to do with Wilde's 'rare | Young slave with his pomegranate mouth', whom his sensualist Sphinx toys with (there is a suggestion in Auden's long draft that the 'sickness' of his own Sphinx is syphilitic), but though the sestet is casting about for associations like these, the answer to the puzzle is more direct and personal.

It makes the most sense to see the final Ouija-board-like dialogue as an interrogation by the poet of his own destiny, and as a condemnation of the writer's pride. He is not an Oedipus, but he does bring all his thirty-one-year-old hopes to this encounter with an ancient Presence who 'does not like the young, nor love, nor learning'. In the long draft Auden stresses the circumstances of his personal confrontation with the Sphinx (he is tired and bored and cross), though he does not go on to write about what questions he might himself have asked it. At this time, Auden was beginning to hate his 'success' and to feel unloved. On the China trip itself, for example, he wept, telling Isherwood that no one would ever love him and that he would never have Isherwood's sexual success. Such feelings would recur throughout his life, and sometimes in more paranoid vocational contexts.

So Auden is asking these questions of himself. In terms of the Jungian division of the psyche that he had come to use, the 'amusement' of the Sphinx is due to the superior knowledge of the Thinking-Intuitive faculties, since in the situation of being unloved it is the Feeling-Sensation faculties who will primarily 'suffer'. The slave amuses the lion, therefore, in much the same symbolic way that Rosetta and Emble 'amuse' Malin and Quant in his psychodrama *The Age of Anxiety*. This is even further from the Theban scenario, but the suggestion is of a gauche defiance in the word 'akimbo' (hands on hips, elbows thrust out) that is the property of all ignorant heroes who issue challenges, and who hope for and perhaps only barely miss the charmed life. Auden knew too much about Freud to think of Oedipus's victory over the Sphinx as anything but pyrrhic. Indeed, as we have seen, Oedipus does not really understand his own answer to the riddle.

If Auden's 'The Sphinx' is itself a kind of riddle, then the answer is in some sense that the Sphinx is the poet himself. The Sphinx is his self-knowledge that tells him that he is not liked and will always suffer. It is Auden who was 'hurt'. It was even Auden who had a vast behind (see 'Letter to Lord Byron', IV. 9). And it was Auden, after all, who eventually reached 'shrill America' by continuing eastwards after his visit to China, though not without hope.

4

'I CAUGHT A TREMENDOUS FISH': SHOULD WE TRUST THE POET?

CLUES: BISHOP'S FISH

Poets can sometimes tell us things about their poems which not only have the air of being helpful, but seem specifically designed to corroborate the truth of what a poem proposes or to explain the circumstances of its writing. Can we trust poets any more than we can their critics?

Perhaps not. When Samuel Taylor Coleridge wrote to William Sotheby on 19 July 1802 that he had been writing a poem to Wordsworth in a period of dejection ('O Wordsworth! We receive but what we give, | And in our Life alone does Nature live,' etc.) he was concealing the fact that the poem was actually written to Sara Hutchinson and in its fullest version is a good deal about the difficulties of their secret relationship. When he came to publish a version of the poem in the *Morning Post* in October, it was addressed to a fictitious 'Edmund'. It was not until 1814 that Sara's gender was acknowledged by his changing the addressee to 'Lady'. But this slightly panicky labelling is the opposite of a clue. It is a smokescreen wafted across the defences of a personal poem, and as such is understandable and common. We really only notice the puzzles in 'Dejection: an Ode' when we compare it with the original manuscript letter to 'Asra'. The philosophical arguments of the truncated version are basically unaffected.

For reasons of this kind we learn to be wary of possibly disingenuous commentary from the poet, but are still nonetheless right to be alert for objective clues that might pass us by. Take Elizabeth Bishop's celebrated poem 'The Fish'. What is the reason for its particular power? Readers feel its dramatic claims on their feelings, but can be puzzled by what sort of feelings these are. It appeared among many fanciful parables in her first collection *North and South*, where its lively specificity suggested that her quest for truth also required negotiations with the actual, and that it is from real experiences that she derives the images that validate their recounting.

'I caught a tremendous fish,' the poem begins, without preparation, almost as though in a dream, but soon to be supported by the vivid documentary details, the authenticity of the thing seen. The fish's brown skin hangs in strips like ancient wallpaper, for example. It is infested with tiny white sea-lice. Its eyes are larger than the poet's, but shallower and yellowed, 'the irises backed and packed | with tarnished tinfoil'. And from its lower lip hang

> . . . five old pieces of fish-line,
> or four and a wire leader
> with the swivel still attached,
> with all their five big hooks
> grown firmly in his mouth.

These hooks are later seen as like 'medals with their ribbons | frayed and wavering, | a five-haired beard of wisdom | trailing from his aching jaw'. The fish is fully imagined, but challengingly actual. The victory of having caught such a veteran is total, but (famously, and pointedly) the poem concludes with the poet letting it go. Victory is described as a kind of transcendence:

> I stared and stared
> and victory filled up
> the little rented boat,
> from the pool of bilge
> where oil had spread a rainbow
> around the rusted engine
> to the bailer rusted orange,
> the sun-cracked thwarts,
> the oarlocks on their strings,
> the gunnels – until everything
> was rainbow, rainbow, rainbow!
> And I let the fish go.

A poet who can fish, and likes to introduce the jargon of fishing, is not so common. Those 'sun-cracked thwarts', as utterly and mysteriously convincing as T. S. Eliot's 'garboard strake' in 'Marina', allow us to believe what otherwise might seem very like a fisherman's tall tale. An interview supplied corroboration: the seed of the poem was the catching of a 60 lb amberjack, and further crucial details belong to the catching of a Caribbean jewfish on a later occasion. Bishop responded enthusiastically to her eager interviewer with something of the fisherman's complex awareness of persuasion and exaggeration: 'With "The Fish", that's *exactly* how it happened,' she said. But then she added, 'Oh, but I did change *one* thing; the poem says he had five hooks hanging from his mouth, but actually he only had three. Sometimes a poem makes its own demands.'

'Actually he only had three' is not necessarily an odd thing to say about a detail in a poem. Whether her poetic fish is an amberjack or a jewfish or indeed any other fish that Bishop had ever encountered is immaterial. The fish in the poem is described and fully realised, but it is not named. All she means is that she never actually saw a fish with *five* hooks in its mouth, and that this is something of significance to an interviewer. The poem needed five hooks. She was giving an interpretative clue. She was saying that the telling details are, in fact, telling *something.*

If we have never been able fully to explain the power of 'The Fish', we may suspect that there is a puzzle here. The following poem in Bishop's *Complete Poems* may help to explain what this is. 'Late Air' is a strange little piece that contrasts the charismatic love songs being broadcast on a late-night radio show (which their listeners lying in erotic receptivity on 'dew-wet lawns' interpret in whatever way suits them) with a better symbol for love that the poet finds on the Navy Yard aerial:

> Five remote red lights
>   keep their nests there; Phoenixes
> burning quietly, where the dew cannot climb.

The parallel with 'The Fish' is a dual one: the symbolism of five, standing for the five wounds of Christ, is in each case matched with a conventional Christian symbol for Christ himself. In 'Late Air' it is the Phoenix, the mythical creature that resurrects itself, while in the first poem it is the Fish, associated with Christ because ἰχθύς ('fish') was an acronym for 'Jesus Christ, Son of God, Saviour', in Greek.

In the myth behind the Crucifixion, which the symbolism of the five hooks alludes to, Christ to be found must first be lost. The Messiah is not recognised. He is even betrayed by one of his disciples (the subject of Bishop's major poem 'Roosters'). In Eliot's 'Marina', for example, the Christian losing and finding is symbolised by the Shakespearean story of *Pericles*, which provides the sea setting which the practised sailor in Eliot so eagerly responded to. That phrase 'The garboard strake leaks' tells us something about the human condition, just as Bishop's similar details remind us that a transcendental iridescence can only issue from a working fishing boat, a shabby little boat that has been rented just as our bodies are rented for the duration of their earthly span. And that iridescence is exhilarating by virtue of the fact that it mysteriously takes the form of a responsive sign from God, the Ark of the Covenant, repeated three times from the rust and oily bilge of the boat: 'rainbow, rainbow, rainbow!' The spirit of the poem is that the mere catching of the fish is enough. It is a 'victory' that has to be graciously yielded.

Bishop's clue leads us to what the poem is up to ('Sometimes a poem makes its own demands'), so that it is worth our paying attention. To believe the poem we are compelled to disbelieve a circumstantial source, and we only come to disbelieve it by believing something else that the poet says, outside the poem. And if we learn from all this that it hardly matters that there were three hooks originally, or that the poet might have made the whole thing up, we accept, because we have to accept the demands of the poem.

Do we feel that she is being a trifle oversensitive about this Christian meaning? A sceptical reader might ask why she does not spell out the religious significance as, say, Gerard Manley Hopkins does in the somewhat related 'The Windhover', where the falcon's scrupulously delineated identity becomes metaphorically indistinguishable from the Christ who seizes souls? One answer might be that she has rediscovered the true baroque by reading Herbert and Crashaw, where the spiritual implications of the everyday are much more matter-of-fact than in the highly orchestrated Hopkins.

DREAMS: DO WE BELIEVE THE POET?

Believing that Hopkins and Bishop are seized in their poems by a revelatory incarnation (or, one might say, mysteriously 'caught' by the creatures they themselves 'catch') is a matter of circumstance and conclusion. As in a case at law, it is all in the evidence. The evidence may be cooked (and the poem a fiction), but it is the verdict that matters. A poem may in this way convince us that a force observed in nature is for these poets a manifestation or at least a symbol of an embodied deity. It is as though our belief in the momentary revelation gives witness to the poet's own belief.

This still doesn't leave us fully prepared for larger leaps of belief, particularly in the case of poems that require not only this kind of suspended assent but also a form of underlying faith as well. It particularly applies to visionary poetry.

One of the greatest puzzles in poetry is where the poem comes from. Where, indeed, do the words of poems come from? Can they ever come from outside the poet, from beyond his own volition? Poets have claimed so, and they have been believed. This is certainly a puzzle.

I said in the case of Bishop's fish that it hardly matters if the poet 'made the whole thing up', and surely most readers will understand poetry to be 'made up' in some sense. The Greek word ποίησις itself means 'something made'. But we know that there is a class of poetry that purports to be 'given', to arrive, even in its verbal details, from somewhere outside the poet's mind, in a dream or vision, perhaps.

Books have been written about one of the most celebrated of

these, Coleridge's startling 'Kubla Khan', which he claimed to
have written straight out after a laudanum reverie, until interrupted by a visitor. There is a consensus of opinion which classes
this poem not as a mysterious gift, but as an aggregate of material that he was already to some extent at work upon, but the
jury is out on the degree to which the unconscious mind can actually compose meaningful verse. Poets may, of course, wake up
possessed of a text. Long before Coleridge and his theories of
the subconscious, the Augustan poet William King was sensibly
interested in the subject:

> The flitting Dreams, that play before the wind,
> Are not by Heav'n for prophecies design'd;
> Nor by ethereal beings sent us down,
> But each man is creator of his *own;*
> For when their weary limbs are sunk in ease,
> The souls essay to wander where they please,
> The scatter'd images have space to play,
> And night repeats the labors of the day.

So much, one might conclude, for epic invocations or the revelation of hitherto unknown truths. The poet finds himself, after
all, on his own. The trouble is that the unalert mind is as likely
to come up with trivialities as with a vision of Xanadu. King's
own example, which follows the unexceptionable theory that I
have just quoted, is 'I Waked Speaking these out of a Dream in
the Morning':

> Nature, a thousand ways complains,
> A thousand words express her pains,
> But, for her laughter, has but three,
> And very small ones, Ha! Ha! He! –

Even this seems rather too neatly organised to have been composed in a state of unconsciousness. But I believe him. I believe him because I have myself woken with verse in my head. Once, for example, I dreamed that I was reading out and explicating a passage of about eight tetrameter couplets. I had the illusion that the text was perfectly there (I was reading it from the page), but seconds after waking could remember no more than the following:

> You think there's no distinction
> As scarlet runs to hoary,
> Forgetting the important theory:
> A sergeant stands between.

Apart from the fact that this is nonsense, it is also not in tetrameter couplets. Everything is wrong with composition unattended by the active intellect. I bring it up simply to show why I believe William King (trusting, too, that you will believe me), and why therefore I am inclined to believe William Hazlitt when he said that 'Kubla Khan' only showed that Coleridge could write better nonsense verses than any man in England. A great poet's nonsense is superior to yours or mine, but he must still examine it carefully to see if it is worth reading.

The process of bringing a dream into words is necessarily reductive, as Coleridge well understood when he described 'the full sharp distinction of Mind from Consciousness – the Consciousness being the narrow *Neck* of the Bottle'. His own dreams were rich and suggestive, all promising subjects for analysis, one would have thought: Duns Scotus making love with the daughter of the King of Truth; Adam murdered by the descendants of Cain; Sir Philip Sidney's wife talking to her maid; a shipwrecked mariner on a deserted island making huge stores of goosequill pens; the dispossessed orphans of a nobleman begging in the streets. But his best-attested example of actually dreaming words is no less trivial than King's:

> Here sleeps at length poor Col., and without screaming,
> Who died, as he had always liv'd, a-dreaming:
> Shot dead, while sleeping, by the Gout within,
> Alone, and all unknown, at E'nbro' in an Inn.

There is a famous intermediate stage between dreamed poems and consciously composed poems that attempts (in terms of Coleridge's above analogy) to get at the contents of the bottle without pouring. Described in this way, automatic writing as cultivated by Mrs Yeats or by Tristan Tzara, Paul Éluard and other surrealists seems as doomed to the reader's disbelief as poetry composed in dreams: the narrow neck of the bottle must, we feel, play its part in channelling the liquid, unless the poet is somehow to be satisfied with semi-spontaneous access to the indiscriminate linguistic garbage of the unconscious mind. There have, by the way, been several later minor schools of poetry (and even some relatively high-profile poets) that have shown little fastidiousness about relying on such access. Their work is ostentatiously unreadable, and offers little pleasure in the decoding of puzzles of the kind that I am concerned with.

A glimpse of one's own subconscious should be different from a vision supplied from elsewhere. I take mediaeval dream-poetry to employ a useful convention that the reader agrees to subscribe to: we do not actually believe that Dante had a vision of Paradise. Yeats, however, really believed that the Communicators (as transcribed by his wife George) had, as they said, 'come to give him metaphors for poetry'. Beliefs are sometimes a necessary preliminary to the making of poetry, and they can be systematised (as Yeats's were systematised in *A Vision*), but for Yeats's readers they issued in poems, not in anything that had itself to be believed in. Mrs Yeats produced more than 3,600 pages of automatic writing in 450 sittings between 1917 and 1920, delighting Yeats and cementing their precarious marriage. It is fair to say that this problematic source of the later Yeats's finest poetry is largely ignored by most readers. The visionary 'source' has been squirrelled away.

But I would like to turn now to one of the most bizarre poetic puzzles of recent years, where the mechanism of the supposed supernatural origin of the poetic text is unignorable: the poetry of the Ouija board.

HOW MAY WE KNOW TRUTH? OUIJA POEMS

Here is an American poem called 'On Truth', written a year after the publication of *The Waste Land*, though very much in a commonplace style which the impact of Eliot helped to outdate:

> How may I know truth? Oh my beloved,
> I would answer thee. Truth is companionable,
> She is never a lady who sighs and languishes—
> Never a knight vainglorious. Truth is
> A simple maid whose tongue is unalloyed.
>
> He who bends his ear confidently
> And listeneth with an ear of self,
> Hears not the voice of truth.
>
> Truth is universal! She sayeth not yea
> Unto one, and nay unto another.
> If thou hast said yea, and thy brother – nay,
> Then one of ye hath lost truth!

Truth is not a lendful wine.
It is as a perfect golden ball, and may not fit
A casket, however cunningly contrived,
Be it not lendful to her curve.

Truth is at the pit of every man's heart,
And ne'er breathed a man, save that he argued
His ain wisdom 'gainst her.

Truth is a just garment, and no man
May hide his nakedness behind it.

The cloth of truth is nay bigger than
A man's palm, yet any man
May hide his wisdom aneath it.

The imagery of this poem is that of a conjuring trick. The first three stanzas claim truth as simple and unarguable. The last four stanzas seem to qualify this by showing truth as something that might be manipulated if you tried cleverly enough with the right equipment, while at the same time pretending that you couldn't possibly be being devious (i.e., 'Look, it must be true: the ball fits the casket exactly' and 'I have nothing up my sleeve').

This mediocre poem is interesting only because it is itself an example of the challengingly disingenuous argument it contains. It is a poem dictated through the Ouija board to a Mrs Pearl Curran of St Louis, Missouri, by a spirit claiming to be a seventeenth-century Dorsetshire woman called Patience Worth. If Mrs Curran already had the poem up *her* sleeve, or if she subconsciously extemporised it at the board, the urge to be a mouthpiece of the truth has been subverted by a text that deliberately asks us to be suspicious of the medium of that truth. It is easy to believe that in a moment of vocational frustration Mrs Curran would rather have been an English country girl of an earlier century than 'a lady who sighs and languishes'. It is harder to think of her maintaining this pretence through fifteen volumes of transcriptions of over 200 pages each and the establishment of the Patience Worth Publishing Company.

The essential puzzle about 'Patience Worth' is not whether she is any good or not, but that believing in her is tantamount to accepting the unlikely continuation and development of the spiritual personality after death. The Ouija board found its fulfilment precisely in the need of the bereaved, particularly after the First World War, to be consoled. It is one of many systems (another is the Tarot pack) designed to give questioners the answers they want. The domestic planchette, first marketed in 1891 and self-confessedly defined as a parlour game, allows the spirit guiding the two or more users' fingers to spell from the twenty-six letters and to count from ten numerals, but also to take frequent short cuts from a 'Yes', an '&', and a 'No'. It's not surprising that Ouija is so named ('Yes' only, in French and German) for this polyglot tautology underlines the convenience of loaded answers to loaded questions, affirmative responses to the serious or ironical hopes of the players: 'Are you a spirit?', 'Are you happy?', 'Is there a life after death?' The answer 'Yes' confirms the hope only at the level of a game in which no player will ever admit to manipulating the device consciously.

If Ouija is only a once-popular game of sentiment and superstition, then it is astonishing that James Merrill, a previously lyric poet of elegant artifice and mannered introspection, should have produced an epic poem of 560 pages largely consisting of material claiming to be transcriptions of spirits dictating through a Ouija board at a top rate of just over one second per letter. To some American critics *The Changing Light at Sandover* (1982) prompts mention of visionary predecessors ('Dante, Homer, Milton, Blake') or takes its place as a centrally important poem of the status of *The Waste Land*. But in this sceptical country publication was abandoned after 'Mirabell', the second of its four parts, appeared. It seemed that an English readership simply could not be guaranteed. The *Times Literary Supplement* reviewer, for example, concluded: 'It is a work of vastly uncertain tone, and I would not trust its playful vision of metaphysical truth one inch.' Since Merrill's tone quite often depends upon a kind of embarrassment in transcribing the information supposedly given him by a variety of spirit voices (including Ephraim, who was a former catamite of the Emperor Tiberius and later turns out to be the Archangel Michael; another, Mirabell, who starts as a hot red-eyed bat and turns into a peacock; and a host of recently deceased human spirits – including the poet Auden – who undergo comparable metamorphoses) it is perhaps no wonder that it is uncertain.

The reviewer was being unfair to the difficult fictional role of 'JM', Merrill's persona in the poem. Even Dante in his *Divine Comedy* sounded uncertain at times, and he had far fewer guides and conductors. As for trusting its vision of the truth (a complex account of material and spiritual purification and reincarnation as a means of avoiding nuclear disaster, a kind of sub-atomic metaphysics of the Elect), we have seen in the case of Yeats, Hopkins and Bishop that the source, occasion or beliefs of a poem are only as convincing as the techniques of the poem make them, and that we do not have to believe in its beliefs. But this perhaps only means that the poem's ideas are localised in the science appropriate to a secular religion in the period of the Cold War. The continued public insistence of Merrill and particularly of his partner David Jackson that the Ouija sessions really occurred without either's connivance lent a unique notoriety to the status of the poem's material and maintained the puzzle. If we seek an answer to the puzzle, one line of inquiry would centre on the fact that in 1955, when the Ouija sessions began, Jackson, like Yeats's wife George, was the poet's new lover, a long-term one after emotional turbulence. And like George, it was Jackson (born with a caul, and evidently superstitious) who claimed second sight. Their sessions similarly cemented a relationship.

Poetry has long been fascinated by the unseen world. Again and again poets return to the Platonic idea of a reality hidden behind the veil of appearances. Jackson's version of this is daily life as a kind of spotlight on the larger field we stand in, which accords rather well with common metaphors of science's gradual illumination of an ambient darkness. Intuitions of what the darkness conceals in the case of *Sandover* read like an eagerness to anticipate scientific discovery by bestowing mythical shape upon it and by reading into it patterns of human destiny (stages of perfectibility and metempsychosis, for example) which scientists are frustratingly unable to provide. Stuffed as it is with dramatic explanations of sub-atomic particles, black holes and what-not, in realistic, scientific terms *Sandover* has to be, in fact, a deeply reactionary work. It is a giant attempt to put man at the centre of his world again, as he comfortably was in the time of Dante.

Perhaps another clue to the puzzle lies in the symbolism of the double 'Yes'. In the game we can only phrase the question in a form which predicates an answer, just as the poet claiming to be inspired can, in fact, only write the poem which, though previously unwritten and unknown, is already latent in his subconscious and in the language and traditions. Merrill continually draws attention to the precious verbal hoard that is the childless poet's equivalent to his untransmitted genes: the summoned spirits are truly the alternatives to the children that Merrill felt that he should have already had as he approached thirty, and the very structure of the poem is based upon the letters, the numbers and the 'Yes & No' of the Ouija board itself.

Are Merrill's Ouija dictations really any different from Pearl Curran's? *Sandover*, of course, contains the process of transcription and not merely its results. But in the world of magical illusion the pretence of revealing its circumstances and machinery merely makes the final illusion all the more mystifying. Merrill's own scepticism about and confessed ignorance of the topics that the board expounds succeed brilliantly in validating its truth with greater credibility. The poem is fashionable in referring to its own creation. In fact, Merrill's spirits require him to write it. It is why they have appeared in the first place, and at the end of the poem we see him sitting down to read it out to them.

In a revealing phrase from an interview with Helen Vendler (in the *New York Review of Books* 3 May 1979), Merrill said that 'the talk and the tone are the candy coating'. But to imply that we are unwilling otherwise to take the medicine of the revealed truth isn't quite the same as implying that this is a poem like any other, nature to advantage dressed, and so forth. We may feel that, in 'Patience Worth''s terms, the cunningly contrived casket of Merrill's art was ready for any golden ball that would fit it, and in that case the talk and the tone have to be part of the game. Not a sugaring of the pill so much as a kind of charming bedside encouragement, while we are slipped a placebo. After all, if it *really* were a pill in the fullest sense, Merrill would have sent the transcriptions to *The Journal for Psychical Research* or asked a scientist if their metaphors concealed any serious propositions. A moment's reflection on this possibility does, I think, restore us to the sanity of sceptical readers suspending our disbelief in a reassuringly conventional way.

Among the many things that *Sandover* manages to be, it is a celebration of rites of passage, a memorial to dead friends and a homage to a dead poetical father in W. H. Auden, transmuted to his own favourite element, the mineral (in a burst of wonderful wordplay Merrill toys with Auden as a kind of quasar, before turning him into something closer to a Blakean grain of sand). The buoyant lift of masquing and celebration prevents the poem from confronting the teasing puzzle of belief in the Ouija board as directly as it might have done if we were centrally considering the case of a questioning of a real father or real disasters. The *desire* to believe Ouija messages is at its greatest when mortality proposes its own puzzle. This is clear, for example, from a book like *Voices from the Void* (1919) by Hester Travers Smith. Smith – the eminently sensible daughter of Professor Edward Dowden – sets up a framework of winning scepticism in order to convey her belief that Ouija does indeed work: tellingly, the clinching cases for her are those involving disasters at sea or soldiers killed in the First World War.

If scepticism fuels a poem using Ouija transcripts, there is, nonetheless, a counterweight in the very capitalised presence of those transcripts. In the case of Sylvia Plath's interesting 'Dialogue over a Ouija Board', their presence, and the presence of Plath's doubt, constitute the poles of the debate between her characters Sibyl and Leroy. Ted Hughes, as editor, consigns the nine-and-a-half-page poem to the 'Notes' of Plath's *Collected Poems*, as though it were merely an oddity, a footnote to the canonical poem 'Ouija'. And he adds his own counterweight in the following comment, which brings readers to a threshold of credulity comparable to the one from which they must view the *Sandover* landscape: 'The spirit named here [Pan] was the one regularly applied to. His news could be accurate. (The first time he was guided through Littlewood's football coupon, he predicted all thirteen of the draws made on the following Saturday – but anticipated them, throughout, by just one match. The first dividend at that time, in 1956, was £75,000. The spirit's later attempts were progressively less accurate and very soon no better than anyone else's).' This is vastly different from the scientific vision of Merrill, but it haunts the scepticism of Sibyl with a similar cunning underwriting of belief:

> LEROY: *How are you, Pan?*
> SIBYL: F-
> I-N-E, he says. You feel him pull
> Under your finger? I mean, you don't push
> Even a little?
> LEROY: You know I don't, and still . . .
> SIBYL: And still I'm skeptic. I know. I'm being foolish
>
> I suppose. If I didn't trust you at this
> I wouldn't trust myself. The fault's my faith
> In Pan: it's been ebbing ever since the mess
> He made of the football pools.

Despite the mess he made of the football pools, Sibyl is soon asking Pan the all-important Ouija question: '*Do you know how my father is?*' This is not only the perennially all-important Ouija question, of course; it is the all-important Plath question. Pan then spells out 'I-N P-L-U-M-A-G-E', and Sibyl is momentarily taken with the authenticity of such a phrase: 'In Plumage,' she says. 'I'd never have thought | To say that. That must be his: his word.' But when she asks Pan to continue, the poem's hermeneutic comedy produces its horrific evidence of being simply a poem after all, an expression of human fear and awe:

Plumage of what, Pan? P . . . He starts again
Tugging us through plumage. I almost feel
Feathers winnowing the room. A thin
Column of dazzle draws my eyes to the wall
As if the air were laboring to produce
An angel. Plumage. O-F-R. He'll
Jog off in jabberwocky now and lose us,

Lapsing into Russian or Serbo-Croat.
A-W-W. He's gone off: what English
Word wears two W's? O-R. Or what?
M-S. Manuscript? He stops. I wish
Those letters separated into sense
Instead of brewing us such a balderdash
Of half-hints.
LEROY: You persist in spelling half-hints

Out of a wholeness. Worms, not wings is what
Pan said. A plumage of raw worms.
SIBYL: How
Tedious. That's what we'd say.

'That's what we'd say.' Plath's simple phrase strikes at the root of
all inspired poetry. Her poem is about the sources and frustrations of the imagination; about, indeed, a singularly Plathian
problem, the dangers of *willing* the imagination. And so, frequently,
is Merrill's more complex poem about just this. How not to be
tedious.

We know, then, that these messages come from ourselves, but
would like to think otherwise. That is why it presents itself as a
puzzle. Even when Ouija is out of fashion there may be comparable situations – for example, in the confident intuitions of the

pianist Rosemary Brown, claiming to transcribe posthumous Liszt. Or more appositely in the problematic field of Facilitated Communication. Here a mother's hand resting under the hand of her disabled child at a keyboard (just as the participants' hands rest on the Ouija pointer) may hope to be thought to have nothing to do with the surprisingly mature words or music that then stream from the child's otherwise locked mind. In these situations, the wish to believe is part of the ennabling process. And the wish to believe is finely balanced with the need to suppress doubt.

The poems of a 'Patience Worth' or a Christopher Nolan cannot escape the sensationalist circumstances of their production, whatever their literary value. But Merrill and Plath work differently. At the core of their Ouija poems somewhere there is acknowledgement of everything that doubting readers must feel: 'Pan's a mere puppet | Of our two intuitions,' says Plath's Sibyl. And Merrill, early on in 'The Book of Ephraim', allows his psychoanalyst Dr Detre to suggest sensibly that what he and David Jackson do is a 'folie à deux', using a mask to speak unspeakable truths and 'sound each other's depths of spirit'. But at the same time, both poems arrange to supply circum-ambient verification of the paranormal (Plath's football pools, JM and DJ learning of George Cotzias's death through the board, etc.) that keeps the reader guessing. This is the dramatic pact between poet and reader, the element of poetic surprise. We never want to read poems which are just what *we'd* say, just as poets never want to write poems which are just what they'd *say*.

HOW DO WE KNOW IF IT MEANS ANYTHING?

It is worth remembering that poems don't mean all that they can mean, only what they can usefully mean. Think of the search mechanism of the computer chess programme, which (unless it is allowed short cuts, such as a repertoire of openings) must evaluate all possible lines, however unpromising. The reader of poetry is in something of the same position, advancing and retreating in the direction of alternative interpretations, discarding the unlikely ones but bearing them in mind until all the meanings have been examined. Readers who have struggled with key words that have alternative grammatical roles, unassimilable epithets, pronouns with multiple antecedents, absent punctuation, unknown names knowingly introduced and so on, will be well aware of this sometimes tedious business of retracing one's steps and starting again. We are reminded of Jane Carlyle's experience of *Sordello* (see p. 1).

Here there might come into play a caveat about meaninglessness, but whether it will act as a consolation to the puzzled reader is doubtful. Take the famous meaningless sentence once proposed by the linguist Noam Chomsky: 'Colourless green ideas sleep furiously.' We see why the sentence was thought to be meaningless (something that is green can't also be colourless, abstract things can't sleep, and could hardly sleep furiously, and so on) but as even moderately obtuse readers of poetry we are probably ready to find meaning in it. Metaphor helps. In fact metaphor can link the unlikeliest bedfellows in a sentence. Colourless green ideas might be the basis of an unappealing ecological policy, for example, and ideas sleeping furiously might be such a policy making its advocates have restless nightmares.

Chomsky's real point, however, lay in his alternative sentence ('Furiously sleep ideas green colourless') which he claimed would

strike readers as inchoate, where the first version at least appears
to be 'grammatical' (if both versions are meaningless, then the
fact that one of them appears to be grammatical supports
Chomsky's theory of innate grammatical structure). But even
here familiar poetic inversion and apposition may guide us to a
point of acceptance. And it is actually quite hard to come up
with words that have no semantic link at all between them. The
BBC's *I'm Sorry I Haven't a Clue* game proves it, since there would
be no dangerous excitement in the cautious chain of such words
created in turn by the contestants, if there were not always a
player who could triumphantly define such a link about to press
his buzzer in objection.

What is it that links words and phrases that give us pause?
Open a book of poems by the American poet Larry Woiwode,
and come to the contents page after the half-title:

> Done.
> Schemes, Lies.
> Half-Love.
> The Rose.
> Both Red and White.
> The Rugged Cross Rotting.
> The Rude.
> Intransigent.
> Jokes I made of Myself.

And so on. Interesting-looking poems, you think? Not so interesting? As your eyes ran down the list you may well have come
to realise that it wasn't, of course, the contents page. The book
has no list of contents, but happens to open with this, the intro-
ductory poem. You may correct my deceitful punctuation to make
sense. Or some sense (the poet's sense, anyway) as follows:

> Done.
> Schemes, lies,
> Half-love,
> The rose,
> Both red and white,
> The rugged cross rotting,
> The rude
> Intransigent
> Jokes I made of myself:

It continues in a mood of half-tolerant self-accusation, and is typical of the poet's drifting manner, though actually much skinnier than most of the poems in his book. When I first read this collection at the time it came out, it reminded me sharply that foreign poetry really is foreign, none more so sometimes than that which uses our own tongue.

This example is intended to enforce my point that the elements of a poem, whatever they may mean in themselves and however good or bad they may be in themselves, require interpretation when they are brought together. The first three lines are no problem. The speaker is finished with all the deceptions that come from his being unable to make a full commitment to someone. He is making a kind of vow. Lines 7 to 9 are part of his self-disgust: he has been able to see himself from the outside well enough to make jokes about himself, but he couldn't get as far as changing his general behaviour. But what are we to make of lines 4 to 6? This is the puzzle. The best we can do is to accept the two roses as two kinds of love, eros and philia, and the cross as neglected religious faith that will prove strong enough to survive his neglect. Obvious, after all, in a way that is perhaps not very interesting poetically.

But attention of this kind to any kind of writing soon accords

it whatever degree of respect it deserves. The stages of acceptance of a meaning or meanings that properly belong to
interpretation are not easily forgotten, even if the reader's appetite
is starved of the ordinary pleasures of poetry: music, structure,
intelligence, figurative surprise. This example will have to stand
for the many minor dull puzzles that arise when reading much
modern poetry. Persistence of interpretation will often be
rewarded, but that process doesn't mean that the poems are any
good. I trust that the puzzles in this book belong to good poems
that attract us, and that the process of solving them is an organic
part of what the poet intends or the poem has come to mean.

Making sense of the paradoxical (sleeping furiously, or a cross
that is both rugged and rotten) is felt by many readers of poetry
to be at the heart of the challenge that faces them. Our immediate attraction to poems that look as though the challenge will
be worthwhile is something of a mystery: there may be a charm
of sound as well as the insinuation of intuited meanings. At other
times we may merely feel that we have a duty to fame. Either
way, the puzzling pleasure in a poem (in the Mallarméan sense)
will only come into play once we have willingly started our
reading.

Gertrude Stein was an American poet who helped to inaugur-
ate the strange tradition of inscrutably ill-connected or oddly
sorted words in poetry. She was much more radical in this respect
than, say, Eliot or Pound, in whose work the difficulties are largely
the result of leaving out what they felt to be inessentials. Stein
actually wanted to make poetry abstract, like painting, so that the
reader could enjoy the collocations of words in their immediate
effect, like coloured pigments. But however spatial or unsen-
tencelike her arrangements and however apparently arbitrary her
choice of words, the Chomskian principle of innate order and
the Mallarméan principle of pleasurable puzzlement means that

her poems can sometimes be teased by interpretation into something that we can recognise as meaning. Or at least we have to try to do this, since this is what reading is.

Her *Tender Buttons* (1914) offers a mesmeric attention to the minutiae of domestic life, where things are described not with attention to their appearance or even their function, but by the guiding light of the poet's playful mind. It is the mind itself which insinuates itself mercilessly into the discrete prose paragraphs of 'Objects', 'Food' and 'Rooms' which make up the tripartite structure of the book. This mind is not that of a modernist painter, choosing shapes and colours that please in their relationship to each other (and intend only incidentally perhaps to evoke a subject), but it is the mind of a writer who has decided to use language in the same way as such a painter chooses his colours. It is often called a Cubist enterprise, because of Stein's associations with that movement, but it will strike the reader as being closer to the programmatic arbitrariness of Dadaism.

The book opens with a paragraph about 'A Carafe, that is a Blind Glass':

> A kind in glass and a cousin, a spectacle and nothing strange a single hurt color and an arrangement in a system to pointing. All this and not ordinary, not unordered in not resembling. The difference is spreading.

Confronted by this, the reader may very well ask my key question, 'How do we know if it means anything?' To T. S. Eliot she was 'quite meaningless' (though he published her in the *Criterion*). Stein's sweetly reasonable tone throughout *Tender Buttons* lends these celebrations of her domestic environment the function of definition and advice, so that she can sound like a deranged Julia Child. But you can never quite catch up with the drift of her syntax, and you will learn nothing that will help you better to keep house. Her objects elude their ordinary appearance, and for much of the time appear to be fighting off a smothering abstraction that makes us search for their outlines all the more keenly.

That carafe, for instance: what is it a cousin to, and what does it not resemble? Is it really not ordinary? What sort of 'difference' does it contribute to? These slightly contradictory elements seem to make it at once familiar and strange (even though it is 'nothing strange') and the sequence of participles that concludes each of the paragraph's three sentences ('pointing', 'not resembling' and 'spreading') emphasises the way in which her method appears to isolate something in order to write about it only to almost immediately blur its identity and restore it to the indiscriminate. The carafe is much less 'there' than you might expect it to be. It is not even clear that its 'single hurt colour' is red wine and not merely the appearance of the glass itself, which may be opaque ('blind'). It hardly even needs to *be* a carafe. Stein's stated purpose is 'intellectual recreation'.

Every reader will have his or her own way of construing writing of this sort, but the amount of construing we do must depend on whether we feel that it is worth it. And on our tolerance of puzzles whose solutions may be infinitely postponed. It brings us back to Jane Carlyle's intolerance of *Sordello*, and the hope that time may solve these puzzles. It may do so because over time persistent reading may make advances of understanding. This is one of the functions of criticism, which at bottom is the sharing of readings. It is beyond question that we now know much more about *Sordello* and *Tender Buttons* than their first readers did, but that does not necessarily mean that either is much read.

INTERLUDE: MERE OBSCURITY

As we have seen, the ordinary difficulty of contemporary poetry arises from the reader's inability to make natural connections between the parts (the relationship of a sentence to its predecessor, the role of an unlikely object in a sentence, the significance of an outlandish epithet, things of that sort). In this it is not very different from the way in which difficult poetry has always been difficult. The poet is inclined to take leaps and short cuts over familiar terrain in pursuit of his conclusion, and he expects the reader to be always at his side. Here is an example of the difficulty of relationship and unlikeliness, from the beginning of a poem by John Ashbery called 'Works on Paper I':

Life in Japan is one of the most famous with all these
chairpeople and night stalls brewing
around a contradiction,
but the fowler knows his business takes him elsewhere,
telephoning, with more time to awake in the crystal pageant
of perplexed symmetries.

The first three lines await elaboration or explanation of a kind that the reader might reasonably expect to occur (something about rickshaws and food bought on the street being unexpected in a high-tech society?). The second three, however, go off in an entirely different direction and also contain their own contradictions. Where is it that the fowler (a hunter of birds) does his telephoning? Is he in a modernist hotel full of mirrors, rather than the duck marshes where he might prefer to be? You will think me being a trifle dogged here, and about to give up unnecessarily, but for me this poem is a good enough example of the brick-wall moment I referred to in my first chapter, since it proceeds like this in largely unrelatable directions. As Gertrude Stein used words and phrases in a move towards verbal abstraction, so Ashbery uses whole sentences. The effect is similarly bewildering and only occasionally meaningful.

What is happening when a poet feels that he has to be obscure? That the poem can't really be doing its stuff if it is perfectly lucid? That a difficult poem is somehow superior to a transparent one? That this is the kind of poem you have to write every time?

There are three reasons for this happening. The first occurs involuntarily when poetry attempts to shake off the semantic dimension of language, and become another kind of art form entirely (like the 'cubism' of Gertrude Stein or the dizzying, slithering collage of Ashbery's non sequiturs).

The second is the honourable, but I think mistaken one that proposes that the world today is somehow more complicated than it ever was before, and that poetry to reflect it (if that indeed is what poetry does) must be equally complicated. The most celebrated expression of this position is T. S. Eliot's in 1921 ('The poet must become more and more comprehensive, more allusive, more indirect, in order to force, to dislocate if necessary, language into his meaning') and the current programmatic adherents of it are still occasionally to be found in small presses and blogs, their work characterised by utter impenetrability of meaning. Eliot's 'dislocation' is a syntactically uncomfortable notion, but it sounds serious and radical. On the whole, though, since those panicky moments in the 1920s, the best poets have tended to accord a greater respect to the naturally supple anatomy of the language. It will move better, that is to say, if you don't twist it out of shape. And why should it move? Because in a poem it has to get somewhere.

The third reason for deliberate obscurity is both more common and less respectable. A beginning poet reads his immediate predecessors and finds them impressively hard to understand. But if this is what poetry is, he is going to have to imitate them. So he produces poetry that he feels he barely needs to understand himself. His ideas and feelings may be in there somewhere, providing a reasonable point of departure, but in the writing there is a suffocating texture of deliberate verbal inconsequence. It is designed to accomplish what poetry already seems to do, to impress above all by its confident parade of the unfathomable.

And in any case poetry is already designed to impress, with aural performance that can insinuate itself prior to understanding. (Swinburne is supposedly a notorious offender here, a hypnotic recycler of accumulated Victorian effects.) To the neophyte, the most challenging phrases can echo like seductive mantras. The hero of John Wain's first novel had a line of Empson's obsessively in his brain ('And I a twister love what I abhor') that he wrestled and dislocated until either all its versions made some kind of weird sense appropriate to the various conflicts in his life, or else it collapsed into absolute nonsense resulting from his drunkenness (*Hurry on Down*, chs. 1, 6 and 10). It is no accident that Wain concurrently produced poems in terza rima with complex Empsonian arguments. And perhaps no accident, either, that Empson was ambitious to sound Swinburnean and to produce what he called 'the singing line'.

Lines of earlier poetry force their shapes and sounds into the creating mind, even when there is no sensible relationship between them. Take Dylan Thomas's 'Incarnate devil in a talking snake', a perfectly sensible first line that turns out to have little syntactical relationship with the rest of its stanza. I have referred to Thomas's compositional intuitions already (see p. 9) and don't find them tedious to interpret at all. But the connections and echoes are frequently subliminal and unaccountable. The striking opening in this case probably comes subliminally from a Swinburne poem about Cromwell ('Incarnate England in his warrior hand | Smote') that is itself full of borrowed Miltonic cadences. The colourful Sitwellisms that spice Thomas's early work were themselves largely versions of the dream visions of Rimbaud.

Such piecemeal lines of imitation are a commonplace in the transmission of poetic traditions, and they are the means whereby unfathomed characteristics like obscurity become exaggerated, like concentrations of undesirable deposits in the frequently reboiled kettles of pensioners. In the modernist period, such concentrations could be wilfully induced. W. H. Auden's *The Orators*, for example, a work of which he professed quite early on to be ashamed, is marvellously rich with borrowed obscurities. The work is saved for the sympathetic reading of posterity because it is equally marvellously rich with a much larger range of constructively parodic effects. And, in any case, Auden was a major orthopædic force in the 1930s, leading 'dislocated' language back into full expressive vigour.

Identifiable practitioners of consistently difficult poetry such as John Ashbery, the L=A=N=G=U=A=G=E poets, or members of the Cambridge School, may owe something to any or all of these causes. The reader may well puzzle over their work, but since pretty much everything in it is a puzzle anyway, it does not really fall within my brief. Nor do surrealist *poèmes-découpages*, or Google-generated flarf. There is much that is inevitably eye-glazing about that sort of thing.

THE ELUSIVE ALLUSION: BORROWING AND STEALING

A pervasive puzzle in poems is the phrase or image that rings a bell. Where have we seen it before? Could it be a memory of an earlier reading of the poem, or has the poet taken it from somewhere else? It might be merely an unusual word that catches our attention, or it might be a whole line. It might be an idea rather than a verbal echo. It might be a character. Is it intended, and what might it therefore mean?

Our earliest reading sticks in our mind and will have the habit of bubbling up where it might be needed. When Edith Sitwell's Soldan sings of his desire for some pastoral maid in her poem 'The Sleeping Beauty':

> Rose and Alice,
> Oh, the pretty lassies,
> With their mouths like a calice

the metre and the interpolated exclamation are borrowed from Mary Howitt, Victorian author of 'The Spider and the Fly' ('Buttercups and daisies – | Oh the pretty flowers'), perhaps quite unconsciously. Such a touch helps to give her poetry its flavour of the nursery, but we wouldn't expect it somehow to import into her poem the buttercups and daisies. The girls' mouths are compared to chalice-shaped blossoms, which these common flowers do not have. So if we notice the borrowing, which surely we are not expected to do, it isn't particularly helpful.

However, when we feel the rhythm of Tennyson's 'The woods decay, the woods decay and fall' in one of the refrains of Empson's 'Missing Dates' ('The waste remains, the waste remains and kills') we may reasonably conclude that an allusion to the living death of Tennyson's Tithonus is somehow in the poet's mind, because it makes thematic sense. Here only the words 'the' and 'and' support a metrical echo, but once we have heard it we can't get it out of our head, rather as Wain's hero couldn't get his Empson line out of his head.

There are other acknowledged echoes of this kind in Empson, who admired the Swinburnean aural mesmerism that often eluded his verbally clotted form of verse composition, sometimes turning to other poets for models. In his 'Notes on Local Flora' there is a dramatic turn (a line of one sentence after a sentence of six lines) which has been described by J. M. Hawthorn as follows: 'No one who heard Empson read the line "I knew the Phoenix was a vegetable", could ever find it anything but humorous – a deliberate anti-climax after the somewhat erudite mythical references earlier on.' On this score, it may actually turn out to *be* the climax. Empson's editor John Haffenden has fifteen lines of mythical and poetical references for this line alone. But he does not note a possible source in one of Siegfried Sassoon's lines in 'Preface' ('Some say the Phoenix dwells in Aethiopia'). It is true that there is a better purely verbal echo in Yeats, but Empson's poem is also about the geographical placing of the tree he wants to identify with the phoenix. Sassoon's line can, therefore, as far as I am concerned, join the complex of allusional sources for the poem. The modern reader has been trained to observe and accumulate them. They are the respectable conscious aspect of the kind of imitation I proposed in the previous section as the source of aggravated obscurity in poetry.

That this should be so is largely due to the modernist neo-classicism of Eliot, who found the practice of allusion in English Augustan poetry and imitated it. Invoking Latin and Greek poets as authentic models was long-established, indeed practised by the classical poets themselves. But after Dryden and Pope it became such a natural habit that supernatural or heroic passages in Virgil could be invoked even as pure comedy, and classical diction then invaded the bloodstream of poetry. Affectionate pastiche of such a recent English 'classic' as Milton joined this available fund of verbal effect that was finally to feed into the blank verse of the Romantic poets and beyond. This is a peculiar and complex process taking a century or more to develop, but it governs a number of verbal puzzles that will crop up in this section and the next.

Straightforward allusion imports significance from an earlier context, or creates an implicit analogy. Here is the beginning of Book II of Pope's *Dunciad Variorum*, where the hero – the critic Lewis Theobald – is to preside over the games instituted by the Goddess of Dullness in his honour:

> High on a gorgeous seat, that far outshone
> Henley's gilt Tub, or Fleckno's Irish Throne,
> Or that, where on her Curlls, the Public pours
> All-bounteous, fragrant grains, and golden show'rs;
> Great Tibbald sate . . .

This is an outright parody of the opening of Book II of *Paradise Lost*:

> High on a throne of royal state, that far
> Outshone the wealth of Ormus and of Ind,
> Or where the gorgeous East with richest hand
> Show'rs on her Kings barbaric pearl and gold,
> Satan exalted sate . . .

We know the practice of crowning Tsars with a literal shower of wealth (vivid for our age from Eisenstein's film *Ivan the Terrible*) and have to convert Pope's 'golden show'rs' into the eggs or contents of chamber pots emptied over the 'curls' of the pilloried Edmund Curll, pirate printer and bookseller, en route to the dubious Miltonic grandeur of his anti-hero, Theobald. Incidentally, readers ever since his friend Swift have found the references in Pope puzzling, and to claim that Milton's 'Ormus' and 'Ind' now probably need footnotes just as 'Henley' and 'Fleckno' do is no real answer. But obscurities of this minor kind are not my real point. Theobald is linked to Satan in the vanity of having a throne at all.

Allusions of this kind can be much more elusive, tempting one to create a category of 'elusions'. Critics are divided, for example, over the degree to which Horace Walpole's celebrated cat Selima, drowned in a vase of goldfish at his house in Arlington Street, is compared to Helen of Troy in the famous poem of condolence written by his friend Gray:

> 'Twas on a lofty vase's side,
> Where China's gayest art had dyed
>   The azure flowers, that blow;
> Demurest of the tabby kind,
> The pensive Selima reclined,
>   Gazed on the lake below.

It was J. C. Maxwell, the great editor of *Notes and Queries* and indefatigable literary bloodhound, who first pointed out that in Pope's translation of the *Iliad* Helen is described as follows, having witnessed the defeat of Paris by Menelaus in single combat:

> Meantime the brightest of the female kind,
> The matchless Helen o'er the walls reclined.

The cause of extensive allusion to Pope was taken up by Geoffrey Tillotson, prompting him to conclude that Helen is a constant presence in the poem, although Gray's best editor, Roger Lonsdale, is more than sceptical, assigning Tillotson's evidence to the categories of common Augustan phrasing and poetic diction, 'elusions' indeed.

Must the reader then be compelled to consult learned editions to discover that Theobald may 'be' Satan, but that Selima may perhaps not 'be' Helen of Troy? It is part of the constant puzzle of poetry that we feel meanings to be not so much concealed from us, as to be offered for discovery. But have we the time or skill to assemble the forensic evidence ourselves? These are show-cased borrowings that make complex points about the relative significance of the subject, mock-heroic moments that evaluate a situation not only through stylistic disproportion but in an open resource to an earlier poem.

It was T. S. Eliot who famously said that immature poets borrow and mature poets steal. You might think that theft would fear discovery, that the poet would feel the reader looking over his shoulder like a detective at the purloined text. In fact, Eliot meant that whereas a timid poet borrows a verbal effect but has no real authority over it, the confident poet makes the borrowing his own, not only by changing it into something else in his own work, but by forever changing the way that we read the original. His quota-tion-riddled poem *The Waste Land* provided numerous examples of this, as in the case of the seduced but indifferent typist:

> When lovely woman stoops to folly and
> Paces about her room again, alone,
> She smoothes her hair with automatic hand,
> And puts a record on the gramophone.

It is likely that most readers today will now know this better than the Goldsmith original, the song from *The Vicar of Wakefield*:

> When lovely woman stoops to folly,
>   And finds too late that men betray,
> What charm can soothe her melancholy,
>   What art can wash her guilt away?

Goldsmith's answer in his song is that all she can do is die, but it is part of the 'charm' of the novel that this fate will not overtake Olivia Primrose, the victim who is also singing the song. Eliot's answer, as we have seen, is the 'charm' of mechanical music that pervades his poem along with a deeper Shakespearean music.

'Stealing' in Eliot's sense means that the line has not been fully returned to Goldsmith if it so happens that we now remember *The Waste Land* when we read him. Outright stealing, on the other hand, adds no value. When the original is discovered like a trophy among the thieving author's possessions without the transfiguring power of the appropriating imagination, we call it plagiarism.

A puzzling example of this can be cited from that excellent writer Angela Carter, in her poetic story 'The Kiss'. An old country woman is selling arum lilies in the market at Samarkand: 'This morning, she came from the mountains, where wild tulips have put out flowers like blown bubbles of blood, and the wheedling turtle doves are nesting among the rocks.' Perhaps nudged by the contrasted setting of the colourful, bustling city and the isolated rural origin of the woman, Carter has appropriated some celebrated lines from Browning's 'Up at a Villa – Down in the City':

> 'Mid the sharp short emerald wheat, scarce risen three
>   fingers well,
> The wild tulip, at the end of its tube, blows out its great
>   red bell,
> Like a thin clear bubble of blood, for the children to pick
>   and sell.

Carter's unthinking borrowing is a mere gesture at what remains in Browning a triumphantly complex image, and is indeed what we might therefore call a plagiarism. It was not, for example, recognised as a borrowing by Tobias Hill when writing about the story in his review of the collection in which it appeared. In fact, he singled it out for praise as an example of Carter's own invention. Could such an image have been invented twice over, perhaps, an example of Théodore Flournoy's cryptomnesia (inadvertent plagiarism)? It's a puzzle.

DARKLING

Single words can often carry the full force of allusion, beyond the ordinary freight of usage and the associations of diction. Here is a puzzle that may be more complex than at first sight appears. Why does Keats – drafting a poem in his friend Charles Brown's Hampstead garden under a plum tree after breakfast – claim that he listens to the eternal song of the nightingale 'darkling'?

The first five stanzas of his 'Ode to a Nightingale' have established that the bird's seductive song has all but drugged him into an empathetic happiness. He would like to disappear and forever join the bird in its innocence of the world's pain, and if drink cannot give him such blessed release, then writing poetry will. The ode now begins the process of enacting this determination. As he loses his sense of the actual flowery ambience of the garden in the darkness, so his imagination begins to be put to work to create it for him. The sixth and seventh stanzas are at the core of this work of the imagination, the high point of Keats's art:

VI

Darkling, I listen; and, for many a time
   I have been half in love with easeful Death,
Called him soft names in many a musèd rhyme,
   To take into the air my quiet breath;
Now more than ever seems it rich to die,
   To cease upon the midnight with no pain,
     While thou art pouring forth thy soul abroad

In such an ecstasy.
Still wouldst thou sing, and I have ears in vain –
To thy high requiem become a sod.

VII

Thou wast not born for death, immortal bird!
No hungry generations tread thee down;
The voice I hear this passing night was heard
In ancient days by emperor and clown:
Perhaps the self-same song that found a path
Through the sad heart of Ruth, when, sick for home,
She stood in tears amid the alien corn;
The same that oft-times hath
Charmed magic casements, opening on the foam
Of perilous seas in fairy lands forlorn.

VIII

Forlorn! The very word is like a bell
To toll me back from thee to my sole self! . . .

'Darkling, I listen': The reader who is sensitive to individual words will want to know more than the fact that the word means 'in the dark'. Keats is indeed listening in darkness *in the poem*, even though he wrote it during a morning, and we perhaps do not need to question the choice of night for his setting. It allows the substitution of the senses of smell and hearing for those of sight, a combination of the heady scent of flowers, the imagined murmur of flies and the song of the bird, that emphasise the withdrawal of the body into its natural surroundings and its declared readiness to die.

It has seemed sufficient to ascribe his use of 'darkling' to Milton (in *Paradise Lost* 'the wakeful Bird | Sings darkling, and in shadiest Covert hid | Tunes her nocturnal note'), for Keats marked these lines in his own copy. His recent conversations about nightingales on a long walk with Coleridge near Highgate would have reminded him that the older poet had made great objections to Milton's presentation in 'Il Penseroso' of the nightingale as a melancholy bird, the raped Philomela of classical myth, and had said so in his conversation poem 'The Nightingale'.

The bird could, however, portend good fortune in love, and Milton alludes to that mediaeval tradition in his sonnet on the nightingale. Keats begins his ode in heartache, envying the nightingale's happiness. He doesn't wish, like Charlotte Smith, for example, in her celebrated sonnet, to be free as the nightingale simply in order to sigh. He wants a world that might somehow bypass the inimical circumstances of fretful human life, a world where beauty and love might have some hope 'beyond tomorrow'.

It is these circumstances that come to the fore in the third stanza of the ode, and they are (perhaps inappropriately) induced by the thought of drinking himself into insensibility. As the ode progresses, the eternally constant song of the nightingale becomes a symbol of persistence in the face of adversity, and more particularly in the face of hunger and alienation, as in the stanzas quoted above. Though generalised and distanced by myth, this adversity is felt by the reader to have a personal application, not least in the allusion to the recent death of his brother Tom from TB.

One hundred years before Wordsworth conceived *The Prelude*, a shy Christ Church wit called John Philips embarked on a poem the subject of which he described as 'my self, a subject never yet handled by any poet'. This apparently proto-Romantic project was in fact a facetious Miltonic pastiche, *The Splendid Shilling*, which was once rightly popular for its devious attainment of real

feeling projected by the speaker's vilely impoverished existence in
his garret. Philips's rambling account of 'griping Penury' soon
reaches its nadir of despondency:

> So pass my days. But when Nocturnal Shades
> This World invelop, and th'inclement Air
> Perswades Men to repel benumbing Frosts,
> With pleasant Wines, and crackling blaze of Wood;
> Me lonely sitting, nor the glimmering light
> Of make-weight Candle, nor the joyous talk
> Of loving friends delights; distress'd, forlorn,
> Amidst the horrors of the tedious night,
> Darkling I sigh, and feed with dismal Thoughts
> My anxious Mind. (ll. 93–102)

Forlorn and *darkling* are significant examples of a whole range of
artificial poetic vocabulary rediscovered by the Romantic poets
from Spenser or Milton through the intermediary agency of
burlesque writers like Philips or Shenstone. Philips's 'Darkling
I sigh' is too like Keats's 'Darkling, I listen' to be accidental,
while the tell-tale 'forlorn' is barely a line away. It is interesting
that in the ode Keats seems to become self-conscious at the very
moment of using this word (which, like 'darkling', was also used
in the invocations in *Paradise Lost*). Does 'forlorn' toll like a bell
from its fairy context because it reminds him of the self-pitying
Philips? Possibly, though there is also an innate shift of meaning
across the stanzas from 'lost' (compare German *verloren*) to
'pitiful'.

It is hard to be at all sure about the borrowing of individual
words. For example, even though *The Splendid Shilling* is
programmed to parody *Paradise Lost*, its candleless speaker might
be thinking for once not of Milton, but of Shakespeare's Fool in

King Lear ('So out went the candle and we were left darkling', I.iv.240). But a whole phrase ('Darkling I sigh') is more likely to hook into the mind. At a crucial moment in his ode, Keats remembers a famous poem about extravagant self-pity, with two colourful words that help to inoculate the ode against the possible charge of feeling too sorry for itself. A fruitful borrowing.

MISTAKES

This book assumes that puzzles have solutions. But how, it may be asked, do we know that difficulty in poetry is not sometimes a product of a misplaced carelessness of effect, some accident at the publisher's or printer's, or even a willed modernist meaninglessness? In cases like these it is likely that the difficulties are insoluble at the level at which we perceive them. And since we are usually unable to look up the answer, how do we ever know what the solution is, or if, in fact, there is one?

It would be easy enough to say that I am not concerned with such cases, since they do not partake of the pleasurable negotiation between poet and reader that sets up puzzles to be solved. But it is true that many of my cases are as much a result of short cuts or diversions taken by the poet as they are of straightforward puzzling. Poets can be guilty of momentarily forgetting their own designs, or of being satisfied with an effect that form or language manages to impose on them through ignorance or unforeseen accident.

Let us look at some examples of these things.

Sometimes, of course, the poet simply makes a mistake that causes us to be momentarily puzzled. Misunderstandings of words can be fairly self-evident, as is the notorious case with Browning's 'twats' in *Pippa Passes*:

> Then, owls and bats,
> Cowls and twats,
> Monks and nuns, in a cloister's moods,
> Adjourn to the oak-stump pantry!

Has Browning turned into Edward Lear? Did he actually know this old word for the female genitals? No, he didn't. He thought it was a kind of wimple (from a couplet he had read in a seventeenth-century poem: 'They talk't of his having a Cardinall's Hat; | They'd send him as soon an Old Nun's Twat'). Incidentally, the word continued to develop. It means an idiot (cf. 'twit' and 'prat') and is now also the acronym for 'The War Against Terror'.

There is a line in one of the most celebrated of Victorian poems about religious doubt and secular affirmation, Matthew Arnold's 'Dover Beach', that brings many readers to a puzzled pause:

> The Sea of Faith
> Was once, too, at the full, and round earth's shore
> Lay like the folds of a bright girdle furl'd.

The folds of a sea suggest waves, gathered and overlapping, which is what you do to a flag or a sail when you are furling it, i.e., rolling it up tightly. So far, complicated enough. But none of this can really apply to a girdle. It defeated Arnold's great editor, Kenneth Allott ('Perhaps the girdle is meant to be visualised as a sash broad enough and soft enough to allow the appearance of parallel wrinkles') and defeats all readers. The Miltonic habit in the poem of incorporating phrases of the formula adjective + noun + adjective is well established ('tremulous cadence slow' and 'vast edges drear' are other examples) so that it really does look as though Arnold intends the girdle to be furled, rather than the folds, though the folds of a religious robe, gathered in by a girdle, would be an appropriate if over-elaborate simile. Sure enough, we discover that for 'girdle' Arnold originally wrote 'garment'. You can wear faith like a garment, like a habit, indeed, though of course it can too easily become a habit. And then when it has to be discarded, you have nothing to protect your nakedness from the weather (as King Lear also discovered at Dover). Arnold's lines continue:

> But now I only hear
> Its melancholy, long, withdrawing roar,
> Retreating, to the breath
> Of the night-wind, down the vast edges drear
> And naked shingles of the world.

The grand quasi-Shakespearean conclusion to this section of the poem is so commanding in its shivering impoverishment, that we forget the puzzle about the monkish girdle, but the concluding rhyme-word is the giveaway. There is little useful that you can rhyme with 'world', however much you may want to use that word in such a plangent end position. He could have got by with 'garment' but not with 'girdle'. And 'furled' is only in the poem for technical reasons, anyway. Rhyme is one of the greatest tyrants of poetry.

Robert Lowell's poem 'Sailing Home from Rapallo', about bringing his mother's body home from Italy in a '*Risorgimento* black and gold casket . . . like Napoleon's at the *Invalides*', is as conscious of dynasty as any of his family poems. It begins with a direct address to his mother ('I could imagine your final week, | and tears ran down my cheeks'), but puts her in the third person for its evocation in the long central part of the poem of the traditions of the Winslow family cemetery. Finally, somehow unable

to modulate back into the emotion of the second person, he tries
for the sort of bizarre details that often validate, with their fierce
but discommoding irrelevance, the authenticity of powerful feelings:

> In the grandiloquent lettering on Mother's coffin,
> *Lowell* had been misspelled LOVEL.
> The corpse
> Was wrapped like *panettone* in Italian tinfoil.

This downbeat ending is perhaps intended as a kind of rebuke
to his own grandiloquence, also with funerary intention, but it
unfortunately ends in error: panettone is wrapped in waxed paper;
it is panforte that is wrapped in tinfoil. Should we puzzle that he
doesn't know the difference? Or has it now become somehow
part of the tender shocking joke, a disproportion between the
container and the contained?

Some mistakes are grandly enshrined in memorable poetic
phrases, and could never be corrected. Tennyson's 'ringing grooves
of change' down which he urges the great world to spin for ever
are the grooves that he imagined the wheels of a train to run in.
He had travelled on the first ever train from Liverpool to
Manchester in 1830; he claimed that it was too dark and that
there were too many people for him to see properly.

Perhaps poets are allowed to mean whatever they want. When
Dylan Thomas writes of a 'capsized' field on 'the uglier side of
a hill', does he mean a flooded or perhaps a merely tilted field,
or does he mean a field *the size of a cap*? Have his readers perhaps
learned to be rather too much on the lookout for concealed
meanings in his work? The most influential critical book written
at the outset of the decade in which Thomas was working
(Empson's *Seven Types of Ambiguity*) seems to claim that poetry is

the richer for being able to mean at least two quite different things at once. We would not now disagree, but always want to test out such strikingly different meanings first, in our head. Can the different meanings be made to work together? Is it helpful to go to the dictionary and consider absolutely every possibility? (You will find an example of this dubious practice when I discuss a title of Hulme's on p. 188). The point is that words always have meanings, but that poets themselves do not always mean them.

Sometimes meanings steal up long afterwards and catch the poet unawares. In his sonnet about the sea-cliffs of Kilkee, Aubrey de Vere appears to be guilty of some Joyce Grenfellish gush ('Awfully beautiful art thou, O sea!') but he is not, of course. Neither is Milton, speaking of Eternity as 'perfectly divine'. Nor, for that matter, is Tennyson, when also looking forward to God's party ('far-off divine event'), and it is perhaps unfair that we are influenced to think here not of Creation but of Revelation, of God as the Host of Hosts welcoming the resurrected to the New Jerusalem (see p. 170 for more on this ambiguity). This change of meaning has become almost exclusively camp, as in Merrill's experience of the Ouija board ('just divine in every sense'). For more on Ouija see p. 89.

Since language changes, a poet doesn't remain forever in charge of his effects, and some puzzles can indeed be simply solved with the dictionary ('There is a green hill far away, | Without a city wall.' Why would you expect a green hill to have a city wall? You wouldn't. 'Without' here means 'Outside'). If no puzzle presents itself, the reader still has to be wary. Shakespeare's Sir Nathaniel was 'a very good bowler', but he had never played cricket. Dryden's 'secular' masque was not meant just for laymen. When Clough sits next to a girl in 'a car', he is not doing what we might at first suppose.

Cousin to misunderstanding is misquotation. Misquotations are absolutely not the fault of the poet, and, of course, no part of his meaning. But a misquotation may show that the reader has tried to solve a puzzle by substitution. It is a form of simple clarification, for example, to imagine that the last line of Milton's 'Lycidas' is 'Tomorrow to fresh Fields, and Pastures new', because the poet has been pretending to be a shepherd and because sheep graze in fields. It is not. The line is 'Tomorrow to fresh Woods, and Pastures new.' The reader has conveniently forgotten the woods and doesn't realise that his mistake has created a tautology (see Google for this universal misquotation).

Substitution of this kind can open up interesting questions that the poet may have thought that he had avoided or disposed of. Take Larkin's celebrated last line of 'An Arundel Tomb': 'What will survive of us is love.' The line is often quoted in any case as a resounding emotional comforter, forgetting that Larkin only introduces it as an 'almost-instinct' that is only 'almost true'. Not much comfort there, then, from the old bachelor, it is commonly said. But what is one to make of Antonia Fraser talking on the radio about her recently published memoir of her marriage to Harold Pinter and quoting the line as 'All that remains of us is love'?

These substitutions raise the interesting puzzle of what Larkin might have thought the survival to consist of (and in particular, *where*). I refer to substitutions in the plural because to begin with Fraser has replaced with an absolute 'all' what in Larkin's poem is something like a question tentatively answered: 'What will survive of us?' 'What will survive of us is love.' Her absolute doesn't seem much, though. 'All that remains' is close in sense to Shelley's 'Nothing beside remains' (see p. 198). The glum sense of her version of the line is, in fact, 'the only thing that remains of us is love.' It is depressingly like a puddle where something has melted, whereas the poet's words deliberately and almost triumphantly invoke survival. To survive is (from the late Latin *supervivere*) to live after death. You might have thought that Antonia Fraser, as a divorced Roman Catholic who needed a ceremony to sanctify her union with the Jewish Pinter, would pick up on the word 'survive', the resurrection of the body, instead of substituting the dismal 'remains'. Larkin is writing about a tomb, after all, where the actual remains were laid. Survival is an altogether grander concept.

But her mistake sends us back to the poet's puzzle. Where *does* love survive, if it does at all? Not in the earl and countess's bodies, clearly. Nor in the tomb itself. Nor in our facile human presumption of it, given that we readers are like the 'altered people' who visit the tomb, no longer the 'friends' who knew them. But it must, if it survives at all, be something that the poem itself recreates, by adopting and elaborating their intended 'blazon'. In that case, the actual words of the poem become of sacred importance. Her mistake might be thought forgivable in a broadcast interview, but it turns out to be there in her book as well.

But let us return to one of the general cases that I began with. Suppose a poet means one thing, and another is actually printed? Who, then, is doing the 'meaning'? Printers, as is well known but not to be forgiven, have strange ideas of their own, which accounts, for example, for the appearance of the bizarrely oxymoronic 'soldier Aristotle' in 'Among School Children' in Yeats's *Collected Poems*. This stood uncorrected (to 'solider Aristotle') until 1947. Some misprints can have more serious consequences. A Bible printed in 1763 gave Psalms 14:1 as 'The fool hath said in his heart there is a God', and the printers were given a swingeing fine. If you think this may have been an accident, consider Psalms 119:161 in a Bible of 1702: 'Printers have persecuted me without cause.' It was clearly tedious and ill-paid work being a printer.

One of the most celebrated misprints in modern poetry occurs at the beginning of Auden's 'Journey to Iceland':

> And the traveller hopes: 'Let me be far from any
> Physician'; And the ports have names for the sea;
>   The citiless, the corroding, the sorrow;
>   And North means to all: 'Reject!'

Every line here except the second line (in which my example occurs) happens to be moderately puzzling, or at least need more interpretative skill. But the phrase 'And the ports have names for the sea' strikes us as both literally and somehow stimulatingly true, underlining the translation that such a journey involves. That is to say, you might embark at Dover across the English Channel and disembark at Calais from La Manche, the same stretch of water. Different names for the same sea can raise political hackles (the Arabian Gulf and the Persian Gulf, for example). But Auden intended something much more nuanced, presumably to do with Greek epithets and their emotional shorthand. It was, in fact, a Faber misprint. However, Auden had time to notice it, decide not to correct it, and even play with the reader's reactions. The poem is on p. 25 of *Letters from Iceland*. On p. 27, there immediately follows his letter to Isherwood: 'Dear Christopher, Thank you for your letter. No, you were wrong. I did not write: "the *ports* have names for the sea" but "the *poets* have names for the sea". However, as so often before, the mistake seems better than the original idea, so I'll leave it.' The reader, therefore, has always known about this, and is in a position to imagine both words at once.

Why is the Faber mistake better in the poem than the word that Auden actually wrote? Because to ascribe human agency to a thing and not to a person requires greater imagination in the reader. And because there is a stronger and more rooted tradition of naming among those who make their living from something than among those for whom it is simply one thing among many that they have to describe. However, in the now unusual circumstances of reading p. 25 and then p. 27 of the original edition, the reader has an ambiguity to play with.

So does the reader of any scholarly edition whose business it is to comment on misprints. Take the case of Shakespeare looking for analogies for Othello's gross mistake in too-readily presuming Desdemona guilty of adultery and therefore murdering her. His abject but still self-dramatising hero wants the record to be set absolutely straight, and therefore feels he needs to illuminate his fatal ignorance with some telling analogy. Let us presume that Shakespeare writes for him the following, or something like it:

> Nothing extenuate,
> Nor set down aught in malice; then must you speak
> Of one that lov'd not wisely but too well:
> Of one not easily jealous, but being wrought,
> Perplex'd in the extreme; of one whose hand,
> Like the base Indian, threw a pearl away
> Richer than all his tribe.

This (though modernised in spelling) is from the earliest printed text that we have, published in a separate quarto in 1622. Give or take a comma or two, or a shuffling of colons and semi-colons, it happens to be what you will be likely to read in any modern edition (the Arden, for example). The printer's source of copy is always a vexed issue. If you were to read the passage in the first collected edition of Shakespeare's plays, published in folio in 1623, it would read like this:

> Nothing extenuate,
> Nor set downe ought in malice.
> Then must you speake,
> Of one that lou'd not wisely, but too well:

> Of one, not easily Iealious, but being wrought,
> Perplexed in the extreame : Of one, whose hand
> (Like the base Iudean) threw a Pearle away
> Richer than all his Tribe:

Any good modern critical edition will point out and explain the difference between 'Indian' and 'Iudean' (it is likely to be a misprint, i.e., a compositor's misreading), but is not likely to resolve such a puzzle if the reader is minded to pursue his own opinions as to which of the two was the poet's intention: (a) if 'Indian' is the word that Shakespeare wrote, then Othello is saying that he is like a primitive tribesman who has no idea of the natural wealth that lies around him; (b) if 'Iudean' is the word, then Othello is saying that he is like Judas who lost his hope of heaven in betraying Jesus (compare his 'I kiss'd thee ere I kill'd thee' ten lines further on, a possible allusion to the kiss of Judas). Any account of the scholarly arguments here will inevitably simplify them, but in support of (b) are such things as the fact that all the other disciples were Galileans; that in Shakespeare's day the word 'tribe' habitually applied to the twelve biblical divisions and wasn't yet associated with primitive peoples; that the 'pearl of great price' of Matthew 13:46 is interpreted as meaning the Kingdom of Heaven; that Judas committed suicide; that the Folio is a better text; and so on. In support of (a) is the fact that Indians' ignorance of the value of gold and pearl had been a commonplace since the time of Pliny; that 'Indian' is metrically preferable; that Othello was not intending to compare himself with someone who made a choice of evil; and so on.

Readers have for many years provided their own counters to these arguments, according to their natural preference (why would an Indian be called base? Why would a compositor change 'Indian' to 'Iudean'? Why should he not have picked out a misdistributed 'u' from the 'n' box in the type-case? and so on). My own feeling is that Shakespeare is already underlining the morality play symbolism in these last scenes by suggesting that Iago is a devil ('If that thou be'st a devil I cannot kill thee' . . . 'I bleed, sir, but not kill'd.' Productions in modern dress keen to emphasise the frustrated NCO careerism of Iago find it hard to communicate the intended thrill at this exchange). For Othello to feel that he himself has thereby become a kind of Judas is perfectly appropriate. He has been weak in the face of temptation. And, like Judas, he kills himself.

5

WHERE HAVE WE SEEN THEM BEFORE?: BORROWED CHARACTERS

TENNYSON'S MARIANA

Here in this chapter are some particular examples of problems that arise when a poet borrows a pre-existing character. It is perhaps a special case of the problems already addressed of how far we trust the poet, or guess what he intends. A new character must be created in all his complexity and significance, but an existing character carries his story and significance with him. Suppose not all of it is needed? Or that the reader is uncertain as to how much of it is meant to be remembered?

A common puzzle in a lyrical poem is how properly to understand the predicament of a character borrowed from elsewhere, when the known outcome of the story would import powerful ironies. You can imagine extreme examples of the difference it would make to the whole point of a poem (if, for instance, Burns's 'O my Luve's like a red, red rose' were to be entitled 'Aeneas to Dido', and we knew that it didn't need the seas to run dry before he found good reasons to abandon her), but some degree of ironical implication results from all such borrowings. In cases where the events of the original story are well known and decisive, to sideline the crucial facts can be problematical. Or, it has to be said, fascinatingly dramatic and significant, as when the 'fact' of the Christian atonement is just beyond the enquiring speculation of Browning's Karshish or Eliot's Magus. In such cases the irony is the whole point of the poem, but our present puzzle is: how can we exclude such irony when it is unlikely to be the whole point? Or how do we decide that it isn't in the first place the point at all?

One of the most celebrated examples of a poem about an existing fictional character in utter ignorance of the peculiar outcome of her original story is Tennyson's 'Mariana'. Tennyson, of course, is not ignorant of it, but does he want *us* to forget it? In Shakespeare's *Measure for Measure* she is the lady who, having once been espoused to the hypocritical magistrate Angelo *per verba de futuro* (with a date already set for the wedding), is abandoned by him when her brother is shipwrecked and all her dowry goes down with him. Angelo's treatment of her is despicably mercenary but perfectly within the letter of that law whose un-Christian character is explored generally in the play. When she is first referred to, Shakespeare goes out of the way to show her cruelly treated:

[Angelo] left her in her tears, and dried not one of them with his comfort; swallowed his vows whole, pretending in her discoveries of dishonour; in few, bestow'd her on her own lamentation, which she yet wears for his sake; and he, a marble to her tears, is washed with them, but relents not.

'This dejected Mariana' has retreated to a lonely farmhouse (a 'moated grange') in the protection of a religious establishment called St Luke's. The setting suited Tennyson's own mood of dank melancholy and his poem characteristically explores the ghostly house and mouldering garden within which Mariana voices her lamentations (which in Shakespeare's wry formulation were Angelo's only gifts to her, and were in any case her own):

> She only said, 'My life is dreary,
>   He cometh not,' she said;
> She said, 'I am aweary, aweary,
>   I would that I were dead!'

A version of this refrain concludes all seven stanzas, turning the poem into a classic statement of stultifying isolation conveyed largely through symbolic and subjective landscape:

> Unlifted was the clinking latch;
> Weeded and worn the ancient thatch
> Upon the lonely moated grange.

In the play Isabella exclaims: 'What a merit were it in death to take this poor maid from the world!' In the poem it is a living death we feel.

However, just as Isabella's own predicament becomes a means to restore Mariana to her life through the bed-trick, so our knowledge of Shakespeare's outcome enables us, indeed compels us, to imagine that restoration as well. Since Angelo will only release the determinedly virginal Isabella's brother from his death sentence if she agrees to sleep with him, the extorted assignation becomes an opportunity both to preserve Isabella's chastity and to restore Mariana to her betrothed by substituting the one for the other in the sexual darkness. At the end of the play Angelo does marry Mariana after all, though it is she who has had to go to him, on a Tuesday night, as Shakespeare bothers to specify, in his garden house.

There are implications of staling virginity in Mariana's own garden ('Unlifted was the clinking latch') that energise the complaints of a jilted woman whose name punningly requires that she should be married. Generations of students have dared to comment on the frustrated insistence of Mariana's refrain ('He cometh not') but the play's requirement that *she go to him* for the legal seal of their consummation is less obvious. What in Tennyson's claustrophobic poem, we feel, could possibly stir her to do so? There is something fulfilling and heroic about the folk-loric bed-trick (more obviously, perhaps, when the adventuring Helena contrives it in *All's Well that Ends Well*) that seems quite beyond the willpower of Tennyson's depressive heroine. We certainly can't imagine her agreeing to do it on any particular Tuesday night.

Do we, then, keep it out of our mind altogether? It is interesting here to compare Tennyson's 'Mariana' with a later Victorian poem that confronts Shakespeare head on. Bessie Craigmyle's 'Mariana and Angelo' was published in her 1886 collection *Poems and Translations*:

> The evening sunbeams, in their crimson glow
>   Fell through the storied Gothic windows bright,
> In flickering rays, that ever to and fro
>   Flecked, now with shadow deep, and now with light,
> The rapt and handlocked pair who sat below.
>   That lady who once mourned in loneliness
> Her heart's one love, her faithless Angelo,
>   Weeping both morn and eve in sore distress,
>   Sat with him hand-in-hand in saintlike loveliness.
>
> And he, her partner, was he worthy her,
>   Who wept within the 'lonely moated grange,'

Where naught but twittering swallows seemed to stir
   'Neath grey-brown lichened eaves? Would he exchange
Her beauty for another's, and would range
   To other faces, for a time more fair,
Resting his head upon a bosom strange?
    Or does the gleam of Isabel's bright hair
    Seem fairer than the silvered chestnut tresses there?

He, turning from the gorgeous, glowing west,
   Rich with the rosy flame of dying day,
And half his stately head averting, lest
   The long-pent tears should find at last their way –
'My bride, my wife, in words I cannot say
   The love and sorrow blent, my heart that fill,
Unworthy of thy love exceeding. Nay,
    After long years of weary waiting, still
    Thy tears, Sweet, fell for me, let mine too have their will.'

She laid her hand on his, a gentle touch,
   Slight, but it thrilled his inmost spirit there.
'Enough, my Angelo; too long, too much,
   Thou hast reproached thyself, and if there were
Cause for it, did I not forgive thee, where
   I waited, praying for thee morn and eve,
Far from the world's rough crowd and empty glare?
    Thine image left me not, nor will it leave,
    Love, *now* you love me best. What need have I to grieve?

'Life is too short for us to mourn and grieve
   O'er that which might have been, and was not, done.
That light has come to me which comes at eve,
    Though not so bright, with chastened radiance won

From tears at morning shed. Beloved one,
Let us wend forth, the sun is well-nigh set,
And lo! From the beech-woods above us, come,
Adown the pleached walk with roses set,
Claudio, with fair and faithful Juliet.'

The differences between Tennyson and Craigmyle are instructive. Tennyson's Mariana hates all sounds and sights, but loathes sunset the most; Craigmyle's Mariana speaks of the reconciliation which sunset brings. Tennyson's Mariana is entirely in the grip of her profound misery and hurt, voicing her refrain even in her sleep; Craigmyle's Mariana is full of moral calculation and the practicalities of forgiveness. You would think there was a gender reversal here: Tennyson simply intuiting feminine feelings and Craigmyle providing a sensible analysis of the couple's odd predicament. There is a sense in which Craigmyle has the harder task, that of reconciling us to the quaint machinations of Shakespeare's plot and humanising the once-thwarted marriage. Yet it is Tennyson who seems to have the profounder insight into what the play has offered. He isolates his Mariana from her original theatrical rescue and leaves her in an existential stasis.

But so, in her own way, does Craigmyle. She has indeed confronted the plot, but her poem nonetheless chooses a moment of stasis. This stasis is common enough in Victorian poetry, through its analogy with the favoured mode of narrative painting, where story is implicit in a moment of necessary stillness. The spectator is required to work out the implications from a frozen moment. But Mariana and Angelo in their tryst after the bed-trick are described as a 'rapt and handlocked pair'. Even before looking up this word in the dictionary we sense its force in marooning the couple within their unique nuptial circumstances (compare 'landlocked'), but are perhaps surprised that the OED tells us that it can actually only mean 'hand-cuffed'. In these circumstances her speculations about Angelo's own erotic preferences and her dismissal of the natural regret that things had not turned out conventionally seem less like mature common sense than part of something imposed on her by forces outside both their wills. 'Life is too short for us to mourn and grieve,' she says, 'O'er that which might have been, and was not, done.' Tennyson's Mariana had endless life to do precisely that, but Craigmyle's Mariana is in a different position. For her it is not quite clear what 'was not done', since all 'doing' has now been performed, including the act that allows the final legality of her espousal. The shadow of doubt remains his illusion that Mariana was Isabella, an uncomfortable fact that her having already long forgiven him does nothing to dispel, since that forgiveness could only refer to his initial jilting of her.

Craigmyle's is a braver poem than Tennyson's in what it tries to do, but it fails to convince us. And yet it is entirely a failing of Shakespeare's that he is unable to convince us of the happiness of Angelo and Mariana. This failing belongs perhaps to the sexual cynicism of the play (the saintly Duke's offer to the chaste Isabella also remains a puzzle for directors in the theatre) and is no doubt the reason why Tennyson has chosen to ignore it entirely. Tennyson's poem is some kind of defiance of Shakespeare's plot, and that is one of the reasons why it is a great poem. But the puzzle remains: we can't forget the bed-trick and therefore read 'he cometh not' as a proleptic and multiple irony.

AUDEN'S MERLIN

Sometimes a familiar fictional character in a poem appears to be acting entirely out of character. A particularly bewildering example occurs at the climax of W. H. Auden's 1932 poem 'O Love, the

interest itself in thoughtless heaven.' In its first ten stanzas, the
poem has apostrophised its redemptive force with a splendid rhet-
oric, urging love to make our 'thought | Alive' in 'the ring where
name and image meet' and to restore our roots. How can we
belong again, the poem asks, not only to our country but to each
other? We have been living in a dream of the past, a confident
version of history that has failed us, leaving us suspicious of each
other. The ironworks at Dumbarton and Rowley have closed. The
conclusion of the poem offers another sort of dream, more adven-
turous and less comforting:

Yet, O, at this very moment of our hopeless sigh

When inland they are thinking their thoughts but are
    watching these islands,
As children in Chester look to Moel Famau to decide
On picnics by the clearness or withdrawal of her treeless
    crown,

Some possible dream, long coiled in the ammonite's
    slumber
Is uncurling, prepared to lay on our talk and kindness
Its military silence, its surgeon's idea of pain;

And out of the Future into actual History,
As when Merlin, tamer of horses, and his lords to whom
Stonehenge was still a thought, the Pillars passed

And into the undared ocean swung north their prow,
Drives through the night and star-concealing dawn
For the virgin roadsteads of our hearts an unwavering keel.

'Merlin, tamer of horses'! The phrase 'tamer of horses' is a
Homeric epithet applied to the Trojan hero Hector. It is, in fact,
in the very last line of *The Iliad*. What can it be doing attached
to Merlin, the legendary wizard first introduced in Geoffrey of
Monmouth's *History of the Kings of Britain* and later to play a significant role in the story of King Arthur?

Auden's poem, though full of bold and colourful gestures, isn't
very easy to follow. There are many incidental obscurities, some
of which are explicable through tracking his sources. The final
lines, for example, lend the adventure an erotic colouring by
picking up on allusions that run throughout the poem to Paul
Claudel's play *The Satin Slipper*, where two lovers are separated by
vast tracts of sea and the journey of union is undertaken through
the Pillars of Hercules. This erotic note was supported by the
'possible dream' being in an earlier version 'some dream, say yes'.
But other allusions suggest that Auden is using Claudel's lovers
as symbols for the 'name' and the 'image' that must come together,
as they are predicted to do in the 'ring' mentioned in that line
in the invocation.

This ring survives from an earlier Auden poem where it represents the psychic field formed by the early Christians at their
agape or love-feast. The final unwavering keel, then, represents
a complex idea of love presided over by the anomalous figure of
an heroic Merlin leaving the Mediterranean for an unnamed
destination. Readers attuned to the solving of puzzles might very
well conclude that despite its magnificent rhetoric and geographical sweep the poem is centered upon a mythical symbol too
muddled to be easily unpicked. When I undertook to do some
unpicking in my book *W. H. Auden: a Commentary* (1998) Merlin
was the major problem (the book contains more details of sources
in the poem, by the way).

Where else did Auden write about Merlin, I wondered, if

anywhere? I could find nothing, except possibly a gnomic reference in his 1929 journal, where he is writing about the Lawrentian theme of mothers treating their sons as lovers and sons treating their girls as mothers. 'How to express this in art?' he writes. 'We are all like <Merlin diving> in full armour.' Auden's handwriting is not at all easy, and I had heavily queried my transcription. Revisiting the MS later, I began to feel that the phrase could just as easily have been 'Morris dancing', which seemed to make no less sense. I was still intrigued by the thought of such an accoutred version of the magician, however. It seemed a kind of parallel to 'Merlin, tamer of horses.' But although Merlin made Arthur's armour (the tradition survives in Spenser's *Faerie Queene*, for example) he isn't known to have worn it himself. Edward Mendelson tells me that he thinks the word is 'dining', and that it cannot be 'Merlin'. This example will have to stand as the single example of the puzzle that arises when the poet's handwriting remains impenetrable. At any rate, if Merlin is to be conflated with Hector, it can only be as a trick of appropriation.

Finding a poet's sources is sometimes a matter of luck. For example, Auden made the Claudel play required reading for a course he taught at Michigan in 1941; a copy of the book-list is in the Auden archives. And, more significantly, he annotated the poem in a copy belonging to Chester Kallman with the word 'Perry'.

Perry turned out to be the cultural anthropologist William James Perry, originator of the theory that the origin of all archaic civilisation was in Egypt, and that megaliths such as Stonehenge evolved by way of the dolmen from the Egyptian mastaba tomb. The reason Perry suggested for this great wave of Egyptian culture is connected with the ritual rebirth of the dead. Such rebirth depended upon the search for life-giving magical substances such as precious metals. In any case, bronze required tin, not available in the eastern Mediterranean. It would account for the presence of dolmen builders in Tintagel, centre both of the Cornish tin-mining region and of the castle of King Arthur, central figure in the myth of the search for the Holy Grail (the cup of the Last Supper, supposedly brought to Britain by Joseph of Arimathea).

Auden was much taken with Perry (his ideas turn up again in 'Spain 1937', the 'Commentary' to 'In Time of War' and other poems). Bearing in mind that another poet much read by Auden in the early 1930s, Pindar, had written in his fourth Isthmian ode: 'And by far-reaching deeds of native valour, did they touch the pillars of Hercules . . . Aye, and they became breeders of horses' (Loeb Classical Library translation, Pindar ii, 461) it is not diffi-cult to begin to see the chain of association, Egypt with its client civilization, Greece; and Greece with Troy through the Homeric subject. Perry's theory about the global development of food-producing cultures depended at certain points on horses (for example, in the opening of the plains of North America to agri-culture). Auden's 'Merlin, tamer of horses' is thus a kind of coded symbol of Perry's ideas, suggesting a dispersal of the megalith-building culture beyond the Pillars of Hercules ('to whom | Stonehenge was still a thought').

The sea-faring adventure is intended to have a high spiritual purpose, perhaps analogous to that of Layamon's Brutus sailing a similar route, leading his Trojan remnant from Greece through 'þan bunnen | þa Hercules makede' in order to create Britain and the earliest manifestation of London, Troy Novant. Layamon also writes of the healing properties of Stonehenge as a burial place, the stones being transferred by Merlin from Ireland. Invoking such magical powers suited Auden at this time, since his Christian beliefs had been put on hold in favour of those of the post-Freudian psychologists, while the new science of anthropology had discovered the widespread practice of magic in initiation into totemic clans and secret societies, one of the major themes in his *The Orators* (also 1932). This is another work of Auden's where emerging social and historical themes are still half-concealed in a kind of excited prophetic mythification.

If we feel that the particularity of the puzzle about Auden's Merlin is not quite solved, does it help to try to put 'O Love, the interest . . .' into a larger tradition of English poems of spiritual voyaging, of which Auden may have been consciously or subliminally aware? He would have read Layamon at Oxford, of course. Dante, who wrote about Ulysses' final voyage beyond the Pillars of Hercules, was one of his three favourite poets in the 1930s, and he quotes from the 'Inferno', canto XXVI, more than once. Although to his high-minded hero Ransom in *The Ascent of F6* Ulysses encouraging his sailors to the voyage was simply 'a crook speaking to crooks' and embarking on little more than a colonial adventure, it is likely that Tennyson's version of this 'typical Romantic Marine Hero' had more spiritual force for Auden. The Victorian Ulysses is hoping to find the 'Happy Isles' and to 'see the great Achilles, whom we knew', which conforms to Tennyson's sense of loss at his friend Hallam's death and his wish to be assured of an afterlife. Ulysses makes no discoveries, founds (and finds) nothing, certainly not the Happy Isles or Atlantis, and drowns in the Atlantic. Whether we are meant to be aware of this known outcome is one of the puzzles of Tennyson's monologue (see the similar problem with his 'Mariana', which I have dealt with at greater length above, p. 130), but the knowledge should not prevent Ulysses from always appearing admirably restless, bold and curious: the question of an actual afterlife is diplomatically postponed at each reading.

A comparable character is found in another key Victorian poem, Matthew Arnold's 'The Scholar-Gipsy'. He is a seventeenth-century Oxford scholar who in an age of significant scientific development escapes into the woods to learn the secret lore of the gipsies. It is not for nothing that the gipsies are etymologically 'Egyptian', and possess such secrets, particularly of divination and prophecy. And it is no coincidence that the scholar, who is seeking 'a spark from heaven', is compared in the famously puzzling metaphorical ending of the poem to a Tyrian trader shunning the profuse but shallow cargo of neighbouring Greek ships and going through the Pillars of Hercules to trade with the more reserved peoples beyond the Mediterranean. Will he by chance discover Atlantis? The poem does not say, but suggests that the scholar-gipsy's ghostly presence is still to be felt, a precursor type of the nineteenth-century disaffected artist.

The honorary Trojan Merlin is analogous to the Trojan prince Brutus, and indeed to the Trojan Aeneas, founder of Lavinium (the precursor of Rome), both successful fathers of great nations. He is seen by Auden in a prophet's role, which had also been emphasised by Layamon. What does he prophesy?

Brutus was given a dream of Albion by the goddess Diana. Auden's 'possible dream' appears to be a new and unsuspected shift in civilisation, uncertainly awaited 'inland' as people look for signs to 'this fortress' and 'these islands' where some decisive change is imminent, accompanied by an efficient excision of disease. To Perry, the world outside the ancient East 'lay in a profound cultural slumber' as the search for commodities went ahead. It was that very search which imported cultural change. Crucially, for Auden, the change can also come from within. The dream that is uncurling has been 'long coiled in the ammonite's slumber'. And even the creators of the England that Auden despaired of had vision of a kind. Indeed, despite their crude sense of glory, they are said to be 'Far-sighted as falcons', a phrase that might possibly have suggested a connection with Merlin, since the Latin name of the bird merlin is *falco columbarius*.

I can't claim that this puzzle is resolved, but there is nothing arbitrary or thoughtless about the difficulty of Auden's poem. It belongs in an existing tradition, and it buys into a number of existing ideas about psychic and social health, trying to make dramatic and persuasive sense of them. It is puzzling because it perhaps tries to do too much, as much modernist poetry did, and Auden in time abandoned the poem and others like it in favour of a greater simplicity.

LOWELL'S AENEAS

There is a puzzle of interpretation in Robert Lowell's 1948 poem 'Falling Asleep over the Aeneid' that forces the reader to engage with a strange twentieth-century practice of American literary attitudinising: seeing yourself as Roman. Lowell's 'old man in Concord' is imagining that he is the founder of Lavinium (indeed, really a Trojan). It is part of the poem's implicit but obscure argument that the poet's distinguished ancestor has some reason to feel as important as Aeneas. The founding fathers of the United States of America were dramatically conscious, too, of creating a vibrant new republic. But, in fact, Lowell's poem is saturated with guilt. The poem is a longish one, but it would be useful to have it before us, with its brief preface:

An old man in Concord forgets to go to morning service.
He falls asleep, while reading Vergil, and dreams that he is
Aeneas at the funeral of Pallas, an Italian prince.

> The sun is blue and scarlet on my page,
> And *yuck-a*, *yuck-a*, *yuck-a*, *yuck-a*, rage
> The yellowhammers mating. Yellow fire
> Blankets the captives dancing on their pyre,

And the scorched lictor screams and drops his rod.
Trojans are singing to their drunken God,
Ares. Their helmets catch on fire. Their files
Clank by the body of my comrade – miles
Of filings! Now the scythe-wheeled chariot rolls
Before their lances long as vaulting poles,
And I stand up and heil the thousand men,
Who carry Pallas to the bird-priest. Then
The bird-priest groans, and as his birds foretold,
I greet the body, lip to lip. I hold
The sword that Dido used. It tries to speak,
A bird with Dido's sworded breast. Its beak
Clangs and ejaculates the Punic word
I hear the bird-priest chirping like a bird.
I groan a little. 'Who am I, and why?'
It asks, a boy's face, though its arrow-eye
Is working from its socket. 'Brother, try,
O Child of Aphrodite, try to die:
To die is life.' His harlots hang his bed
With feathers of his long-tailed birds. His head
Is yawning like a person. The plumes blow;
The beard and eyebrows ruffle. Face of snow,
You are the flower that country girls have caught,
A wild bee-pillaged honey-suckle brought
To the returning bridegroom – the design
Has not yet left it, and the petals shine;
The earth, its mother, has, at last, no help:
It is itself. The broken-winded yelp
Of my Phoenician hounds, that fills the brush
With snapping twigs and flying, cannot flush
The ghost of Pallas. But I take his pall,
Stiff with its gold and purple, and recall

How Dido hugged it to her, while she toiled,
Laughing – her golden threads, a serpent coiled
In cypress. Now I lay it like a sheet;
It clinks and settles down upon his feet,
The careless yellow hair that seemed to burn
Beforehand. Left foot, right foot – as they turn,
More pyres are rising: armored horses, bronze,
And gagged Italians, who must file by ones
Across the bitter river, when my thumb
Tightens into their wind-pipes. The beaks drum;
Their headman's cow-horned death's-head bites its tongue,
And stiffens, as it eyes the hero slung
Inside his feathered hammock on the crossed
Staves of the eagles that we winged. Our cost
Is nothing to the lovers, whoring Mars
And Venus, father's lover. Now his car's
Plumage is ready, and my marshals fetch
His squire, Acoetes, white with age, to hitch
Aethon, the hero's charger, and its ears
Prick, and it steps and steps, and stately tears
Lather its teeth; and then the harlots bring
The hero's charms and baton – but the King,
Vain-glorious Turnus, carried off the rest.
'I was myself, but Ares thought it best
The way it happened.' At the end of time,
He sets his spear, as my descendants climb
The knees of Father Time, his beard of scalps,
His scythe, the arc of steel that crowns the Alps.
The elephants of Carthage hold those snows,
Turms of Numidian horse unsling their bows,
The flaming turkey-feathered arrows swarm
Beyond the Alps. 'Pallas,' I raise my arm

And shout, 'Brother, eternal health. Farewell
Forever.' Church is over, and its bell
Frightens the yellowhammers, as I wake
And watch the whitecaps wrinkle up the lake.
Mother's great-aunt, who died when I was eight,
Stands by our parlor sabre. 'Boy, it's late.
Vergil must keep the Sabbath.' Eighty years!
It all comes back. My Uncle Charles appears.
Blue-capped and bird-like. Phillips Brooks and Grant
Are frowning at his coffin, and my aunt,
Hearing his colored volunteers parade
Through Concord, laughs, and tells her English maid
To clip his yellow nostril hairs, and fold
His colors on him . . . It is I, I hold
His sword to keep from falling, for the dust
On the stuffed birds is breathless, for the bust
Of young Augustus weighs on Vergil's shelf:
It scowls into my glasses at itself.

Perhaps we should be used to modern Europeans pretending to be Romans. When I was a boy you could still find the coins of George III in your change, because they were legal tender: it was a worn shilling of 1816 finding its way into my pocket that set me collecting. What was remarkable about the king's silver head (compared to the one of his reigning great-great-great-grandson that I was used to) was that instead of ending at the neck it extended to a small section of the chest, indicating that he could not possibly be thought to be wearing a shirt collar. Moreover, the head was wearing a laurel wreath, tied with a ribbon that hung down at the nape. Although at the time I was barely conscious of the fact, the mad King George was pretending to be a Roman emperor. A version of the half-crown of the same year shows a good four inches of bull neck and naked back, turning him into a truculent, surly version of an emperor such as Vespasian, Titus or Nerva. I soon discovered that earlier royal portraits on coins went even further, to include shoulder lappets or the folds of a toga. I also noticed as a corollary to all this that even my own George VI's name on his coins was still peculiarly given as 'Georgius', though I knew from newsreels that he spoke English and wore a suit like everyone else.

This imposture began with the first milled coinage after the Restoration of Charles II. It is one of the actual circumstances that help us to see why Pope, addressing his philistine monarch in 1737, could ironically pose as the Roman poet Horace genuinely saluting his patron the Emperor Augustus. George II's second name was, after all, Augustus, and he, too, appeared on his coins in a toga.

The poets of the Augustan age in English poetry consciously venerated their Roman antecedents Horace, Virgil and Ovid, and this is one of the reasons why it is so called. But the age of patronage soon passed, and so, eventually, did classical models for poetry. English poets rediscovered their own mediaeval heritage, for one thing, and soon enough Greece and Rome became merely one source of myth among many. The great poems of the nineteenth and twentieth centuries tend to find their material elsewhere: Wordsworth's *The Prelude*, Byron's *Don Juan*, Tennyson's *Maud*, Whitman's *Song of Myself*, Browning's *The Ring and the Book*, Christina Rossetti's *Goblin Market*, Hopkins's *The Wreck of the Deutschland*, Stevens's *Notes Towards a Supreme Fiction*, Auden's *The Orators*. Such a list is randomly selective, but it includes nothing classical, and perhaps makes my point.

But to some of the American modernists, the Roman world – with its hierarchical society, its militaristic virtues, its sense of impe- rial destiny, and above all its high regard for the epic poem – was still a viable model. The cultural supposition of twentieth-century classicists was put in general terms by T. S. Eliot: 'We are all, so far as we inherit the civilisation of Europe, still citizens of Europe, still citizens of the Roman Empire.'

The *locus classicus* for the more particular analogy is provided by the Aeneas poems of Lowell's mentor Allen Tate. Picnicking by the sea in 1932 with Ford Madox Ford, Tate remembered the Trojans feasting by the Mediterranean and later wrote his strange poem 'The Mediterranean', in which the expanding Roman empire looks at length so far westward that it finally finds Troy once again in Tennessee and its neglected riches. Then there is his 'Aeneas at Washington', where the Trojan speaks by the Potomac of the vigour of prophecy and the rebuilding of cities destroyed by 'the many'. Tate (like other members of the Fugitive Group to which he belonged) found contemporary America a cultural desert created by the profit motive and aggressive Puritanism. Gentlemen of the Old South had always tended to refer to themselves as Romans, and after the Civil War lived their dream of restoring the *res publica*.

In 1937 the young Lowell sought out Tate like a disciple, eager to stay as long as was needed to learn significant truths and the grand manner. (When the Tates with their busy household told the disciple that if he wanted to stay he would have to pitch a tent on the lawn, Lowell could not accept this as a polite rebuff but bought an olive umbrella tent from Sears Roebuck in Nashville and stayed for three months.)

'Falling Asleep over the Aeneid' is a good example of the puzzle that arises when personal attitudes are involuntarily mixed with a public subject. Lowell invents a dreamer in his poem who is old enough to remember the funeral of his Uncle Charles eighty years before, and whose aunt enters the poem as he wakes from his dream, allowing a rich complex of analogies between

Trojan/Italian and Civil War heroism (between Charles Russell Lowell, Jr, for example, the most attractive and illustrious of Lowell's ancestors, and the charismatic Pallas, who also died from a chest wound, and whose funeral is the key episode in Lowell's poem). It is a way of writing about his family's role in American history, and of his own wish to play such a part.

For Lowell, Aeneas was a 'cold man', comparable to George Eliot's Grandcourt. And yet 'pius Aeneas' is capable of both conventional piety (adherence to his duty in bringing the Trojan deities to Italy) and of pity (the powerful sense that Aeneas has at Pallas' funeral of his father Evander's loss). It is this duty that led him to abandon Dido, who amply comes to Aeneas's mind during the funeral. Indeed, Lowell portrays the hero's emotions as puzzlingly more concerned with memories of Dido than of Pallas himself, and the latter seems to be a nightmare surrogate for the former. Epic values are in human terms profoundly ambiguous, as Lowell was well aware when he wrote of Aeneas: 'We know he is leaving a real woman of flesh and blood to follow the empty abstract fantasy of becoming a figurehead in an epic poem.'

There is a two-way traffic here between Lowell's Aeneas fantasising about becoming the hero of Virgil's poem and Lowell himself fantasising about becoming Aeneas. The major functional analogy was already Virgil's: the war between Latins and Trojans, in which the Arcadian Pallas died and was avenged by Aeneas, was intended to put his readers in mind of the recent civil wars generated by the conflict between Caesar and Pompey, wars ended by the *Pax Augusta*. Lowell's dreamer lends the Union a similar role by invoking the American Civil War, but the admiration for Uncle Charles was actually Lowell's own. Charles Russell Lowell has his bravura sonnet (twelve horses killed under him) in Lowell's *Notebook* (1969), where he is likened in his long-haired appearance to the hippy burners of draft cards, a powerful contrast to the poet's own cowardly behaviour at the Vietnam protest march on the Pentagon, nursing his leg-cramps as the MPs moved through the protestors in ominous single file (while the swaggering Norman Mailer was arrested for trying to cross the police line).

A writer who has conceived of himself as a public figure – not only by virtue of his vocation but also by reason of patrician inheritance – will be conscious of the potential power that he wields. This may range all the way from the 'subtle public commitment' of Lowell refusing President Johnson's invitation to a White House Festival of Arts in 1965 (an earlier instance of Vietnam protest) to something quite bizarre like Henry James's dying illusion that he was not only a great novelist, but also Napoleon Bonaparte.

James's illusion was private. Lowell's (if illusion it was) had, of course, to be public, in a public letter, as was his more celebrated declaration to President Roosevelt more than twenty-one years previously ('I very much regret that I must refuse the opportunity you offer me in your communication of August 6, 1943, for service in the Armed Forces'). If not an illusion, it's a notably more arrogant gesture than the burning of a draft card.

Of course, we accept the patrician note in Lowell's refusals with pleased amusement to the degree in which we approve the cause. In 1943 he was outraged by the bombing of Hamburg and the consequent civilian losses. He concluded that 'we intend the permanent destruction of Germany and Japan', and that this will leave 'China and Europe, the two natural power centers of the future, to the mercy of the USSR'. The patrician in Lowell was fearing 'world revolution', and acting already in consonance with Eisenhower's post D-Day objectives and the ensuing Cold War. Lowell's mother was convinced that his greatest objection was a purely cultural one – to the bombing of Rome.

There is no doubt that something of this, too, can be read into 'Falling Asleep over the Aeneid' as a further analogical parallel to the wars of Latins and Trojans and of Pompey and Caesar and of the Union and the Confederate armies. Aeneas' faith is 'that he will ultimately save and establish the state'. Lowell wrote the memory of the rejection of Dido into the episode of Pallas's funeral, because this seemed to him in its sexual force a compelling enough example of the sacrifice that the artist-hero must make, the sacrifice of 'flesh and blood' to 'abstract fantasy'.

Aeneas could have had no idea that he was to be so remembered. As a legendary hero he has no knowledge of the mythic consciousness he inhabits. Such knowledge belongs only to the poet. When Lowell says that the *Aeneid* is 'the story of what one must give up to write a book' he is deliberately confusing Aeneas with Virgil, and teasing us with a concept that comes alive again in 'Falling Asleep over the Aeneid'. Aeneas does not write a poem, but dreaming that you are Aeneas and putting the dream into a poem allows you to make the significant equation of literary with political power, like James's dying dream of becoming Napoleon.

Lowell, one might say, gave up civic obedience in order to write the poem. He gave up the chance to act like a traditional military Lowell in exchange for a monitory political understanding that actually underwrote some of the imperialist attitudes that governed US policy in Vietnam.

The *Pax Americana* may be seen as a conscious version of the *Pax Augusta*, but there is something paradoxical involved in the perception that 'in order to be loyal to his faith that he will ultimately save and establish the state, [Aeneas] is first forced almost to ruin the state'. Heroic as Mailer and Lowell may have appeared to themselves in 1967, it is clear that the US government had no real fear that they could ruin the state, let alone 'establish' it.

In the poem, the old man's copy of Virgil becomes the sword
with which Dido killed herself, and this, in turn, becomes the
'parlor sabre' of 'Beau Sabreur' Lowell, which he holds 'to keep
from falling'. This dream-like metamorphosis leaves undecided
the balance of power between pen and sword. Undecided also
is the balance between sword and turning the other cheek. By
falling asleep over the *Aeneid* instead of taking Holy Communion
the dreamer is emphasising the distinction between 'Union
martyrs' and Christian sacrifice. The pacifist background to
Lowell's politics gives his poem much of this sort of resonance,
and Virgil as the creator of Aeneas was not, for him (whatever
else he was), *anima naturaliter Christiana*.

The great-great-aunt in the poem may well be conscious of
the mediaeval Christianising of Virgil when she comes in and
says 'Vergil must keep the Sabbath'. Admiration of Virgil as a
source of supernatural guidance had indeed been adopted by the
Christian Church, and the Annunciation of his Fourth Eclogue
was not the only proleptic message found in his work. To Dante,
Virgil was '*il dolce maestro mio, alto dottore, virtù somma*' ('my sweet
master, sublime teacher, the sum of human excellence'). And,
after all, falling asleep over Virgil is hardly a new subject when
you think of the *Divine Comedy*.

But what of the subsidiary puzzle which I have already
mentioned, the striking presence of Dido in an episode from the
wars against Turnus? When Lowell came to the writing of his
breakthrough volume of poetry, *Life Studies*, he made a celebrated
and revolutionary discovery. The volume was not called *Life Studies*
for nothing. He was not only consciously turning his back on
twenty years of, as it were, painting in his poems with a rich and
formal palette and returning with a sharpened pencil to the studio
of his memory, but observing a direct fidelity to the voice that in
his phantasmogoric Aeneid poem had said 'It is I'. This pursuit

led to a renewed vigour in seizing upon the raw materials of life for his poetry.

The self is not a construct of tradition, like a boy among ancestors; it is the creation of experience. To be in the hell of one's own behaviour is to feel left alone, the circumstance of 'Skunk Hour', the culminating poem of *Life Studies*, with its redemptive image of the mother skunk and her 'column of kittens' marching up Main Street in the moonlight as though the poet, observing them, is the last man on earth.

More and more in Lowell's work this movement towards an affirming endurance in the face of a suicidal impulse came to rely on documentary evidence. The model for this strategy is history, which must use documents and testimony for its narrative. In writing his own life into his work (even the most intimate aspects of it) Lowell uses the techniques of the historian. This notably led to moral issues. Elizabeth Bishop had objected to William Carlos Williams's use in *Paterson* of a young woman poet's letters to him. In this objection she sharply differed from her friend Lowell, who later made similar use of his second wife Elizabeth Hardwick's letters in his own poems. Can the poet in his guilty sickness, like his persona in 'Skunk Hour', become a kind of voyeur not only of courting couples in cars but also of his own life? It can seem luridly parasitic.

In 'Falling Asleep over the Aeneid' there is guilt, but not quite yet trespass. Written at the time of his divorce from his first wife, Jean Stafford, it makes a redolent symbol of Aeneas's rejection of Dido (the 'real woman of flesh and blood' abandoned, we recall, in order 'to follow the empty abstract fantasy of becoming a figurehead in an epic poem'). What do we remember of Lowell and Stafford? We remember the following. Probably drunk, he drove into a wall with her in the passenger seat. She had months in hospital, 'everything fractured, bits of bone picked out from near the brain', a long series of operations on her broken nose. Then, when it had been carefully repaired, they had an argument and Lowell hit her, breaking it again.

In the poem, Dido has given Aeneas the gold and purple robe with which he wraps the body of Pallas (this is in Virgil); he also holds the sword which she used to kill herself (not in Virgil). Careful attention to the puzzling ambiguities of referential pronouns and unascribed speech might suggest that this beak-like sword has become a symbol of the damaged and abandoned Stafford, which the poet conflates with the speaking corpse of Pallas, and that in a secondary level of meaning is urging the dream-Aeneas to die.

As for the Catholic Lowell's real-life response to the break-up, when Stafford at last after much unhappiness proposed the unthinkable and said, 'I'm sorry, Cal, but it has to be divorce' just as he was walking out of the kitchen, he paused for a moment on the threshold, then, without looking back, said, 'It doesn't really matter. I've got the vocabulary now.' More documentation, in other words: a language for telling their story. This was 'Cal' at his most Caligula-like.

Artistically equipped now with all the language and documents, public and private, that he needed, Lowell became free to write his own epic. In the final text of *History*, there are 368 sonnets, just over one for each day of the year. Calculating the structure on this annual scale, the sonnet about Colonel Lowell having twelve horses shot from under him arrives on 9 May, and a sonnet entitled 'Father' after about six months. Lowell is clearly eager to make his personal entrance on to the stage of 'history'. The pressure of private upon public, of present upon past, is in this way unignorable. To write yourself into history is, after all, perhaps only a megalomaniac form of autobiography, implying that the boy has indeed grown up and joined his ancestors.

In 'Falling Asleep over the Aeneid', Lowell's ancestral heritage was already crucial to his conception of the story. This heritage is equivalent in a sense to Virgil's allusions in the *Aeneid* to Augustus's own supposed descent from Aeneas through Aeneas's son Iulus, and to Lowell's dream-Aeneas imagining his imperial 'descendants' climbing the knees of Father Time. The parallels converge dramatically at the end of the poem, when the dreamer at last appears to wake up:

> . . . It is I, I hold
> His sword to keep from falling, for the dust
> On the stuffed birds is breathless, for the bust
> Of young Augustus weighs on Vergil's shelf:
> It scowls into my glasses at itself.

Just as Augustus was meant to see himself in the *Aeneid*, so Lowell designs his poem to allow him to see himself in *his* own history, mediated through heroes, wearing his own toga.

The brilliance of this final mirror image rests in its animation of the inanimate. Augustus is only a bust, after all. Virgil on the shelf is only a body of poetry. It was all 'only' a dream. And yet the poet himself – his 'old man' persona by now discarded – is metonymised into his glasses and a transferred scowl, an image of quizzical perplexity in the face of the deadness, dustiness, guilt and sheer taxidermy of imagined history.

6

THE TROUBLE WITH TITLES

THE TITLES OF TITLES

If a poet changes a title, he had better be sure that he is not concealing crucial evidence from his jury of readers. Naturally, if a poem turns out to be fit for more than one kind of occasion, a new title can be like this season's hat and we will forget the sort of figure that the poem cut before. Auden has a comic example of time-serving in his poem "'The Truest Poetry Is the Most Feigning'" where a love poem can serve political ends:

> If half-way through such praises of your dear,
> Riot and shooting fill the streets with fear,
> And overnight as in some terror dream
> Poets are suspect with the New Regime,
> Stick at your desk and hold your panic in,
> What you are writing may still save your skin:
> Re-sex the pronouns, add a few details,
> And, lo, a panegyric ode which hails
> (How is the Censor, bless his heart, to know?)
> The new pot-bellied Generalissimo.

> Some epithets, of course, like *lily-breasted*
> Need modifying to, say, *lion-chested*,
> A title *Goddess of wry-necks and wrens*
> To *Great Reticulator of the fens*,
> But in an hour your poem qualifies
> For a State pension or His annual prize . . .

Common changes of title are not so obviously opportunistic. But the effect of a change can be to provide or withdraw a key to understanding. If a change of title results from significant changes in the text (as, for example, in the case of Robert Lowell's *Notebook* becoming *History*, with the 'waste marble' cut from the 'figure') then its purpose may be obvious. Sometimes a change can give with one hand and take away with the other. When Eliot's growing sequence that began as 'Doris's Dream Songs' turned finally into 'The Hollow Men', any reader would have been glad of the guiding theme (with its allusion to Conrad), but might regret the loss of the defining information that the poem began, after all, as a set of lyrics looking for its final size and order. The renaming is a sort of dignified promotion, a process characteristic of Eliot's work generally.

A poet may help or hinder the reader at will. The purchaser of Browning's third number of *Bells and Pomegranates* (1842), containing a collection of 'Dramatic Lyrics', may have paused in perplexity at the volume's title as the *Athenæum* reviewer had done when the first number (consisting of *Pippa Passes*) appeared ('it is reasonable to suppose Mr Browning knows why, but certainly we have not yet found out – Indeed we "give it up"'). Even Elizabeth Barratt needed enlightenment, but she was in the privileged position to 'give up' in a practical sense by asking her suitor the answer to the puzzle. He told her: 'The Rabbis make Bells & Pomegranates symbolical of Pleasure and Profit, the Gay & the

Grave, the Poetry & the Prose, Singing and Sermonizing – such a mixture of effects as in the original hour (that is quarter of an hour) of confidence and creation, I meant the whole should prove at last.' Why did he not explain this to the public? Well, he would eventually do so in the eighth and last number, where the pomegranate is also revealed as a symbol of good works, and the bell implicitly, therefore, of faith.

This is a rather different, theological explanation that fits very well with the investigations of a redemptive force in *Pippa Passes* and would also have had some bearing on one of the monologues in the third number, 'Johannes Agricola'. So, too, might an epigraph which Browning had provided to the latter poem when it had been first run in a magazine nearly seven years earlier but did not reprint, explaining that Agricola was the founder of the sect of Antinomians: 'They say, that good works do not further, nor evil works hinder salvation; that the child of God cannot sin, that God never chastiseth him, that murder, drunkenness, &c. are sins in the wicked but not in him, that the child of grace being once assured of salvation, afterwards never doubteth . . . . that God doth not love any man for his holiness, that sanctification is no evidence of justification, &c.' But the reader of *Bells and Pomegranates* had to make do simply with Johannes Agricola's own self-confessed and outrageous confidence in predestination: he intends 'to get to God'; he has 'God's warrant'; God smiles on him, and as he lies 'smiled-on' he gazes on those equally confident but ungraced Christians in hell whose own genuine striving has inevitably turned to sin:

> Priest, doctor, hermit, monk grown white
> With prayer, the broken-hearted nun,
> The martyr, the wan acolyte,
> The incense-swinging child, – undone
> Before God fashioned star or sun!

'Johannes Agricola' is paired with a second monologue called 'Porphyria', whose speaker also seems to be an Antinomian. He, too, believes that murder may be a sin in the wicked, but not in him, for he recounts how he has just murdered his lover and concludes by claiming, in a curious tone of mingled awe and truculent self-righteousness, 'And yet God has not said a word!'

Our puzzle comes into play when we consider the general title under which these two poems were published in *Bells and Pomegranates* ('Madhouse Cells') and the removal of this title in the three-volume *Poetical Works* of 1863, when 'Johannes Agricola' was re-titled 'Johannes Agricola in Meditation', 'Porphyria' was re-titled 'Porphyria's Lover', and both put into a section entitled 'Romances'. (*Romances*, we incredulously wonder?)

The original Chinese-boxed sequence of titles – *Bells and Pomegranates*/Dramatic Lyrics/Madhouse Cells/I. Johannes Agricola, and II. Porphyria – gives some mileage to the White Knight's pedantry in *Through the Looking Glass* about what a song really is, even though the celebrated passage is usually taken as Carroll's own example of a logician's concept of metalanguages:

'The name of the song is called "*Haddocks' Eyes*".'

'Oh, that's the name of the song, is it?' Alice said, trying to feel interested.

'No, you don't understand,' the Knight said, looking a little vexed. 'That's what the name is *called*. The name really *is* "*The Aged Aged Man*".'

'Then I ought to have said "That's what the *song* is called?"' Alice corrected herself.

'No, you oughtn't: that's quite another thing! The *song* is called "*Ways And Means*": but that's only what it's *called*, you know!'

'Well, what *is* the song, then?' said Alice, who was by this time completely bewildered.

'I was coming to that,' the Knight said. 'The song really *is* "*A-sitting On A Gate*": and the tune's my own invention.'

We may call a title ('Madhouse Cells') by another name ('Dramatic Lyric'), and this helps us to see that what we might overhear outside a prison cell in an asylum is in fact the isolated utterance of a character (not the poet) who might just as well have been in a play. But that is what the title is *called*. The poems really *are* 'Johannes Agricola' and 'Porphyria', though you and I have learned to call *them* 'Johannes Agricola in Meditation' and 'Porphyria's Lover'.

Does any of this matter? I think it does. Agricola's 'meditation' being divorced from any physical setting certainly gives our moral judgement a freer rein. And the anonymous murderer in the second poem is seen more clearly as having very recently committed his crime, rather than endlessly recreating it for the edification of interested visitors. We are not after 1863 in either case overhearing incarcerated madmen rehearsing their respective (if related) manias. We are able to judge their claims objectively. And this is no doubt what Browning finally intended.

In the case of the poem we now know as 'Porphyria's Lover', there is a particular reason for the poet to decide to puzzle us with his textual revisions. The poem itself allows the madman to assert as suddenly realised fact an unnerving situation whose circumstances we almost immediately question:

> The rain set early in to-night,
>   The sullen wind was soon awake,
> It tore the elm-tops down for spite,
>   And did its worst to vex the lake:

I listened with heart fit to break.
When glided in Porphyria; straight
   She shut the cold out and the storm,
And kneeled and made the cheerless grate
   Blaze up, and all the cottage warm;
   Which done, she rose, and from her form
Withdrew the dripping cloak and shawl,
   And laid her soiled gloves by, untied
Her hat, and let the damp hair fall,
   And, last, she sat down by my side
   And called me. When no voice replied,
She put my arm about her waist,
   And made her smooth white shoulder bare,
And all her yellow hair displaced,
   And, stooping, made my cheek lie there,
   And spread, o'er all, her yellow hair,
Murmuring how she loved me – she
   Too weak, for all her heart's endeavour,
To set its struggling passion free
   From pride, and vainer ties dissever,
   And give herself to me for ever.
But passion sometimes would prevail,
   Nor could to-night's gay feast restrain
A sudden thought of one so pale
   For love of her, and all in vain:
   So, she was come through wind and rain.
Be sure I looked up at her eyes
   Happy and proud; at last I knew
Porphyria worshipped me; surprise
   Made my heart swell, and still it grew
   While I debated what to do.
That moment she was mine, mine, fair,

> Perfectly pure and good: I found
> A thing to do, and all her hair
>   In one long yellow string I wound
>   Three times her little throat around,
> And strangled her.

At this point in the poem we are rapt in the man's insane logic: because Porphyria has braved a storm to visit him in his cheerless cottage and light his fire, leaving a formal dinner which he somehow knows about, coming in her grand clothes (she 'glided' in, and her dress is décolleté), coming on foot alone, and therefore getting drenched; because of all this he is finally convinced that she must be in love with him. This is the 'fact' he discovers. The 'moment' is for him overwhelming, and he kills her in order to preserve it. As a 'Romance', it becomes a kind of ghastly *liebestod*, and to readers of Browning generally a parodic example of that 'eternal moment' celebrated in all seriousness in poems like 'Two in the Campagna', 'The Last Ride Together' or 'Now'. To die at the climactic moment of romantic happiness is an extravagant absurdity, but it is one gestured towards by Othello, for example, or actually attempted by characters in Gide's *Les Faux Monnayeurs*. The poem continues:

>   No pain felt she;
>   I am quite sure she felt no pain.
> As a shut bud that holds a bee,
>   I warily oped her lids: again
>   Laughed the blue eyes without a stain.
> And I untightened next the tress
>   About her neck; her cheek once more
> Blushed bright beneath my burning kiss:
>   I propped her head up as before,

> Only, this time my shoulder bore
> Her head, which droops upon it still:
>   The smiling rosy little head,
> So glad it has its utmost will,
>   That all it scorned at once is fled,
>   And I, its love, am gained instead!
> Porphyria's love: she guessed not how
>   Her darling one wish would be heard.
> And thus we sit together now,
>   And all night long we have not stirred,
>   And yet God has not said a word!

His conviction that the aristocratic social world she belongs to ('Porphyria' is a telling name) is something that she really scorns, that her 'ties' with it are 'vain', and that only her pride prevents her from acknowledging an overwhelming passion for him, puts us in mind of the similar story of the mad hero of Tennyson's *Maud*, which must have been influenced by Browning's poem. He, too, neglects himself in cheerless and diminished surroundings. He, too, believes that the high-born heroine loves him, and will leave a grand political dinner to keep a tryst with him. And the fact that he, too, is telling the story induces us to believe him further than our better judgement allows.

A poet's irony governs our interpretation of his poem, and Browning is a master of irony, but readers still need all the help they can get. The change of title is itself ironical, for Porphyria's lover is not her lover at all. He only needs to *be* loved, and this is all he claims. The later title is an obvious code for 'Porphyria's Murderer'. But it is the loss of the general title 'Madhouse Cells' that really concerns us here. It shows very clearly how crucial information can be lost, with apparent carelessness of effect, in the course of a poet's rearrangement of his work. The result is

a literal dislocation of the poem's setting, and the removal of
what many readers feel to be a vital stage of the poem's story.
No one – whatever text they are reading – doubts that Pophyria's
murderer is mad. His catatonic lack of reponsiveness, his inner
excitability, his icy amoral deliberation, and above all his antin-
omianism, are all clear evidence of mania. But the poem as we
now have it does not tell us where he is 'now' or who he might
be explaining himself to. The momentary puzzle is that we do
not therefore know *what happens to him*.

Are Browning's textual changes defensible? He is, of course,
mainly concerned with the murderer's irrational hope of
preserving a moment of time for ever and of escaping conventional moral judgement of his act. We therefore happily accept
this forestalling of narrative outcome, and may well conclude that
the original general title (which also, we must remember, included
'Johannes Agricola') was unnecessarily tidy. Whether it is unnecessarily tidy in the case of Agricola is another matter, however,
since it is not clear that Agricola's peculiar and pathological belief
in personal salvation would automatically get him locked up.
Here, Browning's original general title seems intended merely to
pay lip service to the significance of what 'really' happened: the
historical Agricola was arrested in the middle of the antinomian
controversy in 1540, but broke parole and lived to maintain his
serious theological position in Reformation arguments about faith
and the moral law, an odd fellow-inmate, we might think, of a
jealous murderer. The title 'Madhouse Cells' created as many
puzzles as it solved.

THE TITLE THAT ISN'T A TITLE

The celebrated Auden poem of hypnotic sweep and rhetoric
beginning 'O Love, the interest itself in thoughtless heaven' (see

p. 136) was on its first appearance in 1932 in the *New Statesman* unhelpfully called 'Poem'. A periodical might be forgiven for reminding you that this was not, after all, like most of the contents, a book review or other piece of prose, but it is not difficult to find similar examples in specialist poetry magazines of the period. Reprinted the following year in an anthology, 'Poem' became 'Prologue', a functional title mysterious until, three years further on, it was so collected as the first poem of Auden's volume *Look, Stranger!* which also happened to end with an 'Epilogue'. That might have been the end of it, except that in the 1945 *Collected Poetry of W. H. Auden* it made its final appearance as 'Perhaps', a re-titling that hung over the poem like the sword of Damocles, for Auden never thereafter reprinted it. There was something very perhaps-ish about Auden's retitling in the 1940s.

There are many ways in which the given title of a poem may not look like a title at all, creating puzzles. A poem more particularly headed 'Sonnet' (common in the apprentice work of someone proud to have produced one) is a little more privileged than one headed 'Poem', but the title tells you nothing about it that isn't immediately apparent from a recognition of its form. So what is its real title? It must be presumed not to have one. Such lofty tautology is also found in the work of masters, sometimes as a kind of claim to exclusivity. Ezra Pound's *The Cantos* is perhaps the most notorious example, suggesting not so much that he believed that no one else had ever written in cantos, or that to revive and transcend that mode of epic organisation in the twentieth century is authoritative beyond all competition, but that he had reached that classic status where the activity of a posthumous editor might contribute to the text. An editor might well have called this unfinished series of poems the author's 'cantos' (to distinguish them from his limericks, say, or his translations: the sonnets of Shakespeare procured for the printer

Thomas Thorpe are a common example of such a series, lacking final authorial control). But for the author *himself* so to call them is actually either a carelessly insufficient act of identification or a puzzling challenge to the reader: what true title would you give these poems that have only been generically labelled? Imagine Dante's great work to be called simply *The Cantos*. What a distraction that would have been for the reader who embarked on the vast journey through hell, purgatory and paradise represented by the 100 cantos of his *Divina Commedia*. For the character of a long poem (as opposed to a collection of short ones) is not helpfully identified by reference merely to its form.

There are other ways in which a poet – used to reading scholarly classic texts and wishing, perhaps, to insinuate himself into that company – adopts a titling practice that belongs properly only to the gathering or completing activity of an editor. Most obvious, again in the work of beginning poets, is a title like 'Untitled'. Or even '[Untitled]'. The playful but excoriating Peter Reading is notable for a creative revival of this unpromising ploy, most appositely perhaps in his collection *Last Poems* (1994), itself supposedly 'edited' by another (Reading was only forty-eight at the time, and by no means deceased). There are poems titled '[Untitled]' on the page, but the final poem ('[Untitled]' on the contents page) is *in situ* merely a deliberately unreadable ironical slurry of type. Reading stands outside himself in order to imagine his oeuvre collapsing into the unintelligible.

It makes better sense in a list of contents to use '[Untitled]' only of a poem that is actually discovered to have no title when you come to the page it is on. This absolute absence of a title can, on occasion, create the basic puzzle of just what constitutes the poem's text, since a poem without a title might be mistaken for a continuation of the previous poem in the collection. Its separate identity would only be apparent from the contents page. The reader had better be aware of such pitfalls.

A poem that has no title may sometimes become known by its first line, and this first line can be reprinted above the poem as though it were perhaps, after all, a title, although this irritating practice gives the reader no help whatsoever with a guided entry into the poem. A title should be a signpost, and may be richly exploited as such, so that you have some idea of what to expect. The first line merely tells you that you have arrived, and for it to be also the 'title' turns your reading experience into a little stumbling tic, like Dr Johnson's difficulty in leaving a room.

Of course, in the case of a Shakespeare sonnet from the Thorpe collection, it would take an expert to recognise by number alone any of the 154 (and those who confidently appear to do so sound like the joke about prisoners' jokes). In such a case, the first line is usually necessary for identification. The same is true for any numbered collection, like Housman's *A Shropshire Lad* (sixty-three numbered poems, only sixteen of which have titles). Through this light use of titles, Housman's collection attained a severity and distance that appealed to other modern poets coming after him, particularly the younger Auden. For him, poems could be merely itemised like specimens, as though they had been scientifically collected without the prejudice of the thematic identification that titles might bestow upon them. In this way, the reader might be supposed to be better able to concentrate on what the poem actually *is*, and not what it purports to be. Thus the largely numbered contents of Auden's first three collections of short poems. But it could well be argued that the present-day reader is habituated to titles, and that a poem without one always issues an implicit challenge to remedy the absence. We have already seen Auden's own progressive titling ('Poem', 'Prologue' and 'Perhaps') and should not be surprised by similar sequences of rethought titles of poems most of which in their first book appearance had been simply numbered: 'Pur', 'Like a Dream' and 'This Lunar Beauty'; 'Europe 1936', 'Epilogue', 'As We Like It' and 'Our City'; 'The Territory of the Heart', 'Please Make Yourself at Home' and 'Like a Vocation'. Titles may change according to circumstance, and Auden can move from a chaste impersonality to a cavalier facetiousness and back again in the course of little more than a decade. But he did come to see the need for titles.

Sometimes a poem can remain without a real title and no one much minds, or even notices. But the essential puzzle of what it should really be called never quite disappears. Consider this: you ask a student to go away and read Tennyson's *In Memoriam*, and he happens to find instead his poem 'In Memoriam', written for William George Ward, the Roman Catholic theologian, and published in 1885. Of course, you intended him to read the poem *In Memoriam* written for Arthur Henry Hallam, and published in 1850, but time is short and large editions are confusing. It may even be that he finds Ward a fascinating character, an eventual 'ultramontane' for whom, for a time, John Henry Newman was a sufficient Pope, an 'earnest and pertinacious' confrontationalist who tried to get elected to All Souls' in dirty boots. Is not such a character at the heart of Victorian intellectual life? When he visited Thomas Arnold at Rugby he would sit all day on the sofa reading novels and then weary his host with debate after his long day's teaching. (On Ward's departure, Arnold had to spend a day recovering in bed.) Like many another more conventional subject of elegy, Hallam surely, by comparison, died too young to have achieved anything much.

This hypothetical student vagary takes no account of the primacy of emotion in Tennyson's poetry, of course. Tennyson on Ward is a trivial politeness, though sincerely intended. The reason that he could blithely reuse the 'title' of his most celebrated poem in this

way is that it is not really a title at all but a subtitle, or more properly a phrase attached to a missing title. When this Latin formula
is used, something or other is understood to be 'in memory of' the
person named, implicitly the tribute (wreath or stone or text, whatever) that contains these words.

If we believe that a title should be an appropriate signpost,
then the memorialising of Ward's qualities (his integrity, generosity,
skill in debate and so on) is sufficiently indicated by the heading
we find attached to the modest six lines of the poem, written for
Ward's son to include in a book commemorating his father's long
involvement with the Oxford Movement. But is the same heading
quite enough to encompass all that Tennyson wanted to say in
the 2,902 lines that he wrote for his dearest friend Hallam, dead
at twenty-two, a poet himself, a Cambridge 'Apostle' and, in
Tennyson's view, a sacred harbinger of a higher human type?

From our knowledge of the slow, seventeen-year accumulation
of the 131 sections of the poem (together with a Prologue and
Epilogue) and of Tennyson's habit of calling it 'my book of Elegies'
up to the month before publication, we can see how hard it would
have been to give it a conventional title. How could he both
memorialise Hallam and adequately cover the metaphysical, scientific and theological questionings that arise from his grief?
Tennyson claimed it as 'a poem, *not* an actual biography'. No one
would suppose that it was a biography at all, but the statement
shows the trouble that he was in. Tennyson and Hallam's friend
Gladstone inadvertently identified the problem when, reviewing
the poem, he referred to it as an oblation 'under the title of "In
Memoriam"', like a celebrity travelling furtively in disguise.

The poem succeeds by virtue of an evolving partnership
between the insistent and developing sense of personal loss and
the arguing of philosophical positions. It is an intensely dramatised poem, too, and though it partakes of the conventions of

elegy it also transcends them. Tennyson would have seen at once how it came to be so much more than a 'book of Elegies', without necessarily being able to come up with a title. One possibility he actually considered, *Fragments of an Elegy*, underlines the inter-mittent, abrupted and unschematic lyricism of the poem's arguments, but says nothing of their drift. Another, *The Way of the Soul*, seems more like the real thing. It would have lent encour-agement to the reader to move with a greater confidence from the blind faith in Jesus of the opening lines to the 'one far-off divine event' of the close. That is to say, the poem's lurking despair and doubt would have become not only Tennyson's despair and doubt, but would have been claimed as symptomatic of *the* soul's path to understanding. Actually, the ending is unashamedly ambiguous:

> One God, one law, one element,
> And one far-off divine event,
> To which the whole creation moves.

This could either be a 'Way' in the sense of teleology, or a 'Way' in the sense of a *modus vivendi*. That is to say that if the 'far-off divine event' is in the future, then creation 'moves' towards it, in the light of the amateur evolutionary theories of the poem; if it is in the past, then it is merely the impulse that, as it were, has set creation dancing. Since Tennyson's epilogue is about a wedding, this is not at all inappropriate (if you Google 'divine event', the first two hits are quite different catering services in Georgia and California). It was naturally human and touching to conclude with a celebration of his sister Cecilia's marriage to Edmund Lushington, since Hallam had intended to marry his sister Emily.

But *The Way of the Soul* was a way not taken. We are left with the simple epitaphic formula alone, only a kind of subtitle, and must make up our own minds about what to call the larger substance of the poem.

THE AMBIGUOUS TITLE: ARNOLD AND THE DINNER SERVICE

When the significance of a title is puzzling it may be that it has some private association for the poet, even one of which he is hardly aware. Let us look at a poem by Matthew Arnold, but also turn our investigation into a kind of story.

In 1814 Arnold's Aunt Lydia had surprisingly married Richard Lambart, the seventh Earl of Cavan, a General of the Napoleonic Wars who had whisked her away from the family in Kensington and settled her in his eccentric country seat, Eaglehurst, in Hampshire. When Arnold was first taken to Eaglehurst in 1836 at the age of thirteen he was not at all used to dining off crockery embellished with a coat of arms and heraldic motto, finding a mutton chop on his plate guarded by two bearded heroes, arms akimbo, wearing plumed helmets, scalloped breastplates, swords and sandals. The shield they nonchalantly presented to him on the plate's rim was a complicated affair with dolphins and quartered flowers and goats, surmounted by a coronet and a centaur armed with a bow and arrow. The three six-leaved flowers derived from the three cinquefoils that made the arms of Brabant, used by the Lambart family as far back as 1394 as a claim of descent from the Counts of Brabant. The crest of 1394 was surmounted by a female centaur holding a flower, but since the family reputation was now founded on warfare, the bow and arrow seemed more appropriate.

It made a striking enough distraction from gravy, at any rate, a reminder of the distinction of Aunt Cavan's marital connection. We can imagine his schoolmaster father addressing him by his family nickname and encouraging him to translate the motto which appeared on a scroll leading from the right foot of the left-hand hero to the left foot of the right-hand hero: 'UT QUOCUNQUE PARATUS':

'What does it mean, Crab? "*Quocunque*"? What sort of *Quo*? The indefinite adverb? In any direction? Good. And "*cunque*"? "*Cum*" indicating time? In any direction, at whatever time? Yes? Try "Whithersoever". "*Paratus*"? Indeed – prepared. Prepared for whithersoever. So, we might translate it, by analogy with "Ready for anything", as "Ready for anywhere", Crab, mightn't we? Except that "Ready for anywhere" isn't quite English. Think about it, Crab.'

If Crab did think about it, looking around the room at his uncle's booty snatched from the French in Alexandria in 1801, he understood that a soldier's duty to King and Country would inevitably take him wherever he might be obliged to go, and that he would have to be ready to meet that obligation, particularly if his family motto told him that he should, but that there were many compensations on the way. His father's motto, by the way, if he could really be said to have one, was an obligation in time rather than place: 'It boots not to look backwards. Forwards, forwards, forwards – should be one's motto.'

The Lambarts were a military family for whom the motto was indeed appropriate, but Richard Ford William Lambart was the first member of it to travel so widely in the service: Flanders, Ireland, Holland, Spain, Egypt (where he ended up in command of the entire British Army). He had seen a great deal of action in the first decade of the wars, and had been fully prepared to travel wherever (could one really say 'whithersoever'?) he had been required to go. He was now an old soldier, perhaps retired, though still Governor of Calshot Castle. Old soldiers never die, and they continue to swear horribly.

Ready to go, no matter where: perhaps that was it. Prepared on all sides.

Arnold wrote one of his earliest poems on that visit, inspired by the presiding spirit of his poetry-loving cousin Lydia Gundred. But the material for poetry doesn't often find expression with such immediacy. He knew very well his father's friend Wordsworth's opinion on that subject: poetry is emotion recollected in tranquillity. But the materials of poetry consist of all sorts of odd things that are hoarded up in the mind, to cast their shadows, however slight, at a later date.

All that was represented by the Cavan motto (the conviction of duty, the readiness of both spirit and body, the certitude in absolutes) soon came for Matthew Arnold to be the things he would most question. His characteristic mode is, as he famously phrased it in the Preface to his *Poems* of 1853, 'the dialogue of the mind with itself'. His early poems (such as 'Mycerinus' and 'The New Sirens') represent such dialogue as between studied revelry on the one hand and ennui of the spirit on the other, but the alternatives were to deepen in implication.

One of the earliest poems to benefit from a more considered and philosophically central duality was a poem of 1846 beginning: 'If, in the silent mind of One all-pure, | At first imagined lay | The sacred world ...' The complex hypothesis launched here is of two possible views of the world. One is of the world as imagined by a Plotinean Existence, an emanation gradually taking on physical form from its first idea; the other is of the world as having always existed, with no supernatural origin at all. For human beings to arrive at their self-consciousness in the first kind of world is self-evidently to require them to seek its divine source, however rarely successful such exploration may be; for them to find themselves in the second kind of world is a quite different experience, for they will be continually reminded of and admonished by their kinship with matter. It is only a vain illusion that humanity is unique.

Such a summary suggests that here we have a straightforward
Victorian debate about religious doubt, but the poem is by no
means straightforward:

> If, in the silent mind of One all-pure,
>   At first imagined lay
> The sacred world; and by procession sure
> From those still deeps, in form and colour dressed,
> Seasons alternating, and night and day,
> The long-mused thought to north, south, east, and west,
>   Took then its all-seen way;
>
> O waking on a world which thus-wise springs!
>   Whether it needs thee count
> Betwixt thy waking and the birth of things
> Ages or hours – O waking on life's stream!
> By lonely pureness to the all-pure fount
> (Only by this thou canst) the coloured dream
>   Of life remount!
>
> Thin, thin the pleasant human noises grow,
>   And faint the city gleams;
> Rare the lone pastoral huts – marvel not thou!
> The solemn peaks but to the stars are known,
> But to the stars, and the cold lunar beams;
> Alone the sun rises, and alone
>   Spring the great streams.
>
> But, if the wild unfathered mass no birth
>   In divine seats hath known;
> In the blank, echoing solitude if Earth,
> Rocking her obscure body to and fro,

Ceases not from all time to heave and groan,
Unfruitful oft, and at her happiest throe
    Forms, what she forms, alone;

O seeming sole to awake, thy sun-bathed head
    Piercing the solemn cloud
Round thy still dreaming brother-world outspread!
O man, whom Earth, thy long-vexed mother, bare
Not without joy – so radiant, so endowed
(Such happy issue crowned her painful care) –
    Be not proud!

Oh when most self-exalted most alone,
    Chief dreamer, own thy dream!
Thy brother-world stirs at thy feet unknown,
Who hath a monarch's hath no brother's part;
Yet doth thine inmost soul with yearning teem.
– Oh, what a spasm shakes the dreamer's heart!
    'I, too, but seem.'

It is not as if it is only doubt that leaves man in spasms. The struggle to imagine the imagined and intended world is equally isolating. In the first world he knows he can't be great and pure like a star; in the second world he is disgustingly a brother to things that stir at his feet, like worms. Perhaps Arnold has the third canto of the *Inferno* in mind here, where Dante meets those who were never alive, who have loathsome worms at their feet devouring their blood and tears. They lived without blame and without praise. Man's dual state has been expressed many times in poetry, but perhaps never with so fastidious a sense of isolation. But what does Arnold decide to call this unresolved poem, this poem whose centre hinges on a 'But'? He decides, either with a confidence utterly lacking in the poem itself, or with an irony designed to underline such a lack of confidence, to give it a title of resolve. Here is a puzzle, indeed. He calls it '*In Utrumque Paratus*'.

This title shows him prepared for two alternatives, or more precisely, prepared for either alternative. It reveals, in advance of the poem itself, a reason for not being defeated by ignorance of the profoundest truth that we wish to know about the world. The reason for not being defeated by such ignorance is that to be ready for either possibility to be true is also to be ready to deal with it, to have a philosophical strategy for coping with it once you have learned (if you ever do learn) which it is.

The similarity of the phrase to the Cavan motto can't be accidental, though it was no doubt subliminal. '*Ut Quocunque Paratus*': the Earl himself facing his daily mutton chop would have grown up mindful of his duty to be prepared to go anywhere in defence of his country; '*In Utrumque Paratus*': the poet, adapting the formula, awards himself the appropriate motto of being prepared to do his duty as a metaphorical soldier, a soldier of the metaphysical.

But this is not a solution. There is still something fairly odd going on here. There is an immediate source for the familiar Arnoldian title, which one might imagine has something to do with this serious metaphysical readiness, or could be thought to have such an application when the reader thinks it through with Arnold's intentions in mind. The phrase comes from the second book of the *Aeneid*, where Aeneas is giving his account of the great mistake of taking the Wooden Horse into Troy.

The beleagured Trojans believe that the Greeks have gone. Then they find the horse, and argue about what to do with it. And they also find a Greek with his hands tied behind his back, a young man called Sinon, who turns out to have been planted with the express purpose of convincing the Trojans that he has escaped being sacrificed by the Greeks themselves and that the horse is an offering of atonement left by the instruction of an oracle, by which means the Greeks might get safely home. Before Sinon's lengthy cock-and-bull story is launched, Aeneas explains his motive:

> *Hoc ipsum ut strueret Troiamque aperiret Achivis,*
> *Obtulerat, fidens animi atque in utrumque paratus,*
> *Seu versare dolos seu certae occumbere morti.*

(He had arranged things so as to expose Troy to the Achaeans [i.e., the Greeks], secure in his resolve and ready for either eventuality, whether it be the accomplishment of his trickery or an encounter with certain death)

Now it may be thought that it is indeed suicidal for Sinon to volunteer for a mission like this. How could he be believed? How could the Trojans possibly not realise that he is a double agent?

And equally, how could Arnold's readers, whom he would have expected to pick up his allusion to the Sinon episode, not conclude that the English poet was also facing some sort of risk in the alternatives of his metaphysical position? If you apply the Latin title strictly to the poem, it must mean that one of the Arnoldian hypotheses about the origin of the world is a similar cock-and-bull story that you hope will be believed, and that the other leads to certain death. This is true enough if you consider that the postulated 'One all-pure' of the poem might be as much of a myth as the portents that supposedly led the Greek priest Calchas to offer the Wooden Horse in the first place. The alternative is indeed death, the finality of our individual mortality, for in the unfathered world the yearning soul is finally forced to acknowledge that it has no greater future than the worms ('*I, too, but seem*').

It is a grim motto for what is turning out to be a grimmer and grimmer poem. Must humanity really steel itself to tell elaborate untruths in the hope that they will be believed, in order to circumvent death? If so, then Arnold is proposing something not unlike the wager of Blaise Pascal: that is to say, you might as well believe in Christianity and the afterlife, because if you don't, and it turns out to be true, then you are in trouble. This is a reason for believing in the first kind of world. But it may be impractical to believe nonsense, so that to accept the second kind of world might protect you from a disaster equivalent to the sack of Troy. If so, then you are beautifully saved. If not, then the world is literally an inimical place. 'If not . . .'? That happens to be what Sinon's name means! Is Virgil himself giving a little clue to the puzzle here so that the Trojans might solve it and be saved? The alternatives are puzzlingly twisted, and their symbolic application to the assault on Christian faith by rational doubt leaves Arnold in a satisfying impasse.

Sinon, of course, simply does what he does because he conceives it to be his duty in wartime. For him, '*In Utrumque Paratus*' really is a military motto very like that of Cavan's '*In Quocunque Paratus*', and this may well have been the connecting thread in Arnold's mind between gravy and the classics, his own family-induced if wavering convictions of duty.

COLERIDGE'S MYSTERIOUS PRISON

If explicit titles sometimes do their poems a disservice, only half-explicit ones can be even more distracting. They can refer to circumstances that the poet knows well enough, but which for reasons of delicacy he is unwilling to spell out. It may even be that the poem as it finally stands has cut itself entirely free from those circumstances, and that the poet would have done better not to allude to them at all.

Take Coleridge's 'This Lime-Tree Bower My Prison', a blank-verse meditation of a kind that he invented, first calling it an 'effusion', later a 'conversation poem'. The usual point of such poems was to convey a mystical vision of the unity of created life in a naturalistic setting with the presence of family or friends. The novelty of it lay in the linking of the visionary to its domestic context, the relative informality of the style, and in the way that the closely observing eye conveyed material with symbolic signif-icance. The first two of these characteristics are obvious in the opening of the poem as transcribed in a letter to his brother-in-law of 17 July 1797:

> Well, they are gone, and here must I remain,
> Lam'd by the scathe of fire, lonely and faint,
> This lime-tree bower my prison!

The key phrase from the poem's very first sentence was soon adopted as its title (the poem was first published in the *Annual Anthology* in 1800). The second line (alluding to the fact that his wife had accidentally spilled a pan of boiling milk over his foot) was abandoned before the poem reached print, although a subtitle was added ('A Poem Addressed to Charles Lamb, of the India House, London'), which explained references in the poem to 'my gentle-hearted Charles', who is clearly also one of the 'friends' (in the third person) who are envisaged as enjoying the uplifting walk which the poet regrets being unable to share. The version finally known to the public gave only a generalised reason for the poet's being confined to his bower:

In the June of 1797 some long-expected friends paid a visit to the author's cottage; and on the morning of their arrival, he met with an accident, which disabled him from walking

during the whole time of their stay. One evening, when they
had left him for a few hours, he composed the following
lines in the garden-bower.

But the explanation of his temporary confinement as the 'prison'
of the title is not, in itself, the answer to a puzzle, since the reader
isn't particularly aware of the puzzle I am going to unfold.

The poem, with some brilliance of descriptive conjuring, appears
to describe the very walk that the poet regrets not being able to take.
In his imagination he follows his friends across a hillside and down
a small valley, where a tumbling stream makes a 'dark green file of
long lank weeds . . . nod and drip beneath the dripping edge | Of
the blue clay-stone'. They climb up again to discover a 'magnificent'
view of the Bristol Channel in the sunset, a view 'of such hues | As
veil the Almighty Spirit, when yet he makes | Spirits perceive his
presence'. The poet's pleasure in their imagined pleasure is supported
by his actual observance of the behaviour of the evening sun on the
leaves of his lime tree, and on the other vegetation he can see from
it: a walnut tree, some ancient ivy, elms and bean flowers. He claims
that as long as there is something of Nature to observe, however
little, the heart is kept 'awake to Love and Beauty'.

These compensations for confinement are self-evidently a practical demonstration of a central Romantic belief about the spiritual
value of memory, which at the earliest possible moment in the
final text of the poem Coleridge somewhat self-pityingly complains
about:

> Well, they are gone, and here I must remain,
> This lime-tree bower my prison! I have lost
> Beauties and feelings, such as would have been
> Most sweet to my remembrance even when age
> Had dimm'd mine eyes to blindness!

This is the point of Wordsworth's 'Daffodils', for example, and we cannot feel that it is a cheat when we realise that Coleridge had, of course, taken the identical walk many times before, and so already had these 'beauties and feelings' learned by heart, as the poem proves. He also knew the moral and spiritual value of accepting the natural order and of taking joy in the beneficent holiness of all created things: this reciprocal process is at the heart of his poetry. The poem ends with his blessing of a rook much in the spirit in which his apparently doomed Mariner blesses the water-snakes and is momentarily relieved of his burden of guilt:

> My gentle-hearted Charles! When the last rook
> Beat its straight path along the dusky air
> Homewards, I blest it! Deeming its black wing
> (Now a dim speck, now vanishing in light)
> Had cross'd the mighty Orb's dilated glory,
> While thou stood'st gazing; or, when all was still,
> Flew creeking o'er thy head, and had a charm
> For thee, my gentle-hearted Charles, to whom
> No sound is dissonant which tells of Life.

But there is no particular puzzle about all this, either. It is a sunset version of the creative joy proposed in other conversation poems, such as 'The Nightingale' or 'Frost at Midnight', where his infant son Hartley is the occasion of transfigurations of nature in moonlight. The puzzle still lies in the title.

The little arbour beneath the sheltering, tent-like branches of a lime tree, with its pungent June aroma, was in his neighbour Tom Poole's garden. Coleridge was in the habit of sitting and writing there. But why, really, should it be described as a 'prison'? Readers are inclined, as we have seen, to take the assertions of titles at face value, and there is certainly something in the sense

of confinement and release that structures the poem to accord
with the image of a prison.

But the walk that the poet is unable to share is so insistently
seen as a liberation for his old schoolfellow, collaborator, confidant
and regular correspondent Charles Lamb, who 'hast pined | And
hunger'd after Nature, many a year, | In the great City pent, winning
thy way | With sad yet patient soul, through evil and pain | And
strange calamity!' that we begin to discount the poet's own melo-
dramatised confinement, with its 'scathe of fire'. This alarming
phrase for spilt milk is close to the word 'scathefire' (compare the
German *schadenfeuer*), used when a whole house or town is on fire.

This exaggeration is an instinctive act of sympathy with Lamb,
who had found it almost impossible to get leave from his job at East
India House from the Accountant General. He sometimes had to
work until 7 p.m. without getting any dinner, and his letters are full
of complaints on the subject. The Miltonic phrase 'In the great
City pent' occurs again in 'Frost at Midnight', where Coleridge
refers to himself as 'reared | In the great city, pent 'mid cloisters
dim', and the association of thought is clear. Both Coleridge and
Lamb were Christ's Hospital boys in just that situation – and poor
Lamb *was still there*. He went straight from school into a counting
house, and was now irrevocably a civil servant. London was his
prison, and might be the end of him ('pent' = 'penned', like a lamb).

But none of this explains Coleridge's following words: 'winning
thy way / With sad yet patient soul, through evil and pain | And
strange calamity!' and these have a direct connection with impris-
onment. The strange calamity was a quite specific event, reported
in the *Morning Chronicle* for 26 September 1796:

On Friday afternoon the Coroner and a respectable Jury sat
on the body of a Lady in the neighbourhood of Holborn,
who died in consequence of a wound from her daughter

the preceding day. It appeared by the evidence adduced, that while the family were preparing for dinner, the young lady seized a case knife laying on the table, and in a menacing manner pursued a little girl, her apprentice, round the room; on the eager calls of her helpless infirm mother to forbear, she renounced her first object, and with loud shrieks approached her parent.

The child by her cries quickly brought up the landlord of the house, but too late – the dreadful scene presented to him the mother lifeless, pierced to the heart, on a chair, her daughter yet wildly standing over her with the fatal knife, and the venerable old man, her father, weeping by her side, himself bleeding at the forehead from the effects of a severe blow he received from one of the forks she had been madly hurling about the room.

For a few days prior to this the family had observed some symptoms of insanity in her, which had so much increased on the Wednesday evening, that her brother early the next morning went in quest of Dr Pitcairn – had that gentleman been met with, the fatal catastrophe had, in all probability, been prevented.

It seems the young Lady had been once before, in her earlier years, deranged, from the harassing fatigues of too much business. – As her carriage towards her mother was ever affectionate in the extreme, it is believed that to the increased attentiveness, which her parents' infirmities called for by day and night, is to be attributed the present insanity of this ill-fated young woman.

It has been stated in some of the Morning Papers, that she has an insane brother also in confinement – this is without foundation.

The Jury of course brought in their verdict, *Lunacy*.

This is the official account of Mary Lamb's murder of their mother. Charles himself arrived in the room in time to take the knife out of his sister's hand. The family had been unable to relieve Mary of the burden of caring for her parents. Her paralysed mother needed constant attendance, so that Mary – in her thirties and unmarried – was obliged to share her bed and care for her.

But this was not all. As the *Morning Chronicle* guardedly and charitably allows, Charles was not himself in confinement. But he had been. At the beginning of the year he had been in a madhouse at Hoxton, where he had been kept for six weeks. He spoke of it as his 'prison house'. After the murder Mary was, in turn, confined, apparently with some tact and kindliness, in a house in Islington, lucky to escape being sent to Bedlam. But she, too, was in the same sense in 'prison'.

After all this, Lamb had decided to write no more poetry, and did in fact burn most of his existing literary papers. Coleridge tried to get him to write again, and offered a letter of religious consolation ('They arrive at the largest inheritance who imitate the most difficult parts of [Christ's] character, and, bowed down and crushed underfoot, cry in fullness of faith, "Father, thy will be done"'), but more appropriately wrote that above all he wanted to get Lamb down to Nether Stowey to visit ('You shall be quiet, and your spirit may be healed').

This brings us close to what is supposed to be happening in 'This Lime-Tree Bower my Prison', where we feel the poet willing Lamb's spirit to be healed by the divine afflatus that haunts the Quantocks. This is a Spinozan idea rather than conventionally redemptive like his letter of Christian consolation. The duality is familiar enough in early Coleridge (for example, in the ecstatic unorthodoxies and Christian reproofs of 'The Æolian Harp'). It also involves the active mediation of the poet, who, as someone who is already learning to be sustained by God-in-Nature must show himself able to suffer as well (the symbolic *schadenfeuer* as a kind of truly sensitive *schadenfreude*). The vague priggishness and egotism in the poem are a part of this need to lay himself open in just this way. It is not only that we all do suffer, but also that we are all open to calamity, and are all existentially guilty. Coleridge is trying to express in miniature the scenario of his famous ballad, that only the exercise of the imagination could possibly release him from his life sentence. He is imprisoned, and says that he may never again meet his friends, a predicament precisely analogous to that of the Mariner becalmed among a dead crew, 'alone, alone, all, all alone, | Alone on a wide wide sea'.

His poem 'The Dungeon' explains why the ministrations of Nature would be better for the offender than confinement, and how the 'melodies of woods, and winds, and waters' would 'heal and harmonise' the 'angry spirit'. He naturally suggested that Mary herself should come and stay in Nether Stowey, but this was not possible. What could he do but simply show how the influence of Nature operates *on himself*, and how it induces the lamed ego to turn outwards in an act of benediction? Nature is *the opposite* of a prison.

It is this that explains the exaggerated oddity of the title of this conversation poem, and I think that we can better explain the puzzle if we learn to pronounce it with the right emphasis, if we think of it in a constructive sense as 'This Lime-Tree Bower *my* Prison'.

AGAINST NATURE POETRY: 'CONVERSION'

Of course, it is entirely possible to argue the opposite case to Coleridge's, and claim that Nature can, after all, be something like a prison. Sometimes poets deliberately do this sort of thing

not so much out of sheer bloody-mindedness, but to test out
philosophical alternatives, as when Milton writes 'L'Allegro' (the
Happy Man) and follows it with 'Il Penseroso' (the Melancholy
Man) in such a way as to make the reader feel that these may
very well be aspects of the same poetic personality. Or as when
Tennyson writes first the poem 'Nothing Will Die' and then one
entitled 'All Things Will Die', so that he can explore the common
paradox that we feel is inherent in life and its inevitable changes.
Traditionally, a poem that retracts something proposed in an earlier
one is called a 'palinode', but this deliberate sense of recantation
seems too much of a commitment for the subtle interplay of such
linked pairs as Milton's or Tennyson's.

   T. E. Hulme's poem 'Conversion' argues an opposite case to
the poem by Coleridge that we have been looking at, and it does
so with an air of defying the whole of nineteenth-century nature
poetry and acting as a palinode to Romantic attitudes. Far from
bringing us into a unity with the One Life, as Coleridge believed,
the beauty of Nature in Hulme's poem is a forbidden thing:

> Light-hearted I walked into the valley wood
> In the time of hyacinths,
> Till beauty like a scented cloth
> Cast over, stifled me. I was bound
> Motionless and faint of breath
> By loveliness that is her own eunuch.
>
> Now pass I to the final river
> Ignominiously, in a sack, without sound,
> As any peeping Turk to the Bosphorus.

Immediately we feel that the title embodies a puzzle, and that it
is the sort of puzzle that can only be solved in the light of our

interpretation of the poem itself, which seems to be giving very little away.

One likely reading might be as follows. The metaphor of the eunuch at the end of the first section implies that we can have no fruitful contact with the beauty of the natural world, and it prepares us for the gear shift into the larger metaphor of the Sultan's harem in the second section. In the same way, the simile of the scented cloth is momentarily expanded by the description of the effect it has ('stifled' . . . 'motionless and faint of breath') and then reduced to a 'sack' to corroborate a neat analogy. In our innocent hope of a relationship with the world in which we find ourselves we are suffocated by our own impotence. Our subjective isolation is an indignity, and we die having had only a stolen glimpse of the real world, whose very beauty protects it from us. What the poem is about, then, takes us in this reading into the world of metaphysics.

Hulme was one of the significant presiding midwives of Imagism, a movement dating from about 1908 which sought to get rid of rhetoric and explanations in poetry in favour of the sculpted and unmediated image (see the discussion of Pound, p. 19). One of the consequences of this isolation of images from any discursive context is the relative freedom of interpretation given to the reader. A more detailed and formal analysis of the poem would uncover aspects of its figurative structure about which different readers might well argue. For example, the erotic scenario might equally suggest that the speaker simply becomes habituated to beauty and learns to trivialise it. It is possible to read the 'scented cloth' as a mode of capture, much like the later 'sack'. There is the question of what sort of relationship with beauty is meant by the allusions to an exclusive harem, and whether there is any metaphorical role for the unmentioned Sultan. There is the question of what is meant exactly by 'the final river'. Is it a

symbolic river of death, like Lethe? Or is it more simply the river
that develops from the stream that must, we imagine, run through
the 'valley wood' of the poem's opening?

The poem is to an extent difficult, in the same sort of way
that the slightly later poetry of Pound and Eliot is difficult, but
the title has its own special difficulty. It does not appear in any
obvious way to relate to either the tenor or the vehicle of the
poem's central metaphors, that is to say either to the setting of
a valley with a stream, or the being stupefied by beauty, or the
story of the would-be invader of the harem being thrown into
the Bosphorus. Or does it?

'Conversion' is – in contrast to the delicacy and wry humour
of the poem itself – a severely conceptual word. The OED gives
something like twenty meanings deriving from the idea of turning,
usually from one thing to another (from the Latin *conversionem, con
+ vertere*). The mind, tasked with choice, is sometimes distracted
by the irrelevant. But it must discard the basic meanings as too
simplistic (and, in any case, obsolete). It should probably discard
other obsolete meanings. It must discard specific meanings from
the world of currency or military formations or Rugby football
or the turning of barns into houses, as well as other applications
that were adopted later than the date of the poem (these would
include uses in chemistry and marketing). But there remain cred-
ible options, or options that are sufficiently complex to need some
analysis, and these are still distracting enough:

(1) In logic, inferring a second proposition from a first by using
    the predicate of the first as its subject (OED I.4).
(2) Converting the property of others to one's own uses (OED
    I.7).
(3) Conversion to a particular form of (usually Christian) reli-
    gion, or a less specific spiritual rebirth (OED II.8 and 9).

(4) The action of turning into something else (OED II.11).
(5) The defence mechanism which produces bodily symptoms of
      an internal conflict which has no physical cause (OED III.16c).

How do we deal with this choice? It isn't simply a matter of
deciding which is most appropriate to the meaning of the poem,
since it may be that the title (which is, after all, a part of the text
of the poem) is a significant piece of evidence in deciding that
meaning. Both title and poem must be taken together.

Meaning (4) reminds us that to be stifled with a scented cloth
might even make you think for a moment that you are yourself
being abducted into the harem, the very thing you may long for.
But the cloth 'turns into' a sack, just as the free man turns into
an imprisoned one.

There is a temporal development embodied in the two sections
of the poem ('I walked' in the first section, followed by 'Now pass
I' in the second). This conveys a kind of story at the metaphorical level, which seems appropriate to a version of meaning (3).
It is not exactly the Road to Damascus, but the deprivation
described in the second section, however ignominious, is something like the deprivations of a mature religious discipline adopted
after a 'light-hearted' youth, or at least the profound awareness
of a spiritual rebuke.

The appropriation of beauty by sight, however temporary or
unlicensed, is something that the poem is ambiguous about. The
speaker in his exhilaration and innocence seems to be reduced
to a form of thieving ('any peeping Turk') and yet the appreciation of beauty is presented as involuntary. Meaning (2) seems to
come into play here, and so the title might – in a forensic sense
– tip the balance. That the beauty of the world does not, in fact,
belong to us becomes a legal verdict.

Meaning (5) is given no earlier example than 1909, but this is close enough to the date of the poem, given that the OED isn't entirely reliable on first use. Can we see the swooning at beauty and the breathlessness of the first section of the poem, together with the paralysis of the second section, as being in some sense a manifestation of an internal psychological conflict? The meaning would have to belong to, as it were, a secondary metaphorical level of the poem, and is hard to hold in one's head.

The most unlikely of the five meanings is (1), but can we make any headway with it? A convenient example from a late seventeenth-century logician is given by the OED: 'If A:B::C:D then by Conversion 'twill be as A:A-B::C:C-D.' In Hulme's poem, if A is the world and B is the self, and if C is the harem and D is the voyeur, the correspondences in the first proposition simply demonstrate the basic metaphor. But it is clear that a somewhat subtler explanation of what is going on in the poem is provided by the conversion. Here we see that the parallels appear to enforce the notion of the unlikeliness of a purely autonomous beauty. If the world is to the world without the observing self (A:A-B) as the harem is to the harem without the concealed Turk (C:C-D), what we are being particularly asked to consider is a proof that the world does, after all, exist in our relationship with it, because the Sultan has ordered our death as a result of our peeping. The poem becomes a miniature version of the myth of Paradise lost.

Juggling with these senses of the title may leave the reader quite indecisive, with the puzzle unsolved. Knowing something of Hulme's background (a Cambridge mathematician who became a philosopher of metaphysics) may give more credence to meaning (1) than it deserves. The useful principle of choosing the simplest solution does not here leave us entirely satisfied with meaning (3). None of the other meanings offers itself as anything more than contributory. What is to be done? Perhaps the whole idea of giving an Imagist poem a title is misleading. As Hulme said:

'Thought is prior to language and consists in the simultaneous presentation of two different images.' Insofar as titles tend to be linguistic labels, they may find it hard to partake constructively of the original thought.

GETTING THE TITLE WRONG: *THE WASTE LAND*

Hulme's work was tremendously influential. A handful of poems ironically published in *The New Age* in 1912 as 'The Complete Poetical Works' was immediately reprinted by Pound in his volume *Ripostes* of the same year. T. S. Eliot thought that Hulme was the author of 'two or three of the most beautiful short poems in the English language', and perhaps paid him the compliment of remembering 'Conversion' in his 'The Death of St Narcissus' ('When he walked over the meadows | He was stifled and carried apart | By the river') and in *The Waste Land* ('the hyacinth garden . . . I could not | Speak . . . I was neither | Living nor dead').

  The Waste Land has among its many distinctions the one of being perhaps the best known of the poems that rely heavily on the Imagist experiment. Though it is now almost ninety years old, and generations of readers have digested the accumulated interpretations and discoveries of critics and scholars, it remains a notoriously difficult poem. It would be possible to locate a number of unresolved puzzles throughout the poem, but here I want to confine myself to a strange sort of puzzle connected with the title itself.

  Why is it that this most celebrated of modernist poems is so frequently referred to by the wrong title?

  I'm not referring to the fact that for much of its early existence in Eliot's mind the poem was to be called 'He Do the Police in Different Voices'. It was soon enough known as *The Waste Land*,

and *The Waste Land* is what it assuredly is. Why, then, do so many people call it '*The Wasteland*'? And does this matter?

It is an error more commonly found written than spoken. That is to say, someone who habitually wrote '*The Wasteland*' might in speech give more equal weight to the second and third syllables, so that a listener would mentally transcribe it correctly as '*The Waste Land*'. More often than not, however, the pronunciation of the incorrect title's noun would be the trochee that the spelling suggests. When the error is pointed out, it is often felt to be a venial slip of the pen, as though the two titles were more or less identical. They are not.

It is perhaps worth quantifying the error, or at least giving some idea of its extent not only in common parlance but also in professional and academic contexts. I am not simply referring to the errors of students in their essays and examinations, although the most abundant examples are found there (I would say from my own experience that perhaps three out of ten students habitually perpetrate the erroneous form). In fact, the poem was so miscalled from very early in its existence, as when Bertrand Russell told Ottoline Morrell in 1923 that he was particularly excited to get hold of 'Eliot's *Wasteland*'. The mistitling occurs widely in print, and evidence of it in official contexts could be freely collected, for example, in the promotional leaflet for *Icon Critical Guides to Literature* (distributed by Penguin Books), where in 'Forthcoming Titles for 1999' a poem called '*The Wasteland*' is enthused over by Professor Rachel Bowlby; or in the lively literary periodical *The Devil* (1999, issue unnumbered, p. 22), where Professor Andrew Motion so refers to Eliot's poem (and again, ten years later, in the *Guardian* for 17 February 2009); or in Professor Germaine Greer's lecture 'The Name and Nature of Poetry' (*Guardian Review*, 1 March 2003, p. 6); or in a piece about Henry Reed by Professor Adam Phillips in the *Observer Review* (28 October 2007, p. 28).

Of course, these good professors are in the hands of interviewers, journalists and copy-editors, and are not to be blamed.
Or are they? Probably these interviewers, journalists and copy-
editors were themselves only recently students whose
orthographical errors were silently passed over by their busy
teachers and examiners and therefore continued to be carried,
like undefused bombs, into their unsuspecting literary careers.

Finally, if you want to hear Eliot himself reading his poem in
The Caedmon Treasury of Modern Poets Reading Their Own
Poetry (Caedmon Literary Series TC 0994) you will find it listed
on the record sleeve as – '*The Wasteland*'. Let's see why this
matters, and how much it matters. We shall find that it helps to
solve a puzzle.

It should be possible to end the solecism forever by distinguishing clearly between wasteland (a plot derelict or not yet built
on) and waste land (land laid waste, by an army, perhaps, or by
a failed harvest). A property developer might have his eye on
wasteland, and there is, after all, some of it in Eliot's poetry, as
we shall see. These are the civic interstices across which news-
papers blow or rats scurry. Wasteland is waste as bogland is boggy
or grassland grassy: it is an area of a size unspecified because the
size is unimportant compared with its condition. '*The Wasteland*'
invokes a specific area as yet unspecified. The implied plural,
'*Wastelands*', would have been an interesting alternative title, had
Eliot wished to symbolise the dead souls of his city-dwellers. In
the singular, '*Wasteland*', by contrast, might be a section of a
report on urban conditions. All these alternatives are quite opposed
to the sense of the devastated *patria* inherent in his use of the
singular 'land'. Let us look at this in more detail.

From the beginning, Eliot's poetry was conscious of the bleakness of the city. Its streets are dirty, and beyond the streets are
patches of shabby and undeveloped waste ground. In the second

poem from the long-lost *Inventions of the March Hare* (1909–17) we find 'Bottles and broken glass, | Trampled mud and grass.' The third one begins ironically: 'This charm of vacant lots! | The helpless fields that lie | Sinister, sterile and blind – | . . . | With ashes and tins in piles, | Shattered bricks and tiles | And the debris of a city.' The vacant lots reappear twice in the better-known sequence that survived in Eliot's first published collection as 'Preludes', and fields or yards with dumped metal also put in an appearance. These lots have nothing built on them, but nonetheless contain the abandoned raw material of building. They seem to inform the 'stony rubbish' of the first part of *The Waste Land*, contributing something to the symbolic character of Eliot's urban landscape that might be properly described as 'wasteland' (OED 1.B. 'Land, especially that which is surrounded by developed land, not used or unfit for cultivation or building and allowed to run wild').

So far, so excusable. But this is not what *The Waste Land* is most deeply about. At the centre of the poem there appears its 'most important personage' (in Eliot's words in an appended note), the figure of a blind Greek prophet who famously '*sees*', as Eliot paradoxically put it, 'the substance of the poem'. Readers have been distracted by Eliot's explanatory notes (produced as a space-filler for the Boni and Liveright edition), as much for what they don't explain as for what they do, and the note on Tiresias is possibly the most misleading of them all, since he is an actual witness to relatively little in the poem. The note culminates in a quotation from Ovid, which recounts the reasons for the bisexual Tiresias having been blinded by Juno, but it says nothing at all of the equally relevant roles of Tiresias in Homer's *Odyssey* and Sophocles' *Oedipus Rex*.

It is the last of these that is of most significance here. It is the Sophoclean Tiresias who crucially 'sees' why Thebes is blighted.

It is a punishment, a direct result of the fulfilment of Apollo's oracle that Oedipus shall kill his father and marry his mother. This Oedipus has unwittingly done, and the first scene of the play establishes its effect on the city that he has come to rule:

> You too have seen our city's affliction, caught
> In a tide of death from which there is no escaping –
> Death in the fruitful flowering of her soil;
> Death in the pastures; death in the womb of woman;
> And pestilence, a fiery demon gripping the city . . .

It is Tiresias who is instrumental in compelling King Oedipus to his fatal investigations into the reason for the city being laid waste by famine and plague. His is one of a number of prophetic and admonitory voices in the early drafts of the poem (St John the Divine, Ezekiel, Jeremiah) that lend a tone of rebuke to its analysis of sterility, spiritual death and 'the immense panorama of futility and anarchy which is contemporary history'. And it helps to establish a pattern of devastation in response to involuntary error that borrows the Christian sense of original sin. We find in Eliot's poem an embracing consciousness of frustrated relationships, the waste of war and the haunting difficulty of finding a religious solution to the problems of the afflicted 'city'. The 'O City city' of Tiresias in 'The Fire Sermon' is the despairing 'O polis, polis' of Oedipus when accused by Creon of ruling unjustly, while the Oedipal predicament connects both with the scapegoat Fisher King of the poem's central Grail structure and, through Freud, with Eliot's personal situation, half-disowned by his father and 'broken' by his mother like the 'broken Coriolanus' of 'What the Thunder said'. The arid plain of the final lines of the poem, the kingdom of the wounded Fisher King, is, like Thebes, a land laid waste (OED 2: 'Devastated, ruinous').

The difference between '*The Wasteland*' and '*The Waste Land*' is finally, therefore, the difference between accidental cultural circumstance and a critical and overpowering sense of failure and guilt.

7

WHO IS OZYMANDIAS?:
WHAT'S IN A NAME?

WHO IS OZYMANDIAS?

Shelley's sonnet 'Ozymandias' of 1818 is one of his most celebrated poems (YouTube is currently well-stocked with filmic
settings of it) and is also characteristic of what has always seemed
to be a deceptive scope in the sonnet form itself, its ability both
to focus *and* enlarge. A sonnet is able to make a simple point,
which at the same time reaches beyond the end of the poem with
reverberating consequences to create, as it were, a broad channel
of meditation for the single vessel which is its chosen symbol:

> I met a traveller from an antique land
> Who said: Two vast and trunkless legs of stone
> Stand in the desert . . . Near them, on the sand,
> Half sunk, a shattered visage lies, whose frown,
> And wrinkled lip, and sneer of cold command,
> Tell that its sculptor well those passions read
> Which yet survive, stamped on these lifeless things,
> The hand that mocked them, and the heart that fed:

And on the pedestal these words appear:
'My name is Ozymandias, king of kings:
Look on my works, ye Mighty, and despair!'
Nothing beside remains. Round the decay
Of that colossal wreck, boundless and bare
The lone and level sands stretch far away.

I am concerned with puzzles and not with the niceties of the sonnet's form, but it is worth noting that, like many of the Romantic poets, Shelley is looking for a constructive novelty of rhyme and organisation that might give further force to the seamless and organic effect of the Italian sonnet's structure (where after an initial group of eight lines, the octave, we have one of only six, the sestet, whose rhymes tend to involve rather than expound). 'Ozymandias' has a strange multiplicity of structures. The last three lines of the octave are as closely linked by rhyme to the two tercets of the sestet as they are to the rest of the octave itself, offering the reader a subliminal choice between the traditional 8 + 6 and a new 5 + 9. At the same time, the imposed narrative structure defies each of these latent rhyming structures by insisting upon the 1 + 8 + 2 + 3, which the poet's introduction, the traveller's account and its enclosed words on the pedestal suggest. And this is in a sense mysteriously closer to the Italian structure after all, for the traveller's words form a perfectly traditional descriptive octave, albeit now *within* the sonnet, rather than absolutely introducing it. This corresponds to Shelley's ascribing his information to a 'traveller' in the first place rather than conveying it in his own voice, a distance that is intended to supply credibility.

Our first puzzle is: who is this traveller? The simple answer is that Shelley would have found Ozymandias (which was simply one of the royal names of Rameses II) in the account by Diodorus of Sicily of the Ramesseum at Thebes. So the 'traveller' is really a classical historian. At one of the entrances of the Ramesseum were three enormous statues: Rameses and his mother and daughter. Diodorus transcribes the inscription on the statue of Rameses as follows: 'King of Kings am I, Osymandyas. If anyone would know how great I am and where I lie, let him surpass one of my works' (Loeb translation). Shelley turns the black stone blocks of Diodorus, in which as he would have read 'there is not a single crack or blemish to be seen', into isolated fragments: two stone legs and a broken face ('shattered visage').

This itself may be puzzling. But the adaptation of his source is understandable. Shelley would want his readers to imagine something in accordance with the tradition of Western statuary, rather than with the ritual tombs of Karnak. The great frisson of the poem lies in Shelley's imagining an entirely encroaching desert. There is no hint of other buildings or statues, as are itemised by Diodorus (paraphrasing the third-century BC historian Hecateus of Abdera), and certainly no tourists apart from the traveller himself. The effect is like that of the half-submerged Statue of Liberty in the film *Planet of the Apes*, except that the film played a superb trick upon the viewer, whereby what was thought to be an alien planet turned out to be our own earth after all.

This sort of trick is implicit in Shelley's sonnet, too, for what we take to be something that can only happen in an 'antique land', where outlandish political power makes superhuman claims, may happen closer to home as well. We know that Ozymandias was Rameses II. In the course of enquiring further into the implications of Shelley's sonnet – that is to say, of asking more precisely who Ozymandias *is*, rather than simply who he *was* – let us look at another sonnet on the same subject that makes its own point more plainly.

When Leigh Hunt published Shelley's sonnet 'Ozymandias' in

The Examiner in January 1818, the poet Horace Smith wrote the magazine a letter of enthusiastic praise, and later perhaps ingenuously submitted his own sonnet 'On a Stupendous Leg of Granite', which Hunt saw fit to publish:

On a Stupendous Leg of Granite,

Discovered standing by itself in the Deserts of Egypt, with the Inscription inserted below.

In Egypt's sandy silence, all alone,
   Stands a gigantic Leg, which far off throws
   The only shadow that the Desert knows.
'I am great Ozymandias,' saith the stone,
   'The King of Kings; this mighty city shows
'The wonders of my hand.' The city's gone!
   Nought but the leg remaining to disclose
The site of that forgotten Babylon.
We wonder, and some hunter may express
Wonder like ours, when through the wilderness
   Where London *stood*, holding the wolf in chase,
He meets some fragment huge, and stops to guess
   What wonderful, but unrecorded, race
   Once dwelt in that annihilated place.

Smith spells out everything that in Shelley may be thought to be implied. He unnecessarily names Egypt and its analogue Babylon. He risks evoking the city despite its absence ('The city's gone!' he says, whereas in Shelley there simply *is* nothing). And above all he applies the lesson of the inevitable fall of empires to London. To do this, he has to stress the wonders of the civilisation that has disappeared, and of the comparable wonders of our own that will disappear, whereas Shelley is insistent not only upon the tyranny and arrogance of the relics but upon the privileged insight of the sculptor that conveys them to us. Smith sees no further than the fate of Nash's renovated London, elegant locus of a 'wonderful race' who are in the business of keeping the atlas coloured red. For the anti-imperialist Shelley there is nothing particularly wonderful about the civilisation of Rameses II. For Shelley, the knowledge of the futility of power is already latent in the fragments that survive the pharaoh, because the original artist, the sculptor of the sonnet, possessed that knowledge himself. This is the fruit of irony, whereas Smith's gigantic leg, which somehow must be made to betoken wonders, looks much more like a piece of sentimental bathos.

Of course, Shelley may have wished to imply that all this could happen to London, too, since in his sonnet 'England in 1819' he is even less respectful to the rulers of Regency England than he had been to Ozymandias. However, it is in the nature of poetry to incorporate specific meanings that derive from its material, and whereas Smith's application of his huge fragment in the sestet to England seems merely dutifully logical and perhaps comfortably theoretical, in Shelley's sonnet there is another more appropriately historical meaning, another level of implication.

We may have suspected that Diodorus was not Shelley's only source when we found that his Rameses statue had no crack or blemish. A likelier and closer authority is Vivant Denon, who travelled with the French armies in Egypt in the campaigns of 1798–9 and sketched a ruined colossus at Thebes, resting his paper on the knees of a soldier whose body afforded him a little shade. In his *Voyages dans la Basse et la Haute Egypte* of 1802 he describes this statue as '*méchamment brisé*' (spitefully shattered), gives its enormous dimensions and says that '*dans sa chute il est tombé sur le visage*'. He asks if '*c'étoit-ci la statue de Memnon ou celle d'Ossimandue?*' and concludes that it is more probably Memnon.

When he comes to the actual figures that we have seen described by Diodorus, he mentions the Ozymandias inscription and describes two of the large seated figures, but laconically concludes: '*celle du roi a disparu*'.

This is not only a closer source for Shelley's 'visage' and for the significant 'shattering' or absence of the artefacts described by Diodorus, but it provides us with another parallel for the knowing Egyptian sculptor who was commanded by Ozymandias to construct his statue (and more particularly for the traveller with his tales to tell). It was Vivant Denon whom Napoleon made the first Director of the Louvre and who was instructed to supervise the enormous encyclopædic description of Egypt published from the materials observed or plundered by Napoleon's Imperial army. These cultural monuments were intended to glorify French science, but England had turned the French out of Egypt in 1801 and secured their own booty, including the Rosetta Stone, a sign perhaps that the imperial ambitions of Napoleon could be successfully delimited. In any case, we needn't look far for the obvious Ozymandias of Shelley's day. The tyrant in his sonnet *was* in the most obvious sense Rameses II, but in Shelley's mind Ozymandias *is* in a more applied sense Napoleon, defeated at Waterloo but not yet dead, enisled in exile, and capable of being mocked by the poet's hand.

WHAT IS THE SNARK?

The consciously Freudian implications of a modernist poem like Empson's 'The Scales' (see p. 64) might lead us back through its phallic allusion to the enormous dog in *Alice* to Lewis Carroll's most important poem, *The Hunting of the Snark* (1876), subtitled 'An Agony in Eight Fits'. The excuse would be that nonsense famously frees the conscious mind of a nineteenth-century writer from its usual repression of compulsive sexual material. But although thus liberated, the writer will still not understand quite where his pen is taking him. The *Snark* is an elaborate adventure, with its own internal illogic, but at its core is a puzzle.

Carroll's representative voyagers (the Bellman, the Boots, the Bonnet-maker, the Barrister, the Broker, the Billiard-marker, the Banker, the Beaver, the Baker and the Butcher) contrive in various obsessive ways to pretend that their objective is capable of being apprehended. They have opinions about it, baleful anecdotes and rules of thumb, but are at the same time clearly full of ignorance and fear. They are all, of course, male (the Beaver is an 'it', though Andrew Lang in his review of the poem oddly calls it a 'she', perhaps because it has the habit when on board of sitting and making lace). They are like members of a pack of Happy Families, but without the families.

These males may or may not catch a Snark, but some Snarks are Boojums, and on the way there are other vaguely threatening creatures, Jubjubs and Bandersnatches. We needn't concern ourselves with the comic details of the alliterative adventurers' epic voyage, except to note that they are happy to be distracted by miscellaneous things, which are at once the cherished appurtenances of high Victorian culture and the ordinary building blocks of nonsense. In this context, a creature that can be hunted with forks and hope, who is fond of bathing-machines, whose life can be threatened with a railway share, and may be served with greens, might 'be' almost anything.

This open-endedness has maddened readers eager for an allegory. Carroll was often asked about it. To his child friends he would say things like: 'When you have read the *Snark*, I hope you will write me a little note and tell me how you like it, and if you can *quite* understand it. Some children are puzzled with it. Of course you know what a Snark is? If you do, please tell *me*: for I haven't an idea what it is like.' Martin Gardner in his definitive edition of the poem is rightly dissatisfied with this evasiveness, and is happy to indicate some of the solutions that readers have offered. The Snark may represent 'material wealth' or be a symbol of the North Pole. The poem might be a satire on an unsound business venture or on the Hegelian philosopher's search for the Absolute. Gardner himself proposes that the poem is about the existential dread of death, and (since his edition was first published in 1962) ends with a disquisition on two further 'B's in the news at that time: Brinkmanship and the Bomb.

It is likely that the interpretation of nonsense is more than usually reliant on a reader's circumstances or preconceptions, since the text is by definition independent of coherent evidence. Indeed, in my opinion the best criticism of Carroll's work is to be found in a brilliant book whose very method is itself in the last analysis nonsensical, *The Raven and the Writing Desk* (1976) by the anthropologist Francis Huxley. But I was reminded of this relativity of interpretation when my late friend the resourceful etymologist J. G. Keogh asked me a few years ago how he could find evidence that Carroll might have had early access to W. W. Skeat's 'List of Aryan Roots' prior to the publication of Skeat's *Etymological Dictionary of the English Language* (1879–82) so that he might have made use of it for his poem. Skeat (who had a close association with the family of the Dean of Christ Church to which the original of Carroll's Alice belonged) showed that the Aryan root 'snark' ultimately yielded our word 'snare', and Keogh was supplying Gardner with information for a new edition of the *Snark*.

The connection is thematically appropriate (an etymological noose is enough to hang this poem on or by, after all: 'snare'/'snag'/'snark') but fairly unexciting. I re-read the poem. When I did, it seemed obvious that a sexual meaning lurked in some of the words of the poem. Taking a somewhat tongue-in-cheek leaf out of Huxley's method, I replied to Keogh in more or less the following terms.

Carroll was obsessed by the innocence of little girls, whose evanescent charm always turned out to be contaminated by puberty. He befriended them, teased them, corresponded with them and photographed them (sometimes without their clothes on). Then when they reached the age of twelve they no longer interested him. This is the defining agony of his emotional (indeed of his psychosexual) life. He is besotted by little girls, but drops them when they grow up. He doesn't like sex. He doesn't even like breasts.

The quest for the Snark is an 'agony' most obviously because the old word for a canto was a 'fit' (an 'agon' itself is a public celebration of the Greek games or a contest for the prize at those games). This is a Carrollian literary joke, but his real 'agony' was no joke at all. 'Away, fond thoughts, and vex my soul no more!' he writes in the inscription to 'a dear Child' at the beginning of the *Snark*, a puzzle poem which dares to name her in acrostics. He knows very well that he cannot obtain the 'heart-love' of Gertrude Chataway, and so he writes a symbolic poem for her, to show that such a quest is impossible. The Snark, therefore, must obviously be that elusive thing, the reciprocal love of a girl-child.

There is no reason why the name itself should not be pure nonsense. But many nonsense words in Carroll can be decoded, so it might be worth seeing if 'Snark' can be, too. The theory has been aired that it is simply one of his portmanteau inventions, like the now naturalised 'chortle' (= *ch*uck*le* + sn*ort*) or 'galumph' (= *gal*lop in tri*umph*). The best candidate pair (one provided by Carroll himself) is '*sn*ail' + 'sh*ark*', appropriate to a quest by sea. Too appropriate? Is it a real meaning? It seems obvious to me that we have to adopt a looking-glass method to find the actual meaning, because the blank map that the Bellman provides in Fit the Second is actually a kind of mirror that represents only water without any land. With the help of this sort of reflecting blank map we can see how to look into it, as it were, *cancrizans* (i.e., reading backwards, as Alice read 'Jabberwocky' in *Through the Looking-Glass*). If we do this, we reverse the letters of 'Snark' and reach the true meaning: 'kranS'.

Krans is obviously the German *Kranz* ('innocence' or 'virginity', figuratively from the meaning of 'bridal wreath'). The search for the girl's requited love is bound to be thwarted because of her innocence. When at the end of the poem the Baker seems to have found a Snark, it 'seemed almost too good to be true'. And indeed, it turns out to be only a Boojum. What can a Boojum be but a Bosom in vulgar parlance? Breasts! Carroll can hardly bear to complete this dreadful word: "'It's a Boo—'"

If the Boojum is an unexpected bosom, and therefore a disappointment, the Jubjub ('that desperate bird') is a bosom represented as a threat. The hero of 'Jabberwocky' is enjoined to beware of it. Why? Because, of course, to him it might be a real distraction. The Boojum is merely a childish view of the bosom, something that the child might find comically unlikely in prospect, but the Jubjub is onomatopæically luring to a grown man. A 'jub' is a vessel for liquid, so that a 'jubjub' would be a pair of them. The 'jubjub' is also, like the 'jujube', something to be sucked, and like the 'juju' it can become a fetish.

Another portmanteau beast cropping up not only in *The Hunting of the Snark* but also in 'Jabberwocky' is, as we have seen, the Bandersnatch. This is an indication of the even more greatly feared manifestation of the young innocent's descent into puberty: menstruation. 'Bandersnatch', or 'band[age]' + 'snatch', is a sanitary towel. Which allows us to return to Carroll's portmanteau comment about the Snark itself. We realise that the child's innocence is under an innate threat not only from breasts and menstruation, but from the very nature of her most secret parts, which both attract and repel at the same time. 'Snail' + 'shark' combines the appearance of the clitoris with the traditional horror of the *vagina dentata*. No wonder that Carroll suspected that his little friends had a better idea of what the Snark might actually be like than he did. No wonder that it seems much safer to seek it, like the Gorgon's head, with the assistance of a Huxleyan mirror (which will also, I trust, save me from the charges I myself have made against that lecturer on *Maud*, see p. 58).

WHO IS CRAZY JANE?

W. B. Yeats's Crazy Jane poems (the first seven poems in 'Words for Music Perhaps' appearing in the volume *Words for Music Perhaps* in 1932, together with 'Crazy Jane on the Mountain' from *Last Poems & Plays* of 1940) have intrigued readers for their aggressive mixture of plain and gnomic talk about sex and their defiance of Christian moral authority. On the one hand is Crazy Jane with her passionate memories of her affair with Jack the Journeyman (who is now dead but still calling to her from the blasted oak, like Cathy calling to Heathcliff); on the other is the reproving Bishop. For Jane, love is not polarised as it has become in the Pauline doctrine of the Bishop, but involves the whole body and soul, particularly the body. For her, then, the Bible is merely an 'old book'. Love is a dance that must be danced as long as one may do so, despite the mutual aggression that it involves, for it embodies a truth about life that will outlast time. In the Bishop's equation, spirit is an escape from age; in Jane's it requires the acceptance and resolution of all such antinomies.

Such summaries do little justice to the complexities of these poems, which contain many incidental puzzles of interpretation.

However, I am concerned here with only one of these puzzles: who is Crazy Jane, and why is she 'crazy'?

This is a question that might be easily answered, since unfashionable wisdom has been eloquently possessed by fools and madmen in literature long before Yeats. Jane is an old woman who sleeps rough, who spits at and curses the Bishop, and who is above all defiantly proud of her sexual experience: her body is 'like a road | That men pass over'. Her lover Jack was a journeyman, a hireling or occasional labourer. Their relationship (although Jack has been banished by the Bishop) is a model of the intense but casual encounter ('Men come, men go'). Also, like D. H. Lawrence's Connie, she has learned that 'Love has pitched his mansion in | The place of excrement; | For nothing can be sole or whole | That has not been rent.' And he is still her 'dear Jack', the defining initiator of her experience. By the moral standards of her environment she may well be thought to be mad. She is a kind of senile pariah, giving away her sexual favours, and voicing elemental truths that no one else will dare to utter. A symbol of the late Romantic poet, perhaps? Certainly Yeats has a vested interest in her point of view.

But there is another reason why she is crazy, one that seems to be lightly passed over by many readers. 'Crazy Jane' is the traditional name, in poetry at least, for a jilted girl who has been left by her faithless lover to give birth to her child alone and to become a village outcast. The classic version of this affecting scenario is Matthew Lewis's 'Crazy Jane' ('Henry fled – with him forever | Fled the wits of Crazy Jane'), popular in family albums in the early eighteenth century, and giving its name to the tune of its setting. There ensue poems on her story by William Nicholson, Robert Anderson, John Clare, Eliza Cook and others, while Sidney Dobell has a rather more Havisham-like Scottish version, 'Daft Jean', whose lad enlists and dies before marrying her, though she persists with a fantasy of a white wedding and dies in the snow. Naturally, the sentimentality behind Crazy Jane's predicament barely survived the Victorians, and Yeats's sequence has no mention of a bastard child. Indeed, the relationship between Jack and Jane has moved beyond mere betrayal.

Today, the notion that being abandoned by the father of one's child might itself send you crazy is clearly not as central to such a situation as it once was. For example, the poet George Szirtes in his *Portrait of My Father in an English Landscape* (1998) thinks that Crazy Jane was simply a 'flighty girl' that no one could trust, and links her with 'Wild Alice', 'all flying fur | and impulse'. Yeats himself originally called his character 'Cracked Mary', and so she appears in early printings of the first few poems. He is said to have modelled her in some way on an old woman living near Gort, 'the local satirist' who had 'an amazing power of audacious speech'. Such a character, whose eccentricities he delighted to share with Lady Gregory, seems to exist at some distance from the literary Jane so far delineated. The Gort neighbour doesn't resolve the puzzle, but merely perpetuates it. Did he change the name from 'Cracked Mary' to 'Crazy Jane' in order to incorporate the sentimental tradition launched by Lewis's poem, or was there some other more specific reason? I think that both of these possibilities turn out to be true.

Yeats's 'Cracked Mary and the Bishop', 'Cracked Mary grown old looks at the Dancers' and 'Cracked Mary Reproved' were the earliest to be published, in *The New Republic*, 12 November 1930. But only a few years earlier, and most unusually for the twentieth century, the character Crazy Jane had reappeared, in some poems by W. M. Letts. There is first a passing reference in her book *More Songs from Leinster* (1926): 'I'd rather talk with tinkers by the road, | Or crazy Jane who has fine things to say.' Then in the *Spectator* for 26 March 1927 she has a poem all to herself, called 'Crazy Jane':

Poor crazy Jane
Wanders the roads in wind and rain.
About the countryside she streels,
With tattered skirts about her heels.
With odd, torn gloves on either hand
She dreams that she is someone grand.
For tall she is and haughty-necked,
Her crooked bonnet queerly-decked
With faded roses and a veil
That wisps about her in a gale.

Poor crazy Jane,
To look to her for sense is vain.
Wrapped in a shabby velvet coat
Stravaging round like some old goat.
Her man was gardener, she said,
Upon the boat to Holyhead.
She laughed: 'I'm telling you,' said she,
'There's no one knows – I'm quality.
They'd fall out of their standing, dear,
If they could guess the queen is here!'

Poor crazy Jane.
Would she be happy were she sane,
Robbed of her dreams of rank and state,
When she beneath her rags is great?
The posy that she loves to hold,
May be to her an orb of gold.
Her battered bonnet, ragged gown,
An ermined robe and royal crown.
I wonder is she better so
Than in the dull plain world I know.

Letts's version supplies a further thread of characterisation: her Crazy Jane is distinguished by delusions of grandeur. This would have been attractive to Yeats, for whom an old beggar-woman might well be a queen (*Cathleen ni Houlihan* is the central example) and whose muses were tall and inclined to 'practise a tinker shuffle | Picked up on a street'. His own Crazy Jane has no such delusions (apart from her being on nodding terms with bishops) but the association would have been useful. Letts no doubt had some knowledge of the full nineteenth-century tradition of the character, but it is as neglected in her poem as it appears to be in Yeats's. Even so, a reminder of this tradition would have supplied a cause for the raging and unfulfilled appetite of the old woman: the reckless sexual experience of the unmarried mother that would make her a source of village suspicion, awe and even envy. With a stroke of the pen, therefore, Yeats could change 'Cracked Mary' to 'Crazy Jane' and supply some unearned overtones. Which he did for publication of these poems later in November 1930 in *The London Mercury*, and subsequently for the other poems in the series.

Winifred Letts was not unknown to him. When briefing Horace Plunkett in 1904 for his help in trying to get a theatre patent for the Abbey Theatre, Yeats promised 'a one-act play by a new writer, and . . . other plays by competent writers'. No one-act play by a new writer was performed at the Abbey until Letts's *The Eyes of the Blind* in April 1907, in a triple bill with Augusta Gregory's *The Poorhouse* and Yeats's *Deirdre*. The play, inspired by Synge's *Riders to the Sea*, was badly performed and remained unpublished, but Letts had a second play put on a couple of years later. She had her chances, and it would be strange if Yeats did not remember her work twenty years later if her name happened to catch his eye.

What's in a name? Letts's use of 'Crazy Jane' seems like a rich recovery of something that was in danger of being lost. 'Jane' itself has its own associations, which Yeats's 'Mary' could never have begun to compete with. Lawrence used it for his own earthy version of 'Jane' and 'Jack', the personified genitals 'Lady Jane' and 'John Thomas' in *Lady Chatterley's Lover* (1928), although these names had been in existence since the mid-nineteenth century. A 'jane' was becoming a common name for a girl or a sweetheart, common because simple. But sometimes only deceptively simple. The resourceful heroine of the Gershwins' *Oh, Kay!* (1926) can become more or less invisible by pretending to be Jimmy's maid: 'What a pretty maid! | Simply Jane –.' And Jane in John Crowe Ransom's 'Morning' (1927) is the mysterious agent of enchantment to the waking Ralph, until his masculine role reasserts itself and he perceives her as 'simply Jane'. One of the better-known of Edith Sitwell's housemaids and goose-girls is the Jane of 'Aubade' (1923): 'Jane, Jane, | Tall as a crane, | The morning light creaks down again.' By this – like Letts's 'tall . . . and haughty-necked' Jane – we are reminded of the lines of the Plough Play collected by Chambers in *The English Folk Play* (1933): 'Jane, Old Jane, Dame Jane, Lame Jane, Lady Jane | She has "a neck as long as a crane".' This chain of Janes seems like a small scenario of its own, and may very well have played a part in Geoffrey Grigson's programmed lampooning of the angular Sitwell as a crazed aristocrat, 'the Old Jane', in his magazine *New Verse* from 1936.

WHO IS PIPIT?

Sometimes an evocative name in a poem may be nothing more than that, the quality of the name momentarily suggesting a character. A fleeting personage who is no more than an unelaborated identity can be useful in a poem. The early twentieth-century poets were particularly good at this sort of thing: Edith Sitwell's Captain Fracasse, Auden's Captain Ferguson, Spender's Marston.

Who they are and what they do is little more than an implication of the name, and part of their impact is that nothing else needs to be known about them, and often perhaps nothing can. More than that and they soon become fictional characters.

T. S. Eliot's poems are full of richly grotesque personages, some of them (like Mrs Cammell or Mr Silvero) merely ghosts captured in some vague bodily presence, others (like Bleistein or Sweeney) fully or half-realized characters, whose appearance may be imagined and history partially reconstructed. But in between there may well be a puzzle.

Eliot's poem 'A Cooking Egg' begins, or almost begins, with a notorious puzzle, a female figure described over two stanzas in what is clearly her own room:

> Pipit sate upright in her chair
>   Some distance from where I was sitting;
> *Views of Oxford Colleges*
>   Lay on the table, with the knitting.

> Daguerreotypes and silhouettes,
>   Her grandfather and great great aunts,
> Supported on the mantelpiece
>   An *Invitation to the Dance*.

I say 'almost begins', because there is first of all, as so often in early Eliot, an epigraph intended to give us a clue to what the poem is about. '*En l'an trentiesme de mon aage | Que toutes mes hontes j'ay beues . . .*' ('In the thirtieth year of my age | When I have swallowed all my shames') is from Villon's *Testament*. Eliot, thirty when he wrote the poem, is ironically assessing a life half over but not fully lived, where (as the following four stanzas insinuate) the traditional objectives of the materialist life – itemised as

'Honour', 'Capital' and 'Society' – have been appropriated into a commonplace eternity, so that heaven becomes a kind of club, full of chat with the likes of Sir Philip Sidney, Sir Alfred Mond (founder of ICI) and Lucretia Borgia. Initiation into this club's arcane rules is provided by visionary women with greater expertise than Pipit. But the speaker does not really believe in it. These stanzas of absurd compensation (corralled within the poem by two lines of dots) yield at the close of the poem to a great lament for the loss of true happiness:

> But where is the penny world I bought
>   To eat with Pipit behind the screen?
> The red-eyed scavengers are creeping
>   From Kentish Town and Golder's Green;
>
> Where are the eagles and the trumpets?
>
>   Buried beneath some snow-deep Alps.
> Over buttered scones and crumpets
>   Weeping, weeping multitudes
> Droop in a hundred A.B.C.'s

There are many issues of interpretation in this poem (actually a relatively straightforward example of Eliot's notoriously difficult quatrain poems), but I shall concentrate on the primary puzzle: who is Pipit? I take it that such a puzzle may never be satisfactorily solved, but that the awareness of it as a puzzle is an important part of reading the poem.

There was a memorable Critical Forum in *Essays in Criticism* forty-five years ago which arose from the polite derision poured by its editor F. W. Bateson on the theories of I. A. Richards (that Pipit is the speaker's old nurse) and F. O. Matthiessen (that she is a little girl). Bateson himself claimed that she is 'a sort of Bloomsbury *demi-vierge*, dull but decidedly upper-middle class'. He was trying to prove that criticism had begun to lose a sense of literary context, but it now seems a bit rich that Richards (author of *Practical Criticism*, doyen of context and close reading) should have been his target.

Much of Bateson's argument involved the details of Pipit's room, and he remained obtuse about the italicisation of 'An *Invitation to the Dance*' that rather spoils it as evidence of Pipit's social engagements. Thinking that the poem is about class, he also imagined the screen to be a screen in a restaurant, rather than (as Grover Smith suggested) something like the screen behind which Candide is discovered with Cunegonde. Smith's phrase was 'serves to evoke', acknowledging that not everything in a poem is a precise allusion to something else. When John Hayward felt that the significance of 'autumn' escaped him in the phrase 'autumn weather' in a draft of *Little Gidding*, Eliot was compelled to reply: '. . . because it *was* autumn weather'. He might just as well have said the same about anything in Pipit's room.

But commonsensical interpretation is always necessary at a basic level (there was much argument in the Critical Forum about the word 'supported') and it is surprising to what degree prior assumptions can channel the direction that an individual reading takes. Some strange views found a generous hearing in the correspondence pages of the magazine: the speaker and Pipit have undertaken a marriage of convenience; Pipit is a Victorian maiden lady; she is the child spirit-control of a medium; and so on. Details supporting such readings, together with a multitude of extra-textual assumptions, crowd the mind of the interested reader of Bateson's journal and muddy his own initial response. I. A. Richards was amazed at the certainties of other readers: 'We may "see" Pipit in black silk or give her livelier attire – but her dress is not in the poem.'

The outcome of the *Essays in Criticism* Forum was a general uneasy peace. Richards complained that the 'old nurse' theory (adumbrated in a lecture) was not, after all, his final considered view. It emerged that Eliot himself had told him once that the clue was in another of his poems called 'Dans le Restaurant'. This poem has a seedy, dribbling waiter recounting an overwhelming erotic experience he had had at the age of seven, tickling a little girl in an arbour sheltering from the rain. The pair is then fatally interrupted by a large dog. It is a defining moment of lost ecstasy experienced by a character who is notably more of a 'cooking egg' (i.e., not a fresh one) than Pipit's visitor. But even in possession of this 'clue', Richards remained characteristically loyal to the text: 'I take the speaker to be looking back a long way to a time when something a penny could buy could be all the world to him, and Pipit then (whatever else we care to make her) was a participant.'

'Whatever else we care to make her'. Richards's apparent insouciance is actually a precise challenge. Confronting the poem's initial puzzle, we still have to make a choice between the readings on offer, and these seem essentially to be reducible to three if we accept that the 'penny world' towards the end of the poem is a memory of something shared with Pipit by the speaker of the poem as a child. That is to say, she must be either someone who was (1) also a child at the time, or else (2) the speaker's Nanny, or (3) some other grown person who was willing to unbend with a child 'behind the screen', perhaps an older sister or cousin. That screen (and the later buttered scones of the Aerated Bread Company's cafeterias) distracts many readers into imagining some sort of formal repast. Bateson thought the penny world a cheap meal eaten behind a restaurant screen (whatever that might be). B. C. Southam, in his excellent guide to the *Selected Poems*, unnecessarily points out that late-Victorian children were often concealed at mealtimes from the rest of the family (apparently forgetting that the speaker had bought the 'penny world' himself: surely it must be a treat, a sweetmeat or a piece of confectionery, to be eaten stealthily between meals).

Discussion of the problem has, so far as I am aware, somewhat neglected my third option above. But it may be a way out of an impasse. The nanny theory was determinedly supported by John T. Mayer in *T. S. Eliot's Silent Voices* (1989). Mayer reminded his readers of Eliot's nursemaid Annie Dunne, about whom nothing had previously been revealed except for a photograph of her with the very young Eliot, probably in her late twenties, in a stained skirt, one hand on her hip and wearing the calculated refusal of a smile (reproduced in, for example, Peter Ackroyd's 1984 biography of Eliot). Richards was, after all, correct, Mayer claimed, since Eliot's childhood was the only time that he claimed he was happy, until the period of his second marriage. Bolstering his case by reference to the capitalised abstractions of the four central stanzas of the poem, Mayer declared: 'During his boyhood, Pipit gave him her own society, the penny capital of a treat, and the honour of secretly sharing it "behind the screen", in the privacy so dear to Eliot . . . She is childhood's promise, the Victorian absolutes, and the "penny world" all rolled into one.' This is all very well, but why should a shabby Irish servant in her retirement possess daguerreotypes and silhouettes of her grandfather and great-great-aunts? They were likely to have been agricultural workers not yet emigrated. No, it is clear that whatever limitations the Pipit of the opening of the poem is felt to possess, she is of a quite different social class. It is likely that proponents of the nursemaid theory perhaps not unreasonably have in mind someone like Sebastian Flyte's upmarket Nanny Hawkins, who had 'such a dull life' in *Brideshead Revisited* ('There was a rocking horse in the corner and an oleograph of the Sacred Heart over the mantelpiece'). Not an Annie Dunne by any means.

But this is not all. Mayer, like Lyndall Gordon in *Eliot's Early Years* (1977), had the privilege of working with the drafts of Eliot's early poetry that had been purchased by the collector John Quinn and sold by his niece in 1958 to the New York Public Library, which then kept quiet about them for ten years. Mayer makes no mention of two additional stanzas about Pipit (following the first two) in the draft of 'A Cooking Egg', nor of a reference to Pipit as well as to Grishkin in a draft of 'Whispers of Immortality' (Gordon barely referred at all to the quatrain poems, which she clearly hates). This seems strange, since the discovered material (now published in *Inventions of the March Hare*, 1996) must belong with his argument:

> When Pipit's slipper once fell off
> It interfered with my repose;
> My self-esteem was somewhat strained
> Because her stockings had white toes.
>
> I wanted Peace here on earth,
> While I was still strong and young;
> And Peace was to have been extended
> From the tip of Pipit's tongue.

And in the draft of 'Whispers of Immortality':

> As long as Pipit is alive
> One can be mischievous and brave;
> But where there is no more misbehaviour
> I would like my bones flung into her grave.

The reason, of course, is that this discovered material would upset his argument. We know (from the case of Byron, for example) that servants can have erotic relationships with their charges, but Pipit's slipper falling off, the activity of the tip of her tongue and her contagiously mischievous behaviour surely puts her back in the category of a child, or, if not the younger girl of 'Dans le Restaurant' ('*J'avais sept ans, elle était plus petite*'), the somewhat older playful girl of my third possibility, having now totally outgrown her playfulness and leaving the whole world grown stale.

Although we feel the pressure of a real person behind Pipit, particularly given Eliot's clue to Richards, we have no idea who she might 'be' (a Hinckley cousin, perhaps?) and it does not matter. Some puzzles can live with permanently delayed solutions.

WHO IS BADROULBADOUR?

It is quite possible to read a poem without curiosity. Some crucially intentional fact may easily be passed over, particularly if the general drift of the poem is clear enough. The following poem, 'The Worms at Heaven's Gate' by Wallace Stevens, is a good example:

> Out of the tomb, we bring Badroulbadour,
> Within our bellies, we her chariot.
> Here is an eye. And here are, one by one,
> The lashes of that eye and its white lid.
> Here is the cheek on which that lid declined,
> And, finger after finger, here, the hand,
> The genius of that cheek. Here are the lips,
> The bundle of the body and the feet.
>
> . . . .
>
> Out of the tomb we bring Badroulbadour.

What we are made to feel about beauty and its survival here is immensely qualified by whatever we happen to believe about the afterlife. There is a minor puzzle at this point, because we are uneasy about the thought of worms presenting themselves for admission to heaven. Can we imagine worms having souls, as here they are given voices? Or is the idea a challenge to the very concept of bodily resurrection? How can the corrupted body be reassembled?

Stevens's most celebrated adage, 'Death is the mother of beauty', intends a defining statement about the origin of value in our awareness of transience. The adage both implicitly contains and rebuts a converse truism that death is the murderer of beauty. Conventionally, in the long centuries of the poetic tradition before the practice of cremation, this was perceived to be accomplished by worms upon the beauty of a woman.

We might compare Stevens's poem with another, 'Down Underground', by that stalwart of the Georgian anthologies, the tramp-poet W. H. Davies, nine years older than Stevens:

What work is going on down underground,
Without a sound – without the faintest sound!
The worms have found the place where Beauty lies,
And, entering into her two sparkling eyes,
Have dug their diamonds up; her soft breasts that
Had roses without thorns, are now laid flat;
They find a nest more comfortable there,
Than any bird could make, in her long hair;
Where they can teach their young, from thread to thread,
To leap on her white body, from her head.
This work is going on down underground,
Without a sound – without the faintest sound.

Davies is working in a mode which relishes and dramatises the charnel-house horrors. The conventional images suggest gruesome analogies, such as that between worms and birds: worms, too, build nests for their young and show them how to find food. The similarities of conception and structure in the two poems are striking at first. But this makes the differences all the more crucial. Where Davies's repeated but slightly changed opening lines merely dramatise the reader's uneasiness about such devastation going on unseen and in total silence, Stevens's similarly altered refrain subtly underlines the bold metaphysical claim that his speaking worms are making. The first line is 'Out of the tomb, we bring Badroulbadour'. The comma effectively subordinates Badroulbadour, as though the worms are saying to St Peter: 'We have come out of the tomb and it happens to be our task today to bring you Badroulbadour.' But the last line has no comma, and as a result of the meticulous proof of the worms' ghastly inventory, 'Out of the tomb we bring Badroulbadour' can be seen as a triumphant resurrection: 'Look, we have brought Badroulbadour out of the tomb.'

Such differences proclaim the apparently slight but distinct advance that a modernist poem has made over a Georgian one. Davies has no need to see further than the ultimately *carpe diem* note that his worms evoke. He is borrowing a Jacobean trope as readily as Beddoes did a century before him, suggesting that to find the place where Beauty lies amounts to finding Beauty out, sending her a coded message which insidiously conveys what Marvell said to his coy mistress, that the attentions of the poet should be preferred to the attentions of worms:

> Thy Beauty shall no more be found;
> Nor, in thy marble Vault, shall sound
> My echoing Song; then Worms shall try
> That long preserv'd Virginity:
> And your quaint Honour turn to dust . . .

Stevens's worms, however, are not invasive at all. They are shown not entering the tomb, but leaving it. In Marvell and Davies you could see the worms as surrogate male wooers. In Stevens they are surrogate mothers: 'Within our bellies', they say, as though 'Out of the tomb' were 'Out of the womb', and they finally present what they oddly call 'The bundle of the body', like midwives. In another sense of Stevens's adage, they are indeed the mothers of beauty. They bring beauty to that strange rebirth which the old myth of heaven once licensed and which must be for Stevens, who is a wholly secular poet, principally a statement of value made as a response to the puzzling question of what beauty is.

Another poem of Stevens's, 'Peter Quince at the Clavier', describes beauty as the 'fitful tracing of a portal' and goes on to say: 'The body dies; the body's beauty lives.' In the poem about Badroulbadour this uncertain tracing of the portal is directly replaced by the confidence of the worms at the equivalent portal of heaven. There is the suggestion, too, that the characteristic pose of Badroulbadour, with the fingers of the hand resting against the cheek, is itself a representation of the self-consciousness of beauty. Indeed, each finger, finger after finger, is aware of that cheek's perfection, so that the hand itself is mysteriously metamorphosed into a kind of attendant angel, 'the genius of that cheek'. But the worms' enumeration of her features naturally warns us not to be deceived: this is not Badroulbadour, but bits of Badroulbadour. 'The body dies: the body's beauty lives.' Where does it live, we may ask? Where can it live?

Stevens believed that poetry – 'the supreme fiction' – has the power to eternise the temporal. And it is his belief in the prime effect of analogy in poetry that prompts a return to the puzzling clue in the poem itself for an answer to the question, the clue so easily overlooked in pursuit of the argument.

The most notable, indeed the central fact of the poem occurs before the cautious inventory of the worms. It is the summary of that inventory: 'Out of the tomb, we bring Badroulbadour', and it is also the last word of the poem: 'Out of the tomb we bring Badroulbadour.' The central fact of the poem is an act of naming, or of renaming things which have ceased to have a unitary identity. The worms reclaim a woman called Badroulbadour. Who is she?

On the 731st night of *The Thousand and One Nights*, Shahrazad begins the story of Ala al-Din and the Wonderful Lamp. Badr al-Budur is the name of the Sultan's daughter, whom the humble Ala al-Din first sees when she is passing through the streets to bathe at the hammam. Everyone is ordered to go home, to shut their doors and windows and not look at her, but Ala al-Din hides in the hammam and spies on her through a crack in the door, from which he is able himself to inventorise her beauty:

He had only been in place for a few minutes when a crowd of eunuchs appeared, making way for the princess's train. Ala al-Din saw her among her women, a little moon outshining a host of stars; but, when she came to the threshold, she unveiled her face and he was dazzled with unimagined sunlight. She was fifteen, neither more nor less; when you had seen her, you found the letter alif crooked in your reading, the young branch of the ban a clumsy thing, a crescent moon of no account after her brow. The lids hiding her black eyes were two rose leaves, her nose was as faultless as a king's sword, her neck was as soft as a dove's, her small chin smiled; surely she had been washed to that whiteness in the fountain Salsabil. A poet said of her:

You have decked your hair with a wing torn from the night
     To make the brow white,
You have enchanted your eyes with black kohl
     To trouble the soul,
And have made spells on your cheek with a burnt rose
     To shatter repose.

The blood sang twice as quickly through Ala al-Din's head:
he learnt beauty for the first time . . . [translation by Powys
Mathers]

The voyeuristic undercurrent to this revelation also links it to 'Peter
Quince at the Clavier', where the red-eyed elders of the Apoc-
rypha watching Susanna bathe 'felt | The basses of their beings
throb | In witching chords, and their thin blood | Pulse pizzi-
cati of Hosanna'. The sexuality of that poem is not without a
certain implicit self-disgust, appropriate to the theme of the tran-
scendence of music, but Ala al-Din is not, of course, an elder. I
suggest that he is a representative of that strange Stevensian type,
the figure of the youth as virile poet: 'The poet is a god, or the
young poet is a god. The old poet is a tramp.' Ala al-Din eventually wins the princess entirely through the magic of the lamp,
which enables him to build in an instant the palace of his dreams
for the consummation of their marriage.

    The Aladdin story, which is familiar to us from pantomimes,
is more complex in this source, but its analogical lineaments are
clear enough in Stevens's mind. The magic lamp with its conjured
Ifrit is the poet's genius, his imagination, without which he would
be nothing but a tailor's son (it may be significant that the Man
with the Blue Guitar is also presented by Stevens as a tailor). Badr
al-Budur's palace represents the achieved poem, which eternises
their love. In the story it is Badr al-Budur who, when the wicked

darwish comes offering new lamps for old, unwittingly gives him the magic lamp and is then spirited away with the palace. The analogy would be, then, that the poet wins his beloved through poetry, and then loses her because she can't see its value, even though she remains its inhabiting muse – a situation paralleled by Stevens's relationship with his wife Elsie.

In the story, however, Ala al-Din regains Badr al-Budur, and 'nothing marred their contentment until they, in their turn, were visited by the Destroyer of delights and the separator of friends'. But the story, while acknowledging death, defies it as Shahrazad herself defies it nightly simply in its telling. And as the original story, so the poem. Both *The Thousand and One Nights* and 'The Worms at Heaven's Gate' recreate Badr al-Budur's beauty not only for Ala al-Din, but for the reader, who, like him, 'learns beauty for the first time'. In the source, the princess pauses on the threshold of the hammam; in the poem the worms pause at the gate of heaven. Neither are thresholds over which the reader is permitted to pass. It is only within the short passage of the poem, even challengingly in a state of decomposition, that her beauty is reassembled. It is poetry itself which finally immortalises her.

WHO IS 'YOU'?

Here is a late poem by Ian Hamilton, called 'Ties', unpublished until his posthumous *Collected Poems* (2009):

> You are harvesting dead leaves again
> But don't look up.
> The trees aren't your trees now
> And anyway, white storm birds sing no song.
> Inside the house

> He's playing genealogies again,
> The usual curse:
> His, yours, theirs, everyone's. And hers.

The scrupulous editor of the volume, Alan Jenkins, gives an account of the various typescripts of this poem, including the fact that some lines from it appear among Hamilton's papers with the title 'Second Wife'. It is an extreme example of the puzzle that readers frequently have when faced with naked pronouns: who are all these people, and above all, who is 'you'? An extreme example, yes, but it is a puzzle commonly found in the starkly reduced lyric form favoured by Hamilton.

For example, very early in his work we encounter a poem, 'Windfalls', in which flies, attracted by rotting apples, sleep on 'your' wrist. It is preceded by 'The Recruits' ('"Nothing moves," you say') and followed by 'Birthday Poem' ('Tight in your hands, | Your Empire Exhibition shaving mug'). Even without benefit of editorial comment, the context of these neighbouring poems is more or less clear: the 'you' of 'The Recruits' is a woman shudderingly obsessed by the fear of nuclear attack common in the early 1960s, and the 'you' of 'Birthday Poem' is a man suffering from cancer. It is a small leap of understanding for any reader to conclude that these are the poet's first wife and father (though the veil of anonymity is still a chosen characteristic of Hamilton's method, and precise identification is not crucial). But who is the 'you' of 'Windfalls'? As we move through the volume, remembering the poem we have just read, and mindful of the poem following, we feel a puzzling choice here. The flies of 'Windfalls' also appear in 'The Recruits', but the wrist they settle on belongs to a 'pale, disfigured hand' that seems to look forward to the invalid of 'Birthday Poem'.

Pronouns have always given readers problems, as this stanza

from Lewis Carroll's parody 'She's All My Fancy Painted Him'
suggests:

> If I or she should chance to be
> Involved in this affair,
> He trusts to you to set them free,
> Exactly as we were.

The difficulty indicated here lies in remembering a previously
mentioned name, something with which almost every page of
Browning's *Sordello*, for example, taxes the inattentive reader. But
what if there is no proper name at all in the poem?

Probably the commonest name in poems is 'I', who can easily
be identified as the speaker of a poem (though not necessarily as
the poet in his or her own person). But 'I' is run a close second
these days by 'you', a name capable of very much more ambiguity, when used without an identifying antecedent, as we have
seen.

Is such a pronoun a name at all, you may ask? Nameless creatures may be so addressed. Turning up a mouse's nest with his
plough, Robert Burns speaks to it with the most sympathetic
affection ('That wee-bit heap o' leaves an' stibble | Has cost thee
monie a weary nibble!') even though it necessarily remains anonymous. Well, no, a pronoun isn't always a name, is the answer. But
my special case of 'you' here is the one in which we find a puzzle:
identification is required so that we can know where we are and
who is being addressed. A pronoun is a substitute for a name,
and identification leads us cautiously almost to the point of
naming, though perhaps not quite. A poet may address anything
at all, of course, large or small, visible or invisible, winds, worms,
ghosts, God. Robert Graves addresses his penis ('Down, Wanton,
Down!') and W. H. Auden addresses his body ('You'). You may

think these relationships of greater intimacy even than those with lovers.

It is the unspecified 'you' of modern love poems that I am mostly concerned with here. At least, the addressee is commonly a lover, and the very fact that the name is withheld is offered as a guarantee of the closeness and significance of the relationship. (Before the now archaic second-person pronoun became unusable, that, too, was a fairly reliable indicator, though it was so frequently used of the deity that the reader had to be alert to the kind of devotion professed.)

Before returning to Hamilton's poem, it is worth pointing out that 'you' itself can in general use also mean 'one', and in details of universalised experience serves to link the speaker and reader, even therefore suggesting a sense of 'you' as 'I'. T. S. Eliot's 'Preludes' sets this sort of thing up in the first poem of the sequence:

> And now a gusty shower wraps
> The grimy scraps
> Of withered leaves about your feet

We suppose that he really means (but wishes to avoid) 'my' feet, for the details of the street-scene are reported in order to be shared with the reader, who is assured that if he were there he would therefore see and feel these things too. The second poem emphasises the sheer numbers who have the same experiences:

> One thinks of all the hands
> That are raising dingy shades
> In a thousand furnished rooms.

'One': here is another avoidance of the first person designed to generalise ('you too, reader, would in such a place have such a thought'). The third poem of the sequence appears to continue this relationship with the reader, trying to define for him the common city experience ('thousand . . . rooms'; 'thousand . . . images'):

> You tossed a blanket from the bed,
> You lay upon your back, and waited;
> You dozed, and watched the night revealing
> The thousand sordid images
> Of which your soul was constituted;
> They flickered against the ceiling.
> And when all the world came back
> And the light crept up between the shutters,
> And you heard the sparrows in the gutters,
> You had such a vision of the street
> As the street hardly understands . . .

But no, it turns out that this 'you' is someone else, a prostitute, a character 'borrowed' here from the Parisian novels of Charles-Louis Phillippe. The poem continues:

> Sitting along the bed's edge, where
> You curled the papers from your hair,
> Or clasped the yellow soles of feet
> In the palms of both soiled hands.

There are further puzzles with the pronouns in 'Preludes', but this one is sufficient at the moment. Do we now have to go back and read the leaves as blowing about the feet of a streetwalker? And is the puzzle a deliberate one, to force the reader to *imagine himself as a streetwalker*?

Sometimes a poem simply decides to change tack. Here is the opening of Robert Lowell's 'Sailing Home from Rapallo':

Your nurse could only speak Italian,
But after twenty minutes I could imagine your final week,
And tears ran down my cheeks . . .

When I embarked from Italy with my Mother's body . . .

If this creates a puzzle for the reader, it is momentary, for it is soon plain that 'you' becomes the third-person mother of the rest of the poem. Lowell, incidentally, was a crucial influence on Hamilton's conviction that the personal experience of the poet has an absolute value for the poem, emotionally, as a biographical truth. Such a formula sounds like a commonplace of post-Romantic poetry, but after the impersonality of much modernism it became a distinct trait in the later twentieth century.

Hamilton's 'Ties' relies entirely on this conviction, so that the reader is forced to construct a story. How would it go? The trees that 'you' are gathering dead leaves from beneath (perhaps in a photograph that the speaker has found) are no longer 'your' trees now. Whose are they? They must in a sense belong to the woman referred to in the dramatically crucial final sentence ('And hers'). This woman has not only inherited the trees, but also the curse of the 'genealogies' that the 'he' is 'playing'. In such a baleful context 'playing genealogies' can't simply be the innocent tracing of family trees, but must have the metaphorical force of an obsessive preoccupation with the past, which the 'curse' turns into a matter for rebuke. To imply such a rebuke, Hamilton shifts from the first person of the first four lines to the third person of the last four. The implicit 'I' looking at the photograph is turned into the 'he' criticised for dwelling in the past. So we imagine two women, the one who used to gather the dead leaves, and the other, who appears to have displaced her, the one who resents the past. The dead leaves of the tree (compare the 'family' tree) imply that the first woman may also be dead.

So much is merely logical. The extension of the mysterious pronouns into 'theirs' and 'everyone's' follows naturally from it: the 'curse' of the obsessive memory of the irrevocable past is not only a problem for these individuals as individuals, but it is a problem that they must share, and it is our problem, too, allied to Clym Yeobright's conviction in Hardy's *The Return of the Native* that thought is a disease of the flesh.

I mention this great theme of Hardy here, because Hardy is a presence in Hamilton's poem. We had only got so far with the concealed 'story' of 'Ties', and the characters in the poem remain shadowy. The use of pronouns creates its own problem, and the metaphorical use of 'trees' another. But there is a clue to the remaining puzzle in an allusive quotation in line 4, a reference outwards from the delineated world of the poem to another poem that is likely, therefore, to be a source poem for it. This second poem is Hardy's celebrated account of sacred family moments, seasonal change and death, 'During Wind and Rain':

> They sing their dearest songs –
> He, she, all of them – yea,
> Treble and tenor and bass,
>   And one to play;
> With the candles mooning each face . . .
>   Ah, no; the years O!
> How the sick leaves reel down in throngs!
>
> They clear the creeping moss –
> Elders and juniors – aye,

  Making the pathways neat
   And the garden gay;
  And they build a shady seat . . .
   Ah, no; the years, the years;
See, the white storm-birds wing across!

  They are blithely breakfasting all –
  Men and maidens – yea,
  Under the summer tree,
   With a glimpse of the bay,
  While pet fowl come to the knee . . .
   Ah, no; the years O!
And the rotten rose is ript from the wall.

  They change to a high new house,
  He, she, all of them – aye,
  Clocks and carpets and chairs
   On the lawn all day,
  And brightest things that are theirs . . .
   Ah, no; the years, the years;
Down their carved names the rain-drop ploughs.

Like the 'dearest songs' of the opening, Hardy's poem has become a lyrical performance with pictured scenes, dramatic exclamation and repeated refrain. The white storm birds, like seagulls flying inland from turbulence at sea, presage the natural threat of time and change, as, of course, do the equivalent images in all the stanzas, the finished rose, the eroding rain and the sick leaves (compare the 'dead leaves' in Hamilton's poem). Hardy makes music of all these threatening images. For Hamilton to write 'And anyway, white storm birds sing no song' is somehow to defy the power of poetry to provide any sort of aesthetic compensation for the cruel facts of death. Hardy's family are hurtled through their ephemeral existence, and even their gravestones (like Fanny Robin's in *The Mayor of Casterbridge*) will not escape nature's ravages, but the poem attempts to eternalise them in its familiar details (candlelight, pet hens, furniture on the lawn, etc.) as photographs do. Hamilton's persona is also looking at a photograph and having Hardyish feelings, but the Hardy allusion is part of a bitter argument in the poem which proposes that nostalgia is ultimately useless.

So is Hamilton's poem, then, in any sense 'about' Hardy's remorse after his first wife Emma's death for their long estrangement? Is it 'about' Hardy's second wife Florence's feeling that she was an utter failure if Hardy could still be so obsessed by Emma that he could write the self-laceratingly celebratory poems of '*Veteris vestigia flammae*'? We would have to believe so, if it is a given element of a puzzle that the clue leads directly to a solution. But, of course, the thrust of such a poem as Hamilton's is self-evidently personal and, as we have seen, the allusion to Hardy sets up an argument about nostalgia that after a consideration of 'During Wind and Rain' sends the reader back from that source to the uncompromising bleakness of 'Ties'. Even Hamilton's title argues with itself, being in the plural, since the apparently untieable tie to the first woman should imply that a similar tie to the second will in time prove equally strong, though she may not believe it.

CONCLUSION: THE POEM IN THE HANDS OF THE READER

I have briefly looked at a number of poetic puzzles in this book, rather as they have taken my interest than to illustrate theories. But are there any general lessons to be learned? I have shown how we can – even in the smallest ways – find ourselves reading words that the poet did not write, or importing anachronistic meanings. I have suggested that the very title of a poem may mislead us, and that we had better be careful that we know who is speaking. Poems need not be about people, but when they are we should naturally (being people ourselves) be curious about who they are, particularly if they appear only as a pronoun. The subject, too, whatever it may be, should not be mistaken for its metaphorical treatment; and we shall often need to unscramble riddles in order to discover what the subject actually is. And then we must be mindful of the implications of the 'story' behind the poem. We shall also have to be ready to deal with violations of conventional syntax. Above all, we may find ourselves puzzled by the significance of a subject or the events surrounding it: the merest image may be responsive to our calculating imagination, while symbols (whether allegorical or not) will prove themselves full of poetic meaning, sometimes traditional and sometimes freshly minted.

In all these dealings with the text of a poem, we trust the poet who wrote it. We take it as we find it, whether in the pages of a poet's collected works (which we may already know well, or a little), in an anthology, in a newspaper, or in idleness as we strap-hang in the Underground. But we should understand some of the problems that may attend the transmission of the text, such as errors in the printing house or the poet's own meddling with unsatisfactory earlier versions. These should remind us that the poet minds about his poem, even if he never actually 'finishes' it.

This familiar proposal of Paul Valéry's that a poem is never complete, but only abandoned, may give licence to a reader's belief that a poet simply never has time to tidy up its puzzles. Having seen something of the involving value of puzzles, we know better. But Valéry's investigations into the perfectionism of poets (in *Tel Quel* and elsewhere) give a slightly different slant to the notion as popularised by Auden (to justify his tinkering with early work). Valéry is writing of 'a work whose completion (the judgement that declares it to be complete is entirely subordinate to the proviso that it pleases us) is never reached. There is a basic imbalance of judgement in comparing the latest with the last. The standard of comparison is not the same ... Something successful is a transformation of something imperfect. So something imperfect is only imperfect by being put aside ... A poem is never finished – it is only an accident that terminates it, i.e., that gives it to the public. Such as indolence, the requirements of the publisher – or the emergence of another poem' (my trans-lation). This slightly humorous argument naturally allows for the occasional perfection of a poem when the poet trusts to the idea that it must please, and perhaps tease as well, and is mercifully in Valéry's sense, not 'accident'-prone.

A poem is made to be readable, but not necessarily in the sense that the poet always expects it to be read. The Valéry argument tells us that some poems – for a variety of reasons of accident, privacy or experiment – are kept from readers. Some, indeed, may never have been read by anyone except their creators. Those we naturally know nothing about, and nothing may be said of them. But there is an interesting puzzle common to them all, which touches on one of the perennial questions asked at poetry readings. Why do poets write poems in the first place? The question is often asked by members of the audience who claim to write poems only for themselves, and there is sometimes a slight air of accusation or resentment about even the modest fame of the visiting speaker and the fact that his poems have been published.

There are many common attempted answers to this question, of course, involving the psychological, emotional and cultural uses of poetry and above all the problematic issue of the aesthetic function of mimetic artefacts in human life. But the questioner is not usually bothered with such deep matters. What the question really means are things like 'How can you be aware of the effect of your poem on me?' and 'What effect can my reading of your poem have on you?' and 'What is the nature of this mysterious relationship between poet and reader?' and 'How do I know if I have got it right?' The question is never an aesthetic one. It is always personal.

This quasi-personal relationship that comes to seem possible at poetry readings is a strange thing. People sometimes go to readings in the hope of revelations, rather as they read literary biographies. They also go to them so that they may interrogate the poet. They are looking for clues, perhaps, being used to the presence of footnotes in the edited classics of poetry. But what is it like for the poet?

The poet is conscious of his audience, but he does not often ask questions of them, unless it is to ask if he can be heard at the back. He hardly dare ask if he can be understood. But the smiling (or unsmiling) presence of an audience does make him do a strange thing. This is to introduce a poem with remarks that sometimes give too much away and anticipate the effect of the poem. Or that contain crucial information that the audience will perhaps with justice believe should have been put into the poem in the first place. Offering background information that is clearly an organic part of the poem about to be read is more than a privilege of the occasion or an understandable ingratiation. It is the poet's acknowledgement of what is personal in the relationship to *him*. He is, in a sense, being encouraged to think of rewriting the poem in order to make it more accessible to this particular assembled company. However impossible that may seem, all poets know that they do it to a degree. They pause to gloss an allusion or to distinguish a homophone, they interrupt themselves to chat about sources, they leave embarrassing bits out, or stumble at unforeseen tongue-twisters. Some of these things may be due to the difference between a spoken and a written poem, but most of them show that a poet can, when suddenly face to face with his readers, desperately want to be completely understood.

This book has concentrated on a range of specific puzzles in poetry, some of them notorious cruxes, others things that it is quite tricky for the reader to get right, and a number of them things that might very well remain insoluble. But it has also tried to suggest that it is in the very nature of poetry to be forever setting up problems of meaning that require an alert solving response in the reader. The act of imaginative reading always takes the form of a semantic reward, which cements the bond between the reader and the poet. Setting the poem's puzzles allows the poet to control the reader's involvement; solving the poem's puzzles brings the reader closer to the poet's own involvement. What they are both involved with is, of course, the matter of the poem. The text of the poem is a strangely independent and tenuous linguistic contract between the two parties. Readers are happy to think it immutable, which is why they are some-times put off at readings. They don't want the poem to be instantly changeable at the poet's whim. They don't even want it to be explained away. But they do want to feel that they have got it right.

The normal contract between poet and reader is, in fact, a one-way contract, benefitting one party only. We, as readers, value our intimacy with the minds of the poets we read. The truth of their poems can have a revelatory force. It is like love. But the poet knows nothing of the reader's experience, and it has no satisfaction for him. His own understanding of the text of his poems is fraught with uncertainty, embarrassment and suspicion. Does it work? Do his readers get it? Feedback is mere gossip, even face to face at a reading, nothing like the reader's experience itself. It is not only like love, it is for the poet like unrequited love. Whatever the inadequacies of the completed poem – its obscu-rities, its unnoticed metaphors, its forgotten allusions, its imprecise analogies – all it can do is offer itself on the impersonal page to its eventual reader (for whom, after all, it turns out to have been written) for whatever sympathetic understanding that can be mustered.

And so we see that the poem can escape from the poet with all its cul-de-sacs and loose ends intact and trailing. He has no further authority over interpretation than any other reader, and if he is nailed absolutely unprepared after a reading or quizzed in an interview he is as likely to say 'Search me' or (more politely) 'Make of it what you will' as to provide the hitherto missing foot-note or the Poirot revelation. It is hard to know if the poet is, in fact, secretly pleased or not that there may be residual puzzles. When someone asked Eliot what the first lines of the second section of *Ash Wednesday* meant ('Lady, three white leopards sat under a juniper-tree | In the cool of the day') he gravely replied that it meant 'Lady, three white leopards sat under a juniper-tree | In the cool of the day'. This Delphic obtuseness may conform to theories of the primacy of the text, but it does not satisfy puzzled readers. Nor does it satisfy energetic critics, who will leap in to expound, with reference perhaps to the leopards who accompany Tennyson's Princess Ida, to the Brothers Grimm story 'The Juniper Tree', and to God speaking to Adam in the Garden of Eden. Somehow this doesn't always satisfy puzzled readers either, because they want to experience the poem to the full, directly, and not through its 'sources', whether obvious or less obvious. And they will come to know that the least obvious are likely to remain unexplained. And they will have to live with that likelihood.

The poem has escaped from the hands of the poet, and is in the hands of its readers, who have no authority either, much less than the poet, after all. But it is they who do the reading, and it is the business of reading, among other things, to tackle the poem's puzzles and to solve some of them.

ACKNOWLEDGEMENTS

I would very much like to thank Clara Farmer and Parisa Ebrahimi of Chatto & Windus for all their help with this book.

Lines from 'And the Stars Were Shining' by John Ashbery taken from *And the Stars were Shining* copyright © John Ashbery 2011. All rights reserved. Used by permission of Carcanet for the author. Lines from 'The Sphinx', 'Journey to Iceland' and 'O Love the interest itself in thoughtless heaven' by W.H. Auden taken from *Collected Poems* copyright © The Estate of W.H. Auden 1976, 1991. All rights reserved. Excerpts from 'Chemin de Fer', 'The Fish' and 'Late Air' from *The Complete Poems 1927–1979* by Elizabeth Bishop. Copyright © 1979, 1983 by Alice Helen Methfessel. Reprinted by kind permission of Farrar, Straus & Giroux, LLC. Lines from 'Vergissmeinnicht' by Keith Douglas taken from *Collected Poems* © The Estate of Keith Douglas and reproduced by kind permission of Faber and Faber. Lines from T.S. Eliot's *The Waste Land*, 'The Preludes', 'A Cooking Egg', and 'Whispers of Immortality' taken from *Collected Poems* © The Estate of T.S. Eliot and reproduced by kind permission of Faber and Faber. 'The Scales' from *The Complete Poems* by William Empson, edited with an introduction and notes from John Haffenden (Allen Lane, The Penguin Press, 2000). Copyright © Estate of William Empson, 2000. 'Here Come the Drum Majorettes' by James Fenton from *Out of Danger*, reprinted by kind permission of the author and United Agents. Lines from 'Ties' by Ian Hamilton taken from *Collected Poems*, reprinted by kind permission of Aitken Alexander Associates. 'The Humanist' from *Selected Poems* by Geoffrey Hill (Penguin Books, 2006) Copyright © Geoffrey Hill, 2006. First published in *King Log* copyright © Geoffrey Hill, 1968. Lines from Ralph Hodgson from *Collected Poems*, published by Macmillan. Lines from 'The Death of the Ball Turrett Gunner' taken from *The Complete Poems* copyright © 1945 by Randall Jarrell. Renewed copyright © 2011 by Mrs. Randall Jarrell. 'High Windows' by Philip Larkin taken from *High Windows* © The Estate of Philip Larkin and reproduced by kind permission of Faber and Faber. Lines from 'Crazy Jane' by Winifred Letts taken from *Spectator*, 26 March 1927. 'Falling Asleep over the Aenied' and 'Sailing Home from Rapallo' by Robert Lowell taken from *Collected Poems* © The Estate of Robert Lowell and reproduced by kind permission of Faber and Faber. Lines from 'Dialogue over a Ouija Board' by Sylvia Plath taken from *Collected Poems* © The Estate of Sylvia Plath and reproduced by kind permission of Faber and Faber. 'The Sleeping Beauty' by Edith Sitwell from *Collected Poems* (© Edith Sitwell, 2006) is reproduced by permission of PFD (www.pfd.co.uk) on behalf of the Estate of Edith Sitwell. Extract from *Tender Buttons* by Gertrude Stein, reprinted by kind permission of David Higham Associates. Lines from Wallace Stevens' 'Earthy Anecdote', 'Anecdote of the Jar', 'The Emperor of Ice-Cream', 'The Worms at Heaven's Gate' taken from *Collected Poems* © The Estate of Wallace Stevens and reproduced by kind permission of Faber and Faber. Lines from Larry Woiwode reprinted by kind permission of Farrar, Straus & Giroux.

Every effort has been made to trace and contact all copyright holders prior to publication. If there are any inadvertent omissions or errors, the publishers will be pleased to correct these at the earliest opportunity.

INDEX